THE
URBANIZATION
OF
SOPHIA FIRTH

THE URBANIZATION OF SOPHIA FIRTH

SOPHIA FIRTH

PETER MARTIN ASSOCIATES LIMITED

ISBN 0-88778-082-2

Design: Diana McElroy

Peter Martin Associates Limited
35 Britain Street, Toronto, Canada M5A 1R7

United Kingdom: 17 Cockspur Street, London SW1Y 5BP, England.
United States: 33 East Tupper Street, Buffalo, N.Y. 14203, U.S.A.

Printed and bound in Canada by
T. H. Best Printing Company Limited, Don Mills, Ontario

I dedicate this book to my children.
It is based on real events and real people
as they appeared to me.
The stories, though not pure fiction,
may not be
unvarnished truth either.

THE
URBANIZATION
OF
SOPHIA FIRTH

1

The cold January day began miserably, more miserably than usual; or maybe it was just me, feeling very depressed, sick to death of waiting, struggling, hoping.

At six a.m. the alarm clock rang and I got up. The house was freezing. I could see my way around but I switched on the kitchen light anyway.

There were a few live coals in the old living-room heater. I stirred them up, shook down the ashes, added fresh coal, and adjusted the draughts. Then, confident that that stove would soon be radiating a pleasant heat, I turned my attention to the cooking range in the kitchen.

Lately it had been giving me much trouble. The wood, only partially dry to begin with, had gotten wet and icy during a freezing-rain storm the week before and was very hard to light and keep burning. I had been pestering the Welfare Department for better stuff but they said they had none. In their customary bored tone they kept telling me they were having a hard time getting any kind of wood, let alone dry. I thought the trouble was just that the city officials did not want to pay fairly for the wood, or to hire men to cut it. Certainly there was no lack of good wood in the county.

Well, this morning I expected little trouble. The night before I had broken up an old kitchen chair for kindling. The pieces of long-dry wood, bearing bits of paint and varnish, caught fire at the touch of a match, almost.

Carefully I laid the fire, lit it, and stepped back from the stove.

Phoomphft.

The sound came from behind and startled me.

Nervously I jumped around and ran to the living-room. Clouds of black smoke and soot were billowing above and around the cylindrical stove.

"Damn," I muttered, chagrined. I well knew what had happened. The fresh fuel I had added had settled down and choked the fire; gas had collected and exploded when heat from the struggling flames had increased sufficiently to ignite it.

"What's going on, Mum?" called Billy, my twelve-year-old, from under the blankets on the nearby couch. "How . . . ?"

"Oh, shut up!" I growled. "Just keep your head covered up and I'll have the air cleared in no time."

I checked the stove and saw that it was now drawing well. Yellow-red flames were licking fiercely up over the shiny black lumps of fuel and heavy plumes of smoke were rushing up the pipes to the chimney. I was sure there would be no more explosions.

Smoke was eddying near the ceiling and soot was dropping on everything. I opened the front door, grabbed a large towel and began to swing it about to fan the smoke out while frosty air rushed in around my bare legs. After five minutes I gave up, shut the door and put away the towel.

There was a thin film of ice atop our pail of drinking water. I broke the ice, filled my teakettle with water and set it to boil.

To pass the time while waiting for hot water I lit a cigarette and stood quietly smoking by the living-room heater. The heat from the old coal burner seemed to be going right out through the walls of the shack. Banking the building with snow had not done much good, I thought, like a lot of other things.

Like my husband, Tom Firth, finally quitting the struggle to make a decent living in northern New Brunswick and setting out to try to relocate in Toronto. Not that I had always felt despair about the idea. Indeed not. From the time we married I had tried to talk Tom into making the move, but he had refused. He had insisted for seventeen years that New Brunswick was as good as any place in Canada to live. It was his birthplace and he had a lot of things going for him: he was highly experienced in construction work, held a New Brunswick scaler's license and a stationary engineer's license, and he knew an awful lot of people.

And he knew Canada, he said. "There's nowhere else any damn better than here. Some places are bigger, that's all, but the people are the same. Wherever you go you better have a pocketful of money."

I protested, but not very forcefully. While growing up in a farming section of Gaspé County, Quebec, I had become accustomed to economic conditions being sometimes good, sometimes bad, the same that afflicted Restigouche County, New Brunswick. I was young, optimistic, and willing to give the place a try.

It was during a good time that we met and married. I was twenty-two, the mother of a young son; Tom was forty, and just back from a construction job in British Columbia. For the first decade of our marriage we were quite successful and happy.

The trouble was, eventually a bad time came and stayed so long that even Tom became discouraged. He began to talk of the pros and cons of moving to another province. By then I had five children, three in their teens and starting to talk seriously of quitting school and going to work – somewhere.

Suddenly the oldest, Don, did just that. He dropped out of school and, with the help of a friend, went to Toronto and got a job. He was seventeen. The day he left Tom gave him ten dollars – all the money we had. One long year ago.

Shortly after Don left, Tom lost his temporary job. A week later, I suffered a nervous breakdown and was confined to hospital. Joyce, fifteen, quit school to take care of the house and mind Jenny, five, while Tom looked for work. Our other kids, Johnny, fourteen, and Billy, eleven, did all they could to help.

When I got back to my family it was spring and Tom still had no job.

"What are we going to do?" Tom put the question to me

morosely, a few days after I had returned home.

"You know," I said.

"Go to Toronto, now?" he asked. "You're still crazy! I'd never get a job. At my age and with this crippled leg?"

"Suit yourself," I said, "but I'm going."

"How?"

"Oh, I'll get the money – somehow. There's Don and my brother George up there. There's your brother John and my sister Lois down here. Besides, I have aunts and uncles who'll help. They'll be real glad I finally came to my senses and realized I married a bum."

"Jesus Christ!" Tom shouted, then paused and continued more quietly, "I should have left years ago. It's too late now."

"No, it isn't," I said. "At least not too late to try."

"But, we haven't the money," Tom demurred.

"I'll get some," I assured him, "enough for you to go and look for a job. I'll get it from John or Lois. I'll try John first because I owe Lois a lot already."

"But will you be all right? Will you be able to manage the kids?" Tom asked.

"Sure. I have the doctors and neighbours and relatives. We'll be all right."

"You'll have to get welfare. It isn't much but there's nothing else. Maybe I better not go."

"Oh, take a chance," I said. "What the hell is the good of us all starving together? At least you'll see Don and find out how he's doing. He never writes much. Perhaps you better check up on him. Go on, give it a try."

So with a loan of twenty-five dollars from his brother, Tom set out to try – hard.

The days of trying became weeks, months, then seasons. By summer I was getting discouraged. The kids were out of school and impatient to try life in Toronto, to see their dad and brother again.

Tom's short notes told me he was discouraged too, though he never said it outright. He was getting only temporary one- and two-day jobs. Most of these he got through a company he called "Rent-A-Man-Club". It placed people like Tom in jobs, then took part of the worker's wages for their services. Goddam,

I muttered to myself, where was our Unemployment Insurance Commission? I thought it was set up to get people jobs. Obviously it wasn't working too well.

One July day an old friend, Gloria Dubé, came down on vacation. She visited us and in an attempt to help she said to Joyce, "Why don't you come to Toronto? You'd get work easy. You can stay with us."

Joyce had money due from a mother's helper job. She went to her employer and demanded her pay. When Gloria left again for Toronto, Joyce went along. Jenny and I went to the station to see her off. When we stepped down from the warm train it was raining. We were crying.

Three weeks later I was shocked one sunny afternoon to see Tom arriving home in a taxi.

"What . . . ?" I choked as he came through our kitchen door, his small suitcase in his hand.

"Oh, I'm just getting back from St. John. I've been down to see the Compensation Board. They paid the fare," he explained. "I went right through from Toronto."

"Is your leg worse?" I asked. "What are they going to do?"

"Yes. My leg is worse but they don't care. They won't do anything unless I consent to an operation." Tom spoke in a bitter tone. "I won't consent. They'd really cripple me."

"Well, how is it in Toronto?" I asked.

"Bad! It seems no use. I'm just too old. Perhaps I should try here again."

I felt a shiver in my id.

"Not yet," I told him. "Have you the fare back? You might as well try while the weather is good. We're making out all right. Billy still has his paper route. Johnny is salvaging pulp from the river and he works a bit for the neighbours. Did you see Joyce before you left?"

"Hell, yes. She's got a job. But she won't keep it. She spends money like water. She owes Don and me and Gloria. She'll be coming home."

Next day Tom left us again. For a while I was twice as lonesome as before, but I got over it. The wait continued.

In August Billy's twelfth birthday passed almost unnoticed. There was no money for a present.

Jenny was allowed to start school in September, although she was not yet six. I went with her the first day. She came home at noon with another little girl. She was disgusted with school. She hadn't, she complained, been taught to read or write – the class had just played and a boy had cried for his mother.

Johnny and Billy got a big kick out of Jenny's account of her first day at school. The boys seemed happy to be back themselves.

Jenny's birthday and mine fall in September. I was thirty-nine that fall, and Jenny six. Johnny bought me a small gift and said, "You're getting old, Mum – just as old as Jack Benny." Don sent a little extra money and two dollars especially for Jenny. She and I walked uptown and bought her her first book-bag. It was a big event in our lives.

In October Joyce came home. One rainy, thunder-and-lightning night we awoke to hear her banging on the door and yelling, "Let me in. It's me, Joyce. I'm back."

Jenny was delighted. Joyce had quit her job, just as Tom had predicted. She was going back to school.

"I had to come home," she told me half apologetically. "I was just too lonesome up there. I want to try here again, but I'll save my money just in case. I'll get part-time housework and babysitting."

Winter came with the word from Tom still disheartening. At Christmas, Johnny took some carefully saved money and went to the big city to see for himself how things were. Don was to pay Johnny's way back.

At New Year's, I received a note from Tom. It said his luck had taken an upward swing. He expected to be able to send for us in a week or two. The letter had been written Christmas Day. I read it a couple of times. It looked as if our waiting was almost over. I was afraid to believe it. Oh how I ached to be in Toronto and launched on a New Life.

A sudden sound of hissing steam broke my pensive mood. I turned my attention to the boiling tea kettle and the dull present.

I put a tea bag into one of my two unchipped cups and poured hot water over it. When it had steeped, I added canned milk. It tasted very good.

As I drank the tea my mood lightened. Appreciatively I drank a second cup and smoked more cigarettes.

At seven I made toast and spread the slices with a mixture of margarine and butter. When it was ready I called the kids: Joyce, Billy, and Jenny. They had asked me to get them up for school no matter how cold the house or how bad the weather. Well it was cold for sure but not stormy. Had the situation not changed with Tom, Johnny would have been back too, but to return now for just a few days of school would be a waste of money.

We ate standing around the stoves. As usual Jenny wanted to hear if it would be as cold in Toronto.

"I don't think so," I told her.

"Of course not. It'll be summer by the time we get there," said Billy.

"I don't think we'll ever get there," said Jenny unhappily.

We spoke then of the day's expectations, the bitter weather, and Johnny's good luck at having escaped our lousy life.

Joyce figured it would be quite mild in Toronto. Most of the houses were gas or oil heated. Right now Johnny would likely be asleep in a warm room. His days of shivering in the morning while he injected his insulin were over. A diabetic since the age of nine, he had never let that handicap impede him.

He would be staying at Uncle George's or Gloria Dubé's. George was my brother; he lived in Port Credit with his wife and ten children. Don was boarding there. Gloria had five children and lived in central Toronto. We thought Johnny would prefer to stay at her place where there was more action.

By 8:30 the three had left to walk to their schools one mile away uptown. I arranged my dirty dishes in a large pan and set it on the table. I knew my water pump would be frozen solid. It was the water source for two other families and sometimes we had to assist one another to get it working. This morning I intended to wait for help.

I planned to go back to bed for an hour or two but delayed. I felt caged and isolated. The radio wasn't working – it needed a new tube, I thought. We had no television set, no telephone, and I had not been able to get fresh reading material for over a month. I wanted adult company but it was too early to visit a neighbour.

As I pondered my plight, Harry Doiron knocked at my back door. He wanted a little hot water to finish priming the pump. I threw on a heavy coat and took out my full teakettle and a large empty pot. It took all my hot water to get the pump working. Chivalrously, Harry filled my utensils first. I hurried into the house, put that water on to heat and then rushed back to the pump with another pot and a pail. It was wise to get as much water as possible while the pump was thawed.

I had a few pieces of clothing I wanted to wash by hand in a small tub. Into the tub I poured a pailful of cold water and returned to the pump to refill the pail. I dropped the laundry into the tub to soak while the kettle heated. By the time I was finished lugging water, it was 9:30. I decided to visit the Lanes. They lived just down the hill from me – a short walk. They owned a large house. With most of their children married with homes of their own, the Lanes had converted a lower front room into a canteen. Sometimes I ran up a small bill there and paid it with money Don sent faithfully every week. That fact I deliberately neglected to tell the welfare officer for fear he'd decrease his niggardly help.

Before I could knock at the kitchen door, Grace Lane opened it and invited me in.

"I was watching for you," she said. "I'm glad you took a run down. I just had a phone call for you. I'd have gone up but I thought you'd be down for bread or something so I waited. Guess who called?"

"Lois?" I asked, following Grace into her kitchen. My sister and her husband, James Downe, lived on a farm ten miles south of Campbellton where I lived.

"Not Lois. Guess again. Here's a hint. From Toronto."

"Oh!" Hope rose in me. "Tom – he's sending for us – what did he say?"

"Not Tom, Don. Have a seat, Sophia. Want to take off your coat?"

"No," I said.

"Suit yourself," Grace said. "Don wants to talk to you. He said he'd call back in an hour. You might as well wait here, don't you think?"

"Yes. It's slippery out and cold. I don't care to make many

trips up and down the hill. How long ago did he call?" I asked.

"Oh, maybe twenty minutes. I checked the time. It was a bit after nine."

We looked toward the electric wall clock. It read 9:35.

"It won't be such a long wait," I said. "How are you feeling this morning?"

"Not too bad," she answered. "Ralph isn't too well – his legs. One is worse than the other. The doctor tells him to stay off them but he won't, you know."

Ralph Lane entered the room as his wife spoke. He said, "You know I can't keep off my feet, Grace. I have to help with the store. You're not well. I can't let you do everything. We can't expect the children to keep us and I don't want to live off the Government. Anyway the Government wouldn't give us enough to live decently. How are you, Mrs. Firth?"

"The same. I can't take much more of this lousy life. That shack gets colder by the winter, I'm positive," I told him.

The tinkling of a little bell announced a customer. Mr. Lane shuffled off to serve him. Grace and I talked on, discussing our lives and hopes, and other people. The time sped.

The Lane's phone was on a table in the living-room off the kitchen. At the first ring we hurried in. On the second ring Grace picked up the receiver. It was Don. I was almost trembling when Grace passed the phone to me.

"Hi, Don!" I cried excitedly into the mouthpiece. "How are you?"

"Oh, fine, Mum. How are you? That's what I want to know," I heard Don say.

"Oh, don't ask. We're freezing, starving, lonesome, mad and the stove exploded again this morning. You should see the mess I've got to clean up if I ever get warm enough. The snow is six feet deep and the forecast is for more."

"You want to come up?"

"Do I! Jenny asks every day when we're leaving. How's everyone?"

"Oh, fine I guess. I don't see Dad every day. He works sixteen miles from Uncle George's. Johnny is with him out at the house today. It needs a little cleaning, I think."

"Oh," I said. "Well I suppose we can't talk too long. Are you off today?"

"Yes. I go back tomorrow – but talk all you want. I'm paying."

"I know but I need money for other things. I've got to get some dry wood somewhere or we'll freeze to death. I tell you I feel like Sam Magee."

I heard Don's laugh.

"Are you all ready to come up?" he asked.

"I sure am," I answered. "What's to keep me here except lack of money?"

"I can send you the fare today, if you want."

"Do I want? Oh, Don! Send it, please."

"Well, how much do you need? I'll send it."

Quickly I calculated the four fares, a few taxis, and lunches, maybe a few sundries.

"Seventy dollars should do it. Wire it."

"I will then. But are you sure seventy's enough?"

"Oh, yes. Send it in time so I'll get it this afternoon and we'll leave tonight. Be sure now."

"I will. Don't worry. It'll be there. But are you sure you can make it tonight?"

"You'll see. Just get the money here. Here, talk to Mrs. Lane a minute."

I was, by now, too choked up to speak. I held the phone toward my friend.

She took it quietly from me.

"Oh, she's all right," she told Don. "No she isn't crying. Just too excited to talk that's all. Can you blame her? Oh, Mr. Lane is not too bad. Yes, Arthur is still working, thank God."

She motioned to me to be ready to take the receiver again. I nodded to show I was calming down.

"Yes, fine, Don. I sure hope so. Okay here she is." She passed me the receiver.

"What's the matter?" he asked.

"Oh, I'm just an old woman, Don," I said. "But I'm okay now. You'll be sure to wire the money? The kids are all at school but they'll be home for dinner."

"Okay, I'll let you go. I wanted to be sure you were all right.

We'll expect you then. Someone'll probably be at the station when you arrive. I don't know if Dad works tomorrow or not."

"Well, I'll worry about that when I get there. All right then, I'll start packing right away. So be seeing you soon – good-bye."

I hung up.

"We're leaving for Toronto tonight. Don is sending us the money," I told Mrs. Lane, excitedly.

"That's good," she said, leading the way back to her kitchen. "I hope you'll make out fine. It might be a little hard at first but there's only Jenny really young. I remember Ralph and me, when we moved here. Only George was old enough to get a part-time job. The rest were in school and Henry was five months old."

I was too exhilarated to go home and start packing. I stayed another full hour with Mr. and Mrs. Lane. We talked joyfully together. They seemed to share my elation. They assured me that the bill I owed them could wait a few weeks and insisted I take something home for dinner. I chose canned stew.

The house was still very cold when Joyce and Billy came hurrying in from school. Jenny had taken a lunch of peanut butter sandwiches and an apple.

"Here's a letter from Dad," Joyce cried as she entered. "I took the key and went down to the office. I had a feeling we'd get mail today. Hurry – what's he say?"

"It doesn't matter," I said, ripping the envelope. "We're leaving for Toronto tonight."

"What? Are you kidding, Mum?" cried Billy. "How?"

"Oh, Don's wiring the money. Hey, look kids! Dad sent a money order. That's funny. Oh, wait. He says – 'I don't have a house yet.' Why, he wrote this before the one we got Monday," I exclaimed.

"Well how much did he send? Let me see," Joyce said.

"Are we really going to Toronto tonight?" Billy asked.

"Yes, Billy, we're really going to Toronto tonight. At least some of us are, now I have this from Dad. But Don phoned and I talked to him and he's wiring some money. Well, I expect it'll get here soon enough, but just in case it doesn't I'll save this forty dollars! I wonder if Jenny could go free – but no, she's six."

"But she can pass for a lot younger, she's so small. Give me my fare and I'll take her. I'll tell them she's only four," Joyce urged.

"No. But maybe you and Billy could go. Ahh! Don'll get the money here. Let's plan for that."

"Well, then, I'm not going back to school this afternoon," Billy announced happily.

"We'll need our report cards," Joyce said. "You better go get yours."

"Aw – will you get it, Mum, when you go up town for the money? I want to leave on my paper route early."

"Wait a second," I said. I thought over the request. Joyce could pick up Johnny's books and papers when she got her own. I could phone Billy's and Jenny's schools so the items would be ready when I arrived to pick them up. A taxi to Billy's school, then to Jenny's, and on to the telegraph office wouldn't cost too much and would save a lot of time.

"Okay, Billy," I said. "I'll take these clothes" – motioning to the wet ones in the tub – "and a few others to the laundry. Our sheets should be done. We'll be taking them. We better do some planning together. Joyce, what have you got to do?"

"Just get my report card and things. Then I'll come home to help you pack. The train leaves about 8:30. We've got over seven hours. Billy, will you be done your paper route by then?"

"Oh, sure. That's why I want to get started early."

"But wait," I said. "I might not be here when you get home, Joyce. If I'm not, you go ahead and pack your things. Hey, somebody better run down to Mr. Lane's and see if he has a few boxes. And Billy, I think you'd better not bother coming home after you finish your papers. Go to Grandmother's. We'll meet you there. I'll be taking the trunks to the station as soon as we're packed – after I get Don's money. Pack all you can in the wooden box Dad gave you – it's like a suitcase. Do you want to have it checked through or will you keep it with you?"

"Oh, check it through. It's got about a hundred comic books in it already. I better give it a check – see if the lock's okay," Billy said. He had finished eating, and went off to pack.

"Well, I better get going," Joyce announced. "Mum, what time do you expect the money? Will they phone Mrs. Lane's or will you just go up to the station and ask about it?"

"It could come anytime now. Don's probably wired it already. They phoned before when Dad sent the hundred – they'll do it again I reckon. But I've got to go up town anyway, so I'll call in after I get the school papers and finish the laundry. When I get back home all I'll have to do is pack and go. After you come from school and do your packing leave a note if you go out anywhere, so I'll know where to reach you – in case."

"Well I want to help you to the station. So I'll be home around six anyway. I want to say goodbye to Irene and Gayle. Don't worry, I won't miss the train. I'll call at Gramma's on my way home. I think I'll leave now. Can you get the laundry and everything done by yourself? I'll help if you want me."

"No, I'll manage. You might as well go on to school, because I won't be ready for a bit. Then I'll have to wait on a taxi. You'll probably be coming back when I'm leaving."

"Okay, then I'll see you around suppertime. I wish I had fifty cents – for coffee since I won't be in school. But . . . "

"Oh, I'm glad you mentioned it. You go down to Mrs. Lane's and ask her for the lend of five dollars in change. She knows Don is sending some money but she doesn't know we got Dad's money order. Tell her about it and don't forget to ask for some boxes."

"Oh, good," Joyce cried joyfully. She left on the errand, running. Within a few minutes she was back with the money and some cardboard boxes. I gave her a dollar and she went cheerfully off on her business. Alone again in the still cold house, I was ecstatic.

We didn't have much packing, really, a few personal clothes, bed-clothes, dishes, and odds and ends that added a bit of pleasure to our dull lives.

We were ready to leave two hours before the train got in. It was early evening. Most of the stores were still open and sporting their Christmas trimmings. Joyce met a girlfriend just outside the station and went down the street with her. Billy decided to try selling extra papers. Jenny and I elected to make a final visit to my parents' home.

Dad was just home from the hospital. He was very chipper for his age, eighty, and convalescing after a leg amputation two months before. Mum was overjoyed to have him home again.

Sister Nell was there with her two children. Thankfully, I noted that everybody was well.

"Be sure and write to us now, Sophia," Dad urged, "and let us know how you all make out. Perhaps – you never can tell – we'll get up to see you next summer. Or if I'm not here, Dot can go."

"Oh no, Paul. If you're not here to go with me, you'll not catch me travelling away up there alone. I'm not my sister Martha you know," Mum asserted.

"Oh, Dot, why not go? How do other women live when their old men die? Do you intend to die too?"

"You never know, Paul. I might just go first to spite you – I'm not much younger'n you," Mother told him gruffly.

"Oh well, don't worry," I said. "You've both got many good years left. Who knows? Perhaps we'll all be back next year, though I don't expect such a calamity."

"Well, Dot, better see if there's any turkey left. Give them a lunch. Get the kettle on. What's the matter with you? We can't let them leave hungry. I suppose you won't even miss your old grandad, will you Jen?"

"Sure I will. But I'll write – as soon as I learn to write," piped Jenny.

Mother found turkey enough for all and then some. Jenny and her cousin Ken went to a nearby store for a fruitcake. We were lunching when Billy arrived.

"I didn't go to the station because it's too early," he said. "How are you, Gramps? Here's a paper. Do you miss your leg?"

"Of course I miss it – when I try to walk, you scamp. In fact, it hurts sometimes. So you're off to the big city, eh, boy? Well, I suppose you'll sell lots of papers up there – or shine shoes. Yes, that's a good job for you. When you get rich, will you send your old grandad a dollar or a good cigar?"

"Sure, Gramps, sure. I'll even buy you a car – when I get rich, and I'll hire a man to drive you around. You'll see," Billy promised, pretending all seriousness.

"No, I don't think I'll want to travel very far. A good cigar'll do, or a dozen. I've seen about all of this old world I care to. You're the one to travel now. Well, not too much yet. You're too young. Twelve are you – boy? But in five or six years.

That's the time to start. Do all your travelling before you marry and settle down, boy. That's the wise way," said Dad.

"Marry! Oh-ho, that'll be the day," laughed Billy. "You won't catch me getting married. Never."

"Oh, yes, that's what all boys say. But when they're men, they change their minds," said Dad. He pushed his cup away and reached for his pipe.

I looked at the clock. We had an hour to kill. Near the station, there was a restaurant where three of my friends worked every night. I hoped to see them once more before we left.

"Well, I guess we'd better be going. I want to say goodbye to Hilda and them," I announced. "Bill, will you run over to the store and call a taxi? I'd walk up, but I'm afraid I'll freeze. Gosh, It's cold out."

"I reckon it'll be colder," Dad told us. "The radio said 20° below for tonight."

"Well, it feels like 50° below now. It's a good time to be leaving this old town. But it's going to seem kind of strange to spend the rest of the winter with hardly any snow. Strange, yeah, but now I think about it – kind of fun. I can't wait to get there."

Beep—beep! went a car horn outside. "Here's the taxi," Jenny yelled. "Come on, Mum. We've got to go. 'Bye Gramps, 'bye Gram, 'bye Aunt Nell and Grace and Ken. 'Bye everybody. Let's go."

In a happy mood, we left. I saw my friends at the restaurant. Jen and Bill ordered french fries. Joyce came in just as we were ready to go. We all walked over to the station together. The snow was crisp and crunchy under our heavy overshoes. Overhead the stars and moon shone brightly in a clear sky. In my younger days, I would have enjoyed a two or three mile walk on such a beautiful, calm, winter night. Now, I was glad to enter a warm railroad coach, cozy down in a soft seat with a good book and let myself be hauled over the miles.

2

About 3:30 in the afternoon of the next day, we arrived in Toronto. At least two of us, Jenny and I, were mighty glad to be done with that journey. Eight hundred miles is no little run.

We recognized no one in the waiting crowd milling around as we stepped down. Joyce was familiar with the layout of Union Station. She directed me to a telephone. I dropped in the required coin and dialed my brother's number in Port Credit. It was answered before the second ring.

"Hello," I said. "Lee, this is Sophia. We made it. Is Don there?"

"Yes, he's here. He was just going to work. Here, Don," I heard her say. "It's your mother down at Union Station."

"Mum, so you made it okay? Isn't Dad there? He went to meet you," Don informed me.

"No. I don't see . . . " I said and broke off as Jenny screamed, "Here he is. Here's Daddy."

"Tom found us, Don. Goodbye," I shouted and hung up the phone.

"Hello," said Tom and I simultaneously. Then Tom went on, "You weren't supposed to come so soon. The house isn't quite ready."

"We were pretty cold," I said, piqued. Tom seemed unnecessarily grumpy. "What do you mean, not ready?"

"The stove isn't working yet. We need more furniture. C'mon. Gimme the tickets."

"You mean we've got to go somewhere else? That's okay. There's George's and Gloria's. How long?" I was rummaging in my purse as I spoke.

"Oh, we can stay there now, but Schmidt is still fixing a few things. Johnny's with him."

"So as long as it's fit for us to stay in, what's all the crabbing for? It can't be any worse than that shack in Campbellton," I told him.

"Oh, c'mon! How much luggage you got? Gimme the tickets. You got any money left? This way – the taxis are out here." Tom seemed too impatient. We followed him to the taxi stand.

"Now," he said, "you can all go on ahead. I'll give the driver the address. It's 79 Huron Street. Johnny and Schmidt are there. Just knock and they'll let you in. I'll get the luggage if it's in and come later. Christ – I've got to get to work. I'm late now."

We hurried into the waiting cab. Tom gave instructions to the driver and hurried away as we drove off.

The house Tom had rented was on a one-way street. The driver did not take care to let us off at the right number. I guess he wanted to be rid of us as soon as possible. We weren't the best dressed or most decorous of passengers. Yet he seemed to value our money.

Jenny spotted the house while I was still appraising the city, as much of it as I could see. As we moved to cross the street I said to myself, "Toronto's not so hot – not so hot at all."

Johnny opened the door to us.

"Well, hello! C'mon in. There's me and Mr. Schmidt, the owner, here," he said. Grabbing Jenny around the waist, he lifted her shoulder high. "And how is my little sister? Are you glad to be in Toronto? Glad to see big brother Johnny again?" To his rapid questions, Jenny answered, "Yes, yes." Struggling to get loose, she cried, "Put me down Johnny, I wanta see."

Johnny lowered her to the floor and released her.

"Is Dad waiting for the baggage?" he asked me. "Did you get my report card and my books?"

"Yes, sure, everything we need I brought," I said. We moved behind Jenny and Billy through a narrow dimly-lit hall into a spacious kitchen.

"Mum, this is Mr. Schmidt. Mr. Schmidt, this is my mother, and Joyce and Billy, and the little one is Jenny," said Johnny. To us, he said, "The bathroom's upstairs to your right. Don't go in the other rooms. There's a family renting, but they're moving soon."

Suddenly I understood why Tom was fretting like a wet hen. Well, he should have written a slightly longer letter and perhaps I'd have waited a week or two. Too late. We'd come and we'd have to crowd up a bit. That wouldn't be too hard.

Schmidt had stopped work at the sink and turned to us with a wrench in his hand, saying, "Hello. I'll soon have this all clear and ready to use. Nobody's been living in this part of the house. Your husband told me he'd send for you next week."

"Oh, well. He didn't tell me that, or anything much, except that he had a job and a house. Then, our son called me, said he could send the money right away and so I came as soon as I could. I knew we could stay with relatives and friends if necessary," I said.

"Oh, I have empty rooms on the other side," said Mr. Schmidt. "Your two boys could sleep there for a while, then move back here. I'll give them a key."

While we were discussing where everybody would sleep Tom arrived with the luggage. Johnny went out to help him carry in the trunk, suitcases and cartons.

When that was done, Tom wanted to know how much money I had left.

"Fifteen dollars," I said.

"Is that all?" he grumbled. "Didn't you get the money order?"

"Yes," I answered.

"Well, you must have had over a hundred. What did you do with it?"

"So you think I didn't owe any? There's four of our kids still going to school, remember?" I snarled.

"By Gawd! You'd better learn to look after it up here, or we'll soon be on the roads. It don't grow on trees here either," he warned. Suddenly, he seemed to become aware that a stranger could hear us. Abruptly, he changed his tone and the subject.

"Johnny can get sandwiches at a restaurant on Spadina. He knows where. I've got to go to work, but I'll be back about 11:30. Don't, for Christ's sake, let them kids run wild. It's a big city."

Tom gave Johnny a few dollars, instructed him to get sandwiches and coffee, and turned to go. At the door, he paused and said, "Here's the key. I'll have to get more made. And keep the doors locked. You don't know who might come in. This isn't New Brunswick."

When he was gone, I seethed with suppressed anger for a few moments, but then I reminded myself that he was gruff and bossy because he'd had a hard year and still had a lot of worries, more even than I and I'd had a fair share. Things would improve and life would become smoother, quieter.

Johnny went out and returned in a few minutes with ham sandwiches, buttered cinnamon buns and coffee. We ate gladly.

Finished, Billy asked if he could go out to look over the neighbourhood. "Sure," I told him. "But don't go far. If you do get lost, ask a policeman for directions. There's probably lots of them around."

Joyce asked if she could take Jenny for a walk.

"Of course, but don't rush her around too fast or too far. She'll get too excited. She must be tired because she didn't sleep much on the train. Here's a dollar so you can eat if you get hungry but don't tell Dad. I can't stand his ranting."

Jenny wanted to take off her heavy overshoes to go walking. I let her. The sidewalks were bare.

I left Schmidt and Johnny to finish their work in the kitchen and found a bed to flop on. Boy, did I sleep.

Tom arrived home about 11:30. He found us sitting around the kitchen listening to the radio and discussing our urban centre. Schmidt had gone and we couldn't hear the family upstairs: husband, wife and one child.

The kids had been happily exploring while I rested. Each was delighted with a different aspect of his new environment. For Joyce, it was the Art Gallery, the City Hall and the many stores.

Jenny cheered for the parks. "Slides an' everything," she exclaimed gleefully. "They're just great. But I want to see the mountains. Where are the Rockies?"

"Oh, there are no mountains in this place, honey," we laughed.

"Hills further out, but the Rockies are farther west."

"Ahh," she muttered in disappointment, then cheered up – "Well, maybe we'll go west sometime."

"I'm tired of mountains," Billy said. "They're okay to go picking nuts or hunting rabbits in the fall. But they're hard to climb. Here they've got lots of skating rinks and swimming pools. That's for me."

"Mountains may be hard to climb up, but they're sure great for skiing down. I'm gonna miss that ole ridge back home, you know. But wait'll you see our subway – and the buses and streetcars. You can go miles and miles for almost nothing," said Johnny.

"Is everybody in?" Tom queried as he joined the group. "I was sure half of them would be out gallivanting in the streets. They can't do that here. It's too dangerous. It isn't Campbellton with 10,000 people. This is the largest city in Canada. Out after ten o'clock and they'll be picked up, except maybe Joyce."

"What ages?" I asked.

"Right up to sixteen," Tom said. "I think."

"Humph – just like Campbellton," I said. "Does that curfew work any better here than there?"

"Well, I don't think they enforce it too good. But it'd be just our luck for Johnny or Billy to get caught. Where'd we get the money for a fine?"

"Oh, hell. Stop worrying. They're not gonna run these wild streets at night. But isn't it all right to visit friends at night and come home?" I said.

"Yuh. I guess so. But I tell you, it's too dangerous to be out at night."

"So. It isn't the law you're worrying about. It's the kids' safety. Why didn't you say so? Don is eighteen years old and so far you've never had to go to court with one or pay a fine for one. The only time the police brought one home was when I asked them to hunt up Billy after he first started school and went around hunting up pieces of copper and beer bottles to sell. Do you think they'll be any worse here?"

"They don't have to be worse to get into trouble and cost money we haven't got. They better behave or I'm going."

He'd have gone on laying down the law if George and Lee hadn't arrived to welcome me to their vaunted city. Don was with them.

They didn't intend to stay long so they didn't bother removing coats or hats. They'd have left their shoes at the door and walked in in sock feet but I said, "Don't be silly. You'll ruin your socks. They've been working here all day, and it's pretty dirty."

"Oh you'll get it clean in time," Lee said.

George produced a bottle of whiskey, or rum, or something. The bottle was unfamiliar to me.

"Well, here we are all together again. So let's drink a toast to the new year although it's almost an old year already, and to a better life," said George.

I went to the trunk to search for glasses or cups, whatever came to hand first. Tom offered chairs. Don and Johnny stood by the sink counter. The rest of us were able to sit.

"So, how do you like our city at first glance? You've never seen it before, have you Sophia? You'll find it a big change after the country," said George.

He hasn't changed, I thought. He's still convinced his kind of life is better'n ours.

"We didn't live in the country, George – it was the suburbs," I told him, calmly.

"Suburbs," he laughed. "The whole so-called town was country. What did they have there? Hardly even one taxi stand and that with about six cars when I was down a couple of years ago. Wait'll you see what we've got. Subway, factories."

"Yuh, and polluted air," I scorned.

"They're at it again," Lee cried to Tom. "Let's open that bottle and start toasting before it goes too far."

"I knew it," Tom growled. "Not here twenty-four hours and ready to fight."

"Oh, stow it, Dad," Don said. "It's not much of a person who won't stand up for his hometown. I kind of liked old Campbellton myself."

"Me, too," Johnny sided with him. "It might be small and all that, poor, no work, and things, but there's some great folks living there. Someday, I'll go back – at least to visit my friends."

"Looks like I'm beat," conceded George. "Okay, okay! But you'll see. These Maritimers are pretty hard-headed – and loyal, but some of them are pretty bright. They'll admit the truth eventually."

"I'll admit the truth anytime," I said. "That is as long as it's not incriminating – but I'll wait awhile before I'll concede that Toronto is better than Campbellton. Quite a little while."

"Let it drop, eh?" pleaded Lee. "I want to hear about the rest of the relatives. How are your father and mother? How did he take the loss of his leg?"

"Fine. Both are fine. That operation didn't seem to faze him a bit. Perhaps old soldiers never do die. They either fade away or the doctors kill them piece by piece."

The men laughed at that as I had expected, but Lee wasn't amused. I could see she considered me hopeless. I'd never, ever fit into her group of friends.

It didn't take long to bring her up-to-date on our few New Brunswick relatives, since their lives seemed to remain pretty static, year in and year out, and she saw them in person every summer.

"So, everybody had a fair Christmas. Nell's boyfriend is trying to get up enough money to come up here to look for work, too," I finished that subject.

"I'd send him the money if I thought he could make it," Lee told us, glancing surreptitiously at George. "But that might only put them further in debt. Maybe they're better off on welfare."

I could have told her of the horrors of welfare in New Brunswick and Tom must have feared I was about to. He stood up abruptly.

"Did Schmidt get the taps fixed?" Tom asked.

Everybody glanced at the sink. Tom set his empty glass on the table, rose, and walked over.

"We've got lots of hot water," he said, "a forty gallon tank." He turned on the left tap. "Watch how quick it gets hot."

We watched.

I was about to say that the promise of plenty of hot, running water was one attraction Toronto had for me after lugging freezing water from an outdoor pump to heat on a stove for washing, bathing and scrubbing. I didn't get a chance.

"Now the cold," Tom said, "and you adjust both to the temperature you want and there . . . . "

Splwoosh! A warm geyser shot upward and down as the spout leapt its moorings and, to my dismay, I received an unwanted, unexpected shower over my head.

"Yiiii," I screamed, jumping up and grabbing frantically for a towel or something to wipe my eyes with.

"Here, Mum," choked Johnny. He passed me a towel.

"Thanks," I muttered. Everybody was helpless with laughter except Tom who was getting wet himself as he struggled to shut off the water. For a second he forgot which way to turn the taps.

"So, he didn't get it fixed," he said.

"Mop! Mop!" I cried, recalling as I spoke that we had no mop. I used the towel to dry the sink counter and the chair and floor.

"Well, George! Lee! Tom! Anybody! tell me more about your glorious Toronto and its fine houses," I challenged.

"So – you weren't expected yet," Tom coldly informed me. "But, no, you couldn't wait."

"No, I couldn't. But if you knew the spout was loose, you could have been more careful. At least you could have warned a person."

"Couldn't you get a better house, Tom?" Lee asked, shocked.

"Not in this section, furnished, for my price," Tom told her.

"But why this section?"

"For the schools. Right here we're in the heart of education in Canada," Tom bragged.

"That's what we came to Toronto for, so the kids could get a better education. We could have survived down there, but we couldn't afford to send them through high school. When Don had to quit last year, we decided it was time to move on," I told her.

"When they are educated – or on their own, Tom and I might even go back," I said.

"Go back!" Lee was horrified. "But you'll still need money – even if your kids are finished school. What'll you live on down there?"

"Oh, Lee, you don't understand. Tom can earn a living down there for two or three of us. There is lots of work with poverty wages. We were doing fine until his accident. Even after, even though the Compensation Board short-changed him; until he discovered his boss's double-cross. Even then, he could have done all right if he'd kept his mouth shut about politics and graft and crooked deals. We're here for our kids' sake, not ours." With that I left the room to change my sweater.

"What's this about a double-cross?" George directed the

question to Tom as I returned to the kitchen.

"Oh, that's just her crazy way of looking at things," Tom said. He turned to give me the evil eye which meant, "Don't publish my business or so help me I'll hit you so hard you'll hear your great-grandmother sneeze in Ireland."

"There was no double-cross. He just refused to pay the wage he promised," said Tom.

"Oh-ho! Well, I'd say that was a double-cross," said George. "But wasn't there more to it than that?" I'm sure he'd seen Tom's warning glance at me as I rejoined the group. The set line of my husband's jaw was a sign to any experienced observer that his quitting a boss to whom he'd given the better part of fourteen years was a sore point with him.

Tom was quiet a moment. I guessed he was debating whether to elaborate or let them hear it some other time from me, or the kids who knew it too.

We waited.

At last, he opened up.

"Well, the thing was," he said, "I had been offered a good job scaling before Powell asked me to work for him again. The scaling job was high pay plus expenses and likely to be permanent. At least it would have lasted long enough for me to save some money to come up decently. But when Powell came to me, I didn't know which to take. He was a sort of friend, had done little things for me as I had for him – and I knew he couldn't get another skilled man right away, so finally I said I'd do the job if he raised my pay twenty-five cents an hour. He said he would but the s.o.b. didn't."

"Well, if he didn't, why did you work at all?" asked Lee.

"Oh!" I exclaimed in exasperation. "Down there many men still consider a verbal agreement binding, you see. Tom had to wait two weeks for a pay and only then did he find out Powell hadn't kept the agreement. By then, the other job had been filled. The worst thing was Powell had known about the other offer. So, a rank double-cross, I say, and it hurt Tom pretty bad."

I didn't expect Lee or George to realize just how bad that broken promise and lost opportunity had hurt Tom, and I didn't want sympathy. Tom, I could see, felt bad even at the recollection.

"But that's over," I smiled. "He hurt us, yes – and others too, people you don't know, whom we'd been helping. But he didn't break us, did he, Tom? Did he, boys?"

"Not by a long shot," I heard at least two of our boys say and I felt pride for them. I'm sure Tom did too.

"Here's to the new year, once again," he said cheerily.

3

We had arrived on a Thursday. We didn't bother about school until Monday. Instead, we used the next three days to explore our neighbourhood and sort of get acclimatized. Jenny was the only one who couldn't travel around by herself but Joyce took great pleasure in showing her many interesting things within walking distance that cost very little or no money to see.

Monday – Joyce and Johnny took their report cards and transfer papers and set out to find their schools. They had no trouble at all.

Billy, Jenny and I decided to go to the school at the southern end of our street. I hoped they'd both be enrolled there. But no, we were just outside the zone. Billy was assigned to Lansdowne and Jenny to Orde, public elementary schools.

Once they were enrolled and attending school regularly, life began to take on a somewhat familiar pattern. Except for a few minor family squabbles that arose out of our different interests and opinions, we spent two pleasant weeks before anything deeply upsetting happened.

Then, one bright and sunny day, Jenny was brought home from school early in the forenoon with a note. It said, "Dear Mrs. Firth . . . pediculosis." That's all I remember of it.

Tom was home.

"What's that letter say? What's it about? Give it here!" he shouted.

I gave him the letter.

"I don't know what the matter is. Pediculosis. What kind of a disease is that?" I said, just slightly disturbed.

"Lice! You ignorant clown. She's got lice. You let her get lice!" Tom roared, throwing the offensive letter on the table in disgust.

"Let her? What's the matter with you? How could I stop her? But anyway, there's no need to scream and howl. We can get rid of them," I said.

"Well, you better get at it," Tom said, stomping out of the room. "Lousy," I heard him mutter. "Now it starts."

Luckily, I had learned quite a bit about lice when I was fifteen and got lousy myself – so I wasn't floored. I told Jenny not to worry, lots and lots of people of all ages get pediculosis, left her sitting in a chair pouting and went to the drug store for blue ointment. My parents swore by that and for some reason I believed my father had used it in his lumbering and soldiering days.

I was working on Jenny's hair when a public health nurse arrived.

I didn't find her attitude befitting a person hired to help. I felt she was holding me responsible for letting Jenny get lice, and that she considered me a low-life Maritimer who had no business bringing lice to Toronto, and into their beautiful school. Tom re-entered the room and began disclaiming any responsibility for this heinous crime.

"They've just come up from New Brunswick," he opened.

"Don't try to say she got them in New Brunswick," I cried. "She's been up here over two weeks and if she's had them that long the school must be blind as well as me. Maybe the whole school is lousy." I stopped talking. The remembrance of my own lousy days made my head itch and I started to scratch.

I suppose it was impolite to say the least. The nurse didn't stay long. She left me a bottle of white poison with instructions on the proper, safe use.

For three days Johnny, Joyce and I worked on poor Jenny's

hair. We rubbed in gobs and gobs of ointment, combed, shampooed, combed, and picked out the tiny white nits with our nails; then, repeated.

Eventually, Jenny rebelled. She decided to go back to school. She was sent home. The nurse could still see the eggs. We attacked again. She returned to school. She was sent home again.

We got fed up, all except Tom. "Oh," he insisted, "she must still be lousy or they wouldn't send her home."

"Well, why don't you give a hand?" I challenged.

"No, no!" Jenny screamed. "Not Dad. He's too rough."

"Okay," I said. "One more time. And I'll take you back and let her show me the nits. Else you can quit school."

The next day as Jenny and I arrived at old Orde, I discovered the nurse wouldn't be in until the next day.

"Well," I said, "I'd like to leave her a note to the effect that if Jenny is sent home tomorrow, I'm bringing her back so someone can show me the nits. The nurse better be sure it isn't natural white flecks she sees in her hair – and not nits."

"I'll tell her, Mrs. Firth," said the secretary, trying to be polite but firm.

Jenny was re-admitted the next day. For a week, I waited anxiously. I didn't know where she'd gotten the little parasites. It might have been on the train. As far as I knew, it could have been at school, and if so, how could I be sure she'd not get them again soon? Not one of the rest of us had been infected so we concluded she hadn't had them long. Finally, I began to relax.

The family upstairs moved out and Don moved in. I was glad to have my family together again.

Tom was right. It had started – trouble. Children trouble. Of course, it wasn't as if we weren't used to children trouble. Don hadn't set a perfect example, but so far their scrapes and scraps had seemed to take place at longer intervals.

Johnny was the next to cause us grief. He picked up some virus and his illness was complicated by his diabetes. He had to be hospitalized until he got the old ailment under control. After the crisis had passed, he remained in hospital for two more weeks and went to school from there. With him taken care of, I had more time for the others – and they kept me busy.

Billy came home one day to announce he was quitting school. He was fed up, he said, with that lousy jail.

"What's the trouble?" I asked gently.

"Well, they're bugging me to get gym shoes," he told me angrily, "and I'm not."

"But Billy, gym shoes don't cost too much," I said.

"What happened to your gym shoes?" Tom yelled.

"My gym shoes got stole," Billy yelled back. "That's what happened."

"Why don't you look after your stuff?" another yell. "What in hell is the matter with you? Buy yourself a pair. You found a job."

"I'm not buying a pair. I won't buy a pair. I'm quitting. I've already quit. I'm not going back." More yelling.

"Oh, stop yelling," I growled. "I've got a job with Gloria Dubé. I'll get the gym shoes. She'll lend me the money."

"I've gotta pay for a couple of books too," Billy said.

"Books! Why books?" I asked.

"They got stolen too," he said.

"God damn!" Tom bellowed. "You can't look after your books – you'll pay for them yourself."

"Oh, Billy," I wailed, "why don't you take better care of your stuff?"

"Because I've got no locker," he complained. "I've gotta share with another guy. And I think he hides my things."

"What?" demanded Tom. "You mean they didn't give you your own locker? Then, I'm going to that cocksucking school. They'll get no money out of me until they give you your own locker."

"But, Dad . . . " Billy began.

"Never mind. They are supposed to give you a private locker. If they can't that's their hard luck. I'll put a stop to this – this money-grabbing racket."

"Oh," yelled Billy, "you – you." he stomped off to his room.

The next day Tom went to the school nice and early. I'd have loved to go too, because I don't believe he was as wicked there as he was at home. Still, I've heard him telling other haughty people where to head in. Anyway, Billy complained no more. The school even helped him get gym shoes and a few other things at no direct cost to us.

I started work in a small laundry and dry-cleaning shop. The manager who knew Gloria phoned her at work one day and asked her if she knew of a woman looking for that type of work. She persuaded the man to hire me.

I found a neighbour nearby who was English and was willing to mind Jenny when none of us were home to supervise her after school and Saturdays. Her name was Olga Stanley. She had three children: Andy, the same age as Johnny, Mabel, seven, and Ruth, three. Jenny liked the family. I had few worries about Jenny when I was away. I knew she had a good babysitter and nice playmates.

In March, Joyce celebrated her seventeenth birthday. She quit school and came to work at the laundry shop. She could not take school any more, day after dull day, she explained. I regretted her decision to quit but hoped she'd start night school as Don was planning to do.

A couple of weeks later, to my dismay, Joyce announced she was going to be a hippie.

I had heard the word "hippie" before. Vaguely I understood they were mainly young people in search of a new and better life-style. I thought they were trying to survive without following the ancient method of work and trade. They seemed to have a lot of bad criticism of our social and economic system. They went around hungry and dirty and slept wherever they could lay their stubborn heads.

At the picture of Joyce living like that I felt a cold lump form in my chest.

Tom was home when Joyce told us of her plans.

He roared and cursed. That didn't sway Joyce.

Next payday she left in the evening. Tom's final words were, "And don't come back!"

I overruled him. "Come back as soon as you're ready and if you get in a situation where you need help, please, please let us know."

Next morning she was back early. I was the only one up. "I had to come home to take a bath. I can't stand being dirty," she laughed.

"You're not going to be a half-hippie," I told her. "You can take a bath this time but from now on you'll have to find another bathtub – or go dirty like your idols."

Joyce had cleaned up and was eating breakfast when Tom got up.

"You're not coming here to eat every day, you crazy hippie," he roared.

"Oh shut up, Tom," I roared in turn. "Remember the Dirty Thirties? Did your Dad throw you out when you crawled home after bumming trips?"

"I wasn't a bum and I didn't crawl," he roared.

"Well then, how do you know so much about hoboes? I remember some of your stories! Or were they lies?" I asked.

"Well, perhaps I was a hobo some. But that was different. There was a depression." Tom wasn't roaring anymore.

"C'mon Tom. 'Oh, what a tangled web we weave . . . '" I quoted.

Johnny came into the kitchen. "You better get your stories straight, Dad," he said smiling.

"Oh, go to hell," said Tom, "You're all out to take me for all you can get." He started out of the room.

"You're resisting pretty good," I called to his departing back.

All day Joyce roamed the city as she had the night before. At suppertime she came home. Tom had gone to work.

"I'm not going to be a hippie," she said. I was pretty relieved.

"Well, what happened? What was it like?" Johnny asked her.

"It certainly wasn't much," she said. "Mostly we walked around. When we got tired, we went in for coffee."

"Who's we?" I asked.

"Oh, a couple of girlfriends and a guy."

"I bet you paid for everything," I said.

"Well, yes. They didn't ask me, though. I offered."

"Yes, and that was fine. But what had they to offer?"

"Oh, Mum. Why have you got that attitude? They don't believe in work," she told me fiercely, defensively.

"No, but they need things that only work can produce, don't they? Joyce, face facts. Isn't most of our food produced by someone's hard work? and doesn't it take work to get it here to the city?"

"Oh, I guess you're right," she said. "But some people can't work. They have too many hang-ups and can't stand to be tied down."

"So let them have. But don't admire them for running down the people who feed and clothe them."

"I don't. And I don't want to talk about it anymore. I'm glad I tried it though. I didn't do anything – well I wasn't. . . " She was having trouble expressing herself. In the end she cried, "I didn't try drugs or sex yet. So I don't feel any different."

Another day Bill's old habit of throwing stones up the mountain or into the river came back. Unthinking, he picked up a pebble and tossed it away. It broke the glass in a neighbour's door. The people, Finnish, came over. The whole family came over. Only the fourteen-year-old could speak English. She pointed at Billy. He'd already told me. I tried to assure her we'd have it fixed. Silently, I thanked God and Gloria for my job. Tom came home. He had to be told. There was hell to pay. Tom took the broken door in its aluminum frame to a glazier's. It cost six dollars to fix. A few days later, another boy and Billy were wrestling on their verandah. Billy got pushed against the same door window. It broke. Repeat scene. Some of us wanted Tom to pay just half. The other culprit had disappeared. Tom shelled out. He said he couldn't take any more; as soon as school closed, he was shipping us back to New Brunswick. I merely said, "Like hell."

I had contacted a doctor and was getting tranquilizers without trouble. They were really good and did I need them! After the window trouble, I hoped for smooth sailing. I was disappointed.

One day, Billy's school called. Could I go to see them soon? Sure I could. Well, I was told they couldn't understand Billy. He was above average but he wasn't adjusting. Sometimes, he seemed to be looking right through the teachers. They wondered if Toronto had stunned him. I laughed.

"He's not stunned," I said, "he's mad. Make some of those bullies leave him alone. Two or three at a time fight him. They call him 'tramp'. They won't let him join their games. Make them leave him alone. He's doing fine away from school. He has a job and his boss seems to like him."

"He told us he didn't know who was boss in his family. Then, he said he guessed it was his mother," the counsellor said.

"Oh, that's because I can handle words better and win most of the arguments. But on the very serious problems, Tom and I usually agree and we don't want Billy pushed around or pushed to make good grades. He'll be okay if you make his schoolmates respect his rights." They must have cracked down on the other students. Billy changed subtly, became more cheerful and playful.

One lonely May evening I sat on the verandah railing and lazily watched Jenny happily skipping rope with four other children in the lane.

The strip of dusty, hard, hot, gray cement on which the children played was a sad change from the large, gently sloping, grassy field where Jenny and her other friends could sprawl in happy abandon between games.

Would Jenny ever enjoy that old playground again, I wondered, or would it be covered with buildings soon?

Familiar voices broke on my ears. I glanced away from the laughing children.

Johnny and Owen Clark were coming down the street, arguing fiercely. Owen was carrying a large transistor radio. As usual he had the volume too loud to suit me. Johnny turned in our gate. "See you around, Owen," he said.

"Yuh, sure," Owen answered. He went on a little farther.

Johnny bounded up our steps. "Hi, Maw."

"Hi," I answered. "What were you and Owen debating?" Johnny perched on the broad window sill to my right.

"Oh, nothing much. Owen's got some stupid ideas. Up at Yorkville last night he stole a policeman's helmet and his belt and billy club. Well I didn't see him take them but I saw him with them. He thinks that's a big thing. I tried to make him see this country'd be in a bad mess without police but for some reason he thinks the police make the trouble, not the crazy kids. I think he'd have really liked to see those officers badly beaten or killed." As the words registered I felt a flicker of alarm. I looked sharply at my son.

Yorkville! I had heard the name along with group names: hippies, greasers, long-hairs, motorcycle gangs. From the small talk of the neighbours I knew they considered it a serious trouble spot, a place where intractable kids hung out. The night before, as all of us were well aware, there had been some trouble there. Police sent in to quell a riot had been viciously attacked, their lives endangered. I had not dreamed a child of mine had been near the place.

"Oh Johnny," I exclaimed, "were you at that riot last night? Good heavens! I thought you and Owen went to a show."

"Well we started out for the show but Owen wanted to go to Yorkville. I'd never been there so I said okay. That was about 9:30. We wanted to see if anything was happening."

"You just watched, I hope. You didn't get in a fight."

"No, I didn't fight. Well I had nothing to fight about. I thought for a while I might love to help the police, when they were cornered on top of their cruiser with a guy in handcuffs, but just as I was making up my mind what to do more police got there so I didn't get in it."

"How did Owen get the policeman's gear? Did he join the attack?"

"I don't know. I saw him with the things. So many were grabbing at the police that I can't say who got the stuff. You see, they arrested a guy and started to drive away but the crowd was blocking the street so they stopped. Then some stupid maniacs began banging on the cruiser trying to break the windows, perhaps to get the prisoner. Then the police got out and got him on the roof of the car. They wouldn't use their guns. They just tried to fend off the blows without really hurting anyone and hang on to their prisoner. He was handcuffed to one policeman. But two men against that crowd were almost helpless. Probably it would have been worse only the crowd was packed so tight it was damn hard to move. After the extra police came the crowd broke up some and I moved away. Owen and I had got separated but when the crowd began to disperse we got together again. He showed me the stuff."

"Johnny, what did Owen do with those things? His father won't let him keep them. He wouldn't even know he was up in Yorkville."

Johnny laughed. "Oh, Mr. Clark knows all right. He came and got us about two o'clock. When everything seemed over we started home but the subway was closed and no streetcars were coming. I didn't know the way. Oh, I could have found out, it isn't far I know now. Anyway Owen had a dime left so he called his father. When he came, Owen had got rid of the stuff. A friend is keeping the police belt and the rest he gave away, I think. Boy, Mr. Clark was mad. He told Owen, 'Get in that car and shut up.' And to me, 'You too,' so I got in. I wasn't scared, of course, but Owen was. He had been warned not to go there at all. Well Mr. Clark growled all the way home. He said to me, 'Your mother shouldn't allow you out this late.' He didn't know you didn't know I had gone there and Dad's at work so you had to be blamed. I didn't want to make him any madder for Owen's sake so I politely agreed with all he said. Owen got slapped around some anyway in the house after they got home."

"I don't doubt that but it'll probably just make Owen sneakier next time."

"He's pretty sneaky now. He's scared of his father but he doesn't obey very good. He had orders to stay clear of Yorkville. I didn't."

Johnny stood up, a sign he was bored. "Well, what's there to eat? I'm pretty hungry."

"Some sort of goulash with steak. Dish yourself up some. I'm gonna rest here awhile. And Tom brought in an apple pie. It's in the fridge."

Johnny went into the house. I sat on, pondering the problems of parenthood.

4

In June our three kids who had stayed in school were promoted to higher grades. When school closed Johnny began to look for a job that would last all summer.

Gloria's young brother, Harold Leblanc, came up hoping to find a summer job also. He was a few years older than Johnny and a diabetic. The two boys had been friends for years.

Gloria's husband Bob got both of them jobs at the gravel pit where he worked, let them both board at his house and gave them drives to and from work with him.

At the end of June, Tom got word from the New Brunswick Workmen's Compensation Board to report to the hospital. Tom did. He decided he might as well have an operation on his leg. The doctors would take a bone from his hip and put it in his heel, Tom explained to me. He came through the operation fine.

All went well while he was in hospital but compensation cheques didn't start coming. Even after he was home a week there was no sign of a cheque.

Rent got behind. Our grocery bill went up. Tom began to growl. The landlord began to worry. He'd been suckered before. He talked to Tom. Tom talked to me. Something was wrong, he said.

He took a few of our scarce dollars and wired the NBCB. The answer came back that they hadn't received the doctor's report. Tom couldn't believe it. He called the doctor. The report had gotten stuck away in a drawer and been forgotten.

A few more days of waiting, then the first cheque arrived. Schmidt and others developed a more respectful attitude toward us. I smiled to myself.

One warm summer evening Jenny and I were visiting Mrs. Stanley. Olga and I sat on an old couch by the side of the house and talked while we watched Jenny, Ruth and Mabel play. We were in the front yard. From there we had a better view of the street than my front yard gave. A few cars and people went slowly by as we sat there.

Suddenly, Mrs. Stanley nudged my arm.

"Look there, Sophia, coming up the street. See that man and woman with two children? They're people Bill and I know. I bet they're looking for a place to sleep. They're on welfare. They have eight children and I hear they're going to lose those two. They can't look after them. Don't let on I told you, if they stop to talk."

They stopped to talk.

"Hello, Olga," the woman said. "I see you're taking it easy. I wish I could."

"Hello yourself, Jane," Olga replied. "How are you Harry? This is my friend Sophia Firth. They live just across the street. Sophia, that's Jane and Harry Blane. The boy is Dick and the little girl is Mary. Have you time to visit awhile Jane?"

Jane and Harry looked at each other. The children were trying to loosen their parents' grips on their little hands. The boy was five, the girl three.

"Well, we've no place else to go," Harry said. "We're just walking. Is Bill in?"

"Yes. He was tuning his guitar when I came out. Come. I'll take you in. Coming Sophia?"

"No. I'll stay here. It's too hot in there. That's why we came out. Maybe Mrs. Blane would like to sit here awhile."

"The kids are thirsty. I'll come out after," the woman said.

Olga escorted the newcomers into the house. Shortly the children came out and joined the other three in the yard. A little later Olga came back to her seat. She began to speak in very low tones. "They're looking for a room all right. They haven't a cent. Bill and I can't put them up tonight. We did before in another house when they got down and out. They don't deserve sympathy. He gets a good job and loses it over drink. As soon as he gets hold of a dollar, he drinks it. She didn't used to but she does now. She's getting as bad as him. The Children's Aid Society has threatened to take Dick and Mary too. That's why they're walking with them instead of bumming drinks, I think."

Olga stopped talking as Jane came from the house to join us in the cooler yard.

"It's hot weather," she commented.

"Yes," agreed Olga. "Sophia, there's Tom on your verandah looking up and down the street."

"Oh he must want me. He probably can't find something and wants to ask me where it is. Not that I'm likely to know. I'll go see. Will Jenny be okay?"

"Sure, I'll keep an eye on them all," Olga promised.

Tom couldn't find the scissors. Neither could I.

"Them damn careless kids," growled Tom. "They never put anything back. Just leave it dragging behind their ass. A fine pack you raised." His voice changed. "Who's that other woman at Stanley's? Is she a relation?"

"No. Just people they know. She and her husband just arrived with two kids. They haven't a room or money to rent a bed. And the CAS is after those kids. It's taking care of six of their kids already."

"Eight kids!" Tom said. "Who are they? What work does he do?"

"They're Jane and Harry Blane, Olga told me. That's all I know. They just arrived a few minutes ago. I didn't have time to get all their history. I'll go back and get another chapter," I said.

"Don't go now. You mind the house. Is Bill there? I want to see if he has a saw."

"Go on over. I know you're dying of curiosity. I wanted a cup of my own tea anyway."

Tom left and I went into the house. When he came back I had finished two cups of tea and two cigarettes.

"Well, did you satisfy your curiosity?" I asked.

"Oh I'm not curious. Olga said they've been having hard luck. They all used to be good friends a few years ago but the Stanleys moved. Both of the Blanes drink a lot but they're not cruel to their kids. They just neglect them."

"I feel sorry for them but if they can't straighten themselves up nobody can. The CAS is helping and so is the Welfare. What kind of work can Harry do, or doesn't he want to work?"

"He's a good worker when he's sober, Olga said. He paints, works on construction, drives a truck. He's willing to try anything he can get, I guess."

"He'd have to, I suppose, to support his liquor habits," I said. "They must know they can't afford everything any more'n we can. To support our reading habit we have to give up new clothes."

"Is Olga going to take them in?"

"She can't. They haven't the room. Anyway Bill is fed up keeping them. I wonder if . . . "

"If we should offer them a bed? Tom do you think we should?"

"I don't know. Maybe not. Still, those poor kids. What if it turns cold and they can't find a room? I'll go and talk to Olga, see what kind of people they are–whether they've ever been in police trouble."

Tom walked purposefully over to the Stanley's. I waited on the verandah. It was growing dark. I waited half an hour.

Tom came back with Jenny.

"Olga says they're honest. I was talking to Blane. He seems all right. Down on his luck but looking for work. Do you want to offer them a place to sleep tonight? Make it clear it's just for tonight for the kids' sake," Tom told me.

"A room for who?" Jenny cried standing beside me. "Them new kids at Mabel's house? I like the little girl. She can sleep in our room."

"Well both kids can sleep in your room, I think. On the old couch. It won't matter if they wet it. Schmidt told me I could throw it out anyway. The adults can sleep in Johnny's room. It's lucky they came tonight because Johnny'll probably be home tomorrow night. By then I can have it all disinfected–just in case. I have the day off tomorrow luckily."

So the Blanes stayed one night with us. In the morning, after breakfast, as they prepared to leave, Jenny gave Mary an almost-new doll. The little girl was overjoyed.

They hadn't been gone long before Jane returned with the children. She was excited. Outside they had run into Schmidt. They had never met him before but he had greeted the children kindly. They had all got to talking and had discovered that Schmidt had empty rooms. In fact the whole of No. 81 was empty except for him. Harry had boldly asked him to rent them a room with kitchen privileges if he found a job that very day and let them pay later. Schmidt had considered carefully, then agreed. Now Jane wanted to know if she and the kids would be welcome at my house until Harry returned from seeking work.

"Sure," I said, "but I can't offer you a room tonight. My boy is coming home after work today."

Harry returned at noon. He had a job at least for a week. They had a few possessions at a friend's. The little family left to get them, then came back and moved into 81 Huron.

At the end of a week Harry drew his pay. He had told his employer of his straitened circumstances and the man had paid him up though it was the rule to keep a week's pay back until the end of the job.

That evening, I heard loud voices at 81. Before dark I saw the Blanes drive away in a taxi with all their possessions. Schmidt voluntarily explained that they had refused to pay their second week's rent in advance. "People have to pay in advance," he said. "I helped them. Now they should help me. But they wanted to go drinking. He was drunk when he got home. No good. No good."

"No damn good," Tom said. "We helped them too and didn't ask a cent. Now where'll they go?"

"To skid row," I said. "Isn't that where lots of people with problems end up?"

"So I've got problems," Schmidt said. "You got problems, no? You going to skid row?"

"No, she'll go to 999 Queen if she keeps on," Tom said. "You can't help everybody."

"I don't try to help everybody," I said, "but all kids are society's problem. So the Blanes wanted to drink—to have a little fun. Hell, so do you. But . . . " and I tried to sound sarcastic " . . . you guys can afford to drink. And pay your rent and taxes. How come?"

"We make the money," Schmidt said. "We're smart."

"Sure you're smart," I said. "But just tell me how you make the money. Tell me—do you get your money from other people?"

"Oh shut up," snarled Tom. "Blane has money. Why don't he spend it right?"

"So what is right? Blane told you his wages. You know he's getting less than you. Is his work not as important? Should he pay the same prices?" I asked.

"Well they pay the same for beer. Is that right?" Schmidt asked.

"No it isn't right. Not a damn bit right. Part of Blane's trouble and yours and mine is the fault of our economic system. This dog-eat-dog bit and profiting off one another is no damn good. I'm for people—not the system," I said.

"Oh there she goes again," Tom said. "I'm gonna have a beer. Schmidt, want a beer?" He went into the house.

"See, there you go, Tom. Poor Blane can't even afford a beer for himself let alone give one away," I said.

Schmidt looked at me thoughtfully. "No. I have to go," he said. He started down the street.

Don bought himself a good used car. It was big and a real gas-burner. Billy bought a bicycle, rather a bike-and-a-half. The first buy had poor wheels but a good frame. Billy kept the frame, painted it and attached brand new wheels he had bought separately. He figured the bike would save him bus fare to school.

Within two weeks the bicycle was stolen. Billy was, to say the least, upset. He threatened mayhem, then murder.

With police help, he got it back in good condition. No charges were laid, partly because it was sneaked back during the night and we didn't bother searching any further for the thief. We decided the culprit had become scared, or else had been forced by his parents to get rid of it. "He's lucky," Don said. "Leave well enough alone." Case closed.

A month later, the bicycle disappeared again. A search was made, but Billy never saw bar nor wheel of it again—so far as he could prove. He became suspicious of various student acquaintances. He didn't seem to bear the second loss so hard.

At the end of August, Johnny, Joyce and I quit our jobs. Right away I got taken on as order-filler in a warehouse and retail store for a stationery company. Johnny and Joyce went back to school, as of course did my younger ones. Joyce also became a volunteer worker with underprivileged kids.

Johnny had managed to save enough money for a battery-operated combination radio and record player. Many evenings he and I sat around and listened to country-and-western songs or read rather than go out or watch television.

It was a little past suppertime, Johnny and Billy were in their rooms. Don hadn't returned from work. Joyce and Jenny were out enjoying the evening air. I was washing my dishes. Tom was lying on his bed with a book. The house was calm.

"Get to hell out of my room!" I heard Billy roar, shattering my quiet mood. I moved quickly toward the stairs hoping to prevent a donnybrook. I was not quick enough. From over my head there came a tremendous crash, a thump and the sound of hurrying feet. Startled into momentary inertia, I saw Tom dash through the bedroom door and leap up the stairs, two steps at a time, his heavy cane at the ready.

"I'll kill them!" he roared. "Always fighting! Breaking up the goddamn furniture! I'll kill them!"

"No you won't," I said quietly, running behind him. "Give me that bloody cane. You'll do no murder while I'm here."

"There you go," he roared, without a pause in his hurried ascent. "You don't give a damn how soon we land out on the street. Bastards."

Then we were in Don's and Billy's room, the site of the racket. There on the floor before us lay Don's suitcase surrounded by large pieces of broken glass from the dresser mirror. Tom uttered a strangled sound and raised the cane to strike at Billy. Johnny had gone.

"Tom! Don't!" I screamed in his ear. "It's no good. We can buy a new mirror."

Tom lowered the cane, his rage receding. "Yes. And where will we get the money?" To Johnny who had arrived back at the scene, "You little s.o.b., look what you've done. Broke Schmidt's mirror. That'll cost twenty-five or thirty dollars."

"Don't blame me!" cried Johnny. "I didn't throw the suitcase. He did."

"It's your fault," Billy howled. "You made me. You wouldn't get out of my room."

"It's not just your room. It's Don's too. I have the right to come in and get the books Don borrowed from me," Johnny defended.

"Bastards!" Tom roared. "I'll kill you both." He raised his cane again.

"Hold it!" I yelled. "Johnny get to your room." Johnny retreated. "Tom get downstairs. I'll clean it up. It's only an old mirror."

Tom lowered his cane once again and walked dejectedly downstairs. He was muttering. "An old mirror! The only decent piece of furniture in the house. Well. It's no use—it's just no use. We'll never get ahead. Not with a gang like that."

Tom disappeared into his room and became silent. I cleaned up the mess, then went to talk to Johnny.

"You have got to respect Billy's rights more," I said.

"I wasn't doing anything—just looking for a book."

"Well you had no business looking for it when he told you to get out."

"But it's my book. Don had it and it's Don's room too."

"Johnny, you don't like anyone coming into your room without permission. You like privacy. Why couldn't you have asked me to look for the book?"

"Well, I didn't know Billy'd get so mad."

"No? Well how would you have acted in his place? Just remember Billy can't beat you or Don. If you order him out of your room he knows you have the strength to put him out—so how do you think he feels?"

"All right. I won't go into his room again when he's there."

"But that isn't enough. You must recognize his rights and try to help him. You can show respect by asking permission to enter his room and call me to help settle disputes. It isn't right to boss him around now when your strength is greater, because it won't always be. When he's twenty-one how will you make him respect your wishes? By beating him or threatening maybe? It won't be so easy."

"All right, I said. I'll leave him alone. You don't have to talk all night."

"Okay Johnny. I'll stop haranguing, but only because I respect your needs and rights."

I left his room and closed the door. I planned to talk to Billy later. Tom remained silently in our room. I finished my dishes in peace.

Certain of Billy's actions began to worry me. I watched curiously as he brought good skates, wallets and books to his room, kept them a few days and then went away with them. One day as he brought in a new-looking pair of skates, I asked him about his project.

"Oh, they're collateral," he said.

"What?" I gasped.

"Col-lat-er-al. This guy borrowed forty-five cents from me. When he pays it he gets his skates. But I can use them till he does," Billy explained.

"You mean," I asked, "you've started a loan company? This boy—does his mother know what he's doing?"

"Oh, sure. She doesn't care. He has his paper route and can spend his money the way he likes. He bought his own skates so it don't cost his mother or father."

"Well—but," I murmured and was at a loss for more to say.

Billy's enterprise prospered. Tom called him Mr. Beaverbrook. Billy's best customers were Joyce and Marge Williams.

Marge lived a short way down the street on the other side. She was fourteen, the youngest of a family of six children. I had seen some of the others and was acquainted with the mother and the only other daughter, Doreen, eighteen. Marge worked after school at a restaurant. Joyce had a part-time job, too.

It was Marge who got Joyce to ask me to take a hand in Billy's loan business. He was, they complained, Charging them 100 percent interest for a week's loan. "It isn't fair," Joyce opined. "After all, I'm his sister and Marge is my friend."

Well, I didn't think Billy's rates were decently low but the girls were older than he. I thought they should be able to work out a deal by themselves, but just for fun I decided to see what I could do.

"Fair," Billy said. "What's fair in business? They ask me to lend. I don't ask them to borrow."

"Billy's right, Maw," Johnny told me. "Those girls should learn to manage their money better. Perhaps they'll learn."

"But you can't look at this thing from a strictly business point of view, boys. You're cheating your sister and her friend. It isn't very nice."

"It's nice for me," Billy laughed. "I don't care if she is my sister. She wants my money, she'll pay."

"If they don't want to be cheated they shouldn't make those kind of deals," said Johnny.

"Now look. Those girls came to you as friends. Surely you could lend them money at a cheaper rate," I argued.

"Sure I could but I don't want to. I'm not gonna treat them as friends in a business deal. All businessmen are out to make a profit. If they weren't they'd go bankrupt," said Billy.

"But there's another side . . . " I started. Johnny interrupted me.

"Yes," he laughed, "and that's the stupid side. Joyce and Marge are suckers and deserve to be taken."

"Oh Johnny, that's a damn poor attitude. You surely don't agree with all the business practices," I cried.

"Not fraud, no. But Billy is quite open and honest with his customers. They make the deal with their eyes wide open, and that's their privilege. Some day they'll learn."

"Okay, Johnny. I see your point and Billy's too. But there's one more I'd like you to consider and that's our responsibility to one another," I said.

"What responsibility have I got to them?" Billy asked. "I'm not making them do anything. They're doing it to themselves. I couldn't cheat them if they didn't let me could I?"

"I suppose not, Billy. But why are you cheating them? Do you go around beating babies just because you can do it?"

"No," said Billy.

"Mum, that's a different case. It's not the same thing at all," Johnny protested.

"Well the principle is the same," I said. "We don't go around doing all the mean things to people we can do. We have a responsibility to treat people with respect for their weaknesses and—and needs."

"Not in business. Not me!" said Billy.

"Why not, Billy? Why do you want to take advantage of people's stupidity and weakness to get rich?" I asked.

"Businessmen do it. They have to, to keep their business going. You just can't afford to be kind in business," Billy answered.

"Then stay out of business, Billy. There's ways and means of making a good living without gypping the people as many businessmen do."

"Oh sure. By working your ass off and taking all the shit," Johnny cried.

"You're right, Johnny," Billy said. "See, Mum, he understands."

"Oh I understand too, Billy. It's just that I think there are more important and satisfying things than getting rich. One is being strong enough not to need to use people and being big enough to help them instead. I suppose I can't stop you from being crooks, but I don't like it."

"Well there's more crooked people in the world than any other kind," Johnny told me. "A person just about has to be nowadays unless he wants to starve or do without everything."

"I know, Johnny," I said. "You have to be pretty strong to stay poor when you have the ability to get rich. You have to have principles, like being a fair dealer."

"Okay, Mum. You talked me into it. You can tell Joyce they only have to pay fifty percent interest from now on," Billy smiled.

I gave up in defeat. Later I told the girls they would just have to do without borrowing and save their money.

"Well I don't think it's right for Billy to charge us so much for the loan of a few dollars," Joyce cried.

"I don't either, but is it smart for you to borrow from him?" I asked.

"Well, I guess not," said Marge. "It's our own fault, Joyce. We make the deal too."

"But we're stuck," Joyce protested. "We have to agree to his terms if we want the money."

"Well, Joyce, I can't help you," I said. "You know, there are three kinds of people: the suckers, the ones who take them, and people like me who try to get the first to be less gullible and the second to be less exploitive."

"What do you mean, Mum? Who's gullible?" Joyce asked.

"Oh hell, Joyce, I don't know anymore what I mean. I'm tired of trying to keep peace between you kids. You'll just have to tend to your deals yourselves. Now I'm going outside."

I left the problem to the girls. They must have learned. They stopped borrowing from Billy. His other customers must have too, or Billy lost interest. He went out of business a few weeks later.

In November, Joyce brought an unhappy young girl, Sandra Berube, home one quiet evening. Sandra was only fifteen but she was much better developed than many full-grown women; that is physically. But while she had a very nice shape, her face was not beautiful.

It seemed as if they stayed but a minute, then were gone again. Later that night when Joyce returned she asked if I had a minute to talk before going to bed.

"Okay," I said. "But we'll have to be quiet, the rest are in bed."

"I'll be quiet," Joyce said, getting out cups and teabags. "Mum, what do you think of Sandra?"

"She certainly has a good figure," I said. "Where does Sandra live?"

"Over on Madison. That's close. Her family's from St. John. Her father's still down there. Her mother's left him. Sandra has no sisters, but two brothers. They're up here. Buddy's seventeen, Timmy's twelve. Sandra doesn't get along with them or her mother. Timmy hides her stuff to make her mad and Buddy beats her. Sandra wants to go back with her father."

"Will her father take her? Can he support her?" I asked.

"He can support her all right. He has a good job. But her mother wants her to stay here. She says Sandra'll only get in worse trouble there."

"Oh, is she in trouble here? Is she going to school?"

"Yes but she skips a lot. She's in grade nine. Mrs. Berube got a call from Sandra's teacher last week. Her mother's threatened to put Sandra in a home."

"I think Sandra must be doing more than skipping school, Joyce. Does she smoke?"

"Well, yeah, some. And she stays out late sometimes without her mother's permission. Her mother thinks she drinks."

"How did you come to know her?"

"At school. She's a nice kid but kind of mixed-up. I like her and am trying to help her. She has no sister to talk to and when she tries to talk to her mother Buddy butts in and so Sandra can't explain what she wants."

"Does she know what she wants? I mean what she wants to do when she's grown-up, in the way of a job, or career?"

"I mean what she wants now, besides school and work. You want things when you're young, too."

"I know, dear. But when you're young you should think a bit about the future and plan for it. That's probably what Mrs. Berube tells Sandra."

"Yes, she does. Mum, I wonder if you talked to Sandra's mother would it help?"

"It might. Then again it might not. Maybe Sandra's got to find things out the hard way. Maybe she doesn't want to listen to old folk. If she doesn't care what we think we can't help her."

"Maybe you're right. Anyway I'm going to try to keep her going to school."

Around the middle of December Joyce told me Sandra had been picked up by the police for prostitution or vagrancy, been made a ward of the court, and sent to training school.

"It's her mother's fault she's locked up," Joyce added bitterly. "She told the judge she has no control over Sandra. She thinks Sandra will be better off in a training school, but training schools aren't all nice. Some guards are real cruel and dirty too. Some kids come out worse than they went in."

"I know," I said. "But what do you think skipping school, drinking and sexing it up would lead to for your friend? She isn't in training school just for punishment. She's there for protection from the men and women who were just using her without a care for her future."

"Yes, but what protection has she got from the ones in there who'll just use her too? Training school and jail can be pretty awful. They're run by some awful people. So are our regular schools. This society is just terrible."

"Not in every way. There are lots of good people around. Some are just lucky enough to meet more of the good kind. Maybe Sandra'll be lucky."

"Maybe. She wasn't meeting many of the good ones out here. Those who cared and tried to understand, I mean."

"Who do you think is to blame for that? Do you think Sandra really tried to meet those who understand and care?"

"I don't know. I feel mixed-up too. Well, I'm really glad I have you to talk to. I'm going to write to Sandra and let her know I still care."

"Good, Joyce. And try to look on the good side. At least Buddy won't be able to beat Sandra in there."

Joyce smiled. "That's right. At least she's clear of him. Well I'm going to bed now. Good-night, Mum. And thanks."

5

As a Christmas bonus Tom's company gave him a five-dollar coupon toward a turkey or other food item. The day before Christmas Eve, Tom brought home a large turkey. That created a problem. I had no oven. The stove belonged to Schmidt and Tom would not demand that Schmidt fix it nor would he let me do so. Neither would Tom let me call in a service man. We couldn't afford to fight with our landlord because he might throw us out. Well with my job and the kids I had little energy left to fight with both Tom and Schmidt, so I turned to the neighbours. When Mrs. Stanley heard of my predicament she offered to let me roast our turkey at her house. I gladly accepted her offer.

My job lasted right to Christmas. On the afternoon of December 24, I was paid in full and laid off.

That evening while Tom was at his job Jenny and I took our turkey to the Stanley's. While it roasted Olga and I talked in the kitchen. Jenny watched TV with Bill and the kids in the living-room. By the time Tom got home at 11:45 the turkey had been roasted and brought home. I was alone in the house when Tom arrived.

"Where are all the kids?" Tom asked as he entered the kitchen.

I put down my cigarette and said, "Well, I don't know where the big ones are, but Billy and Jenny are out with Howie Dubé, carol-singing. Howie said they'd make a lot of money and– "

"Damn! You let them go out this time of night?" he roared. "You must be crazy!"

"Now, just a minute. I may be crazy–I never said I wasn't. But Howie and Billy are both past thirteen and they promised not to go wandering far away. We've been here almost a year. Anyway, I expect them back in about thirty minutes," I roared back.

"You expect them back. That's all you ever do–but you don't know. I tell you, the police'll be here any minute and they'll be in jail. You can't trust them boys together. They're liable to go to Yorkville."

"Yorkville, hah! And who has money there? Doom and gloom–why are you such a pessimist? They'll be back. So you might as well shut up."

He didn't shut up, or even sit down. "It's always been like this," he growled. "Just when things seem to be getting better, something happens to set us back." For a few minutes, he puttered around growling, swearing, and calling me, plus most of my relatives, derogatory names. I watched him calmly while an uneasiness grew in me. I wished the kids would hurry back. Tom's mood changed. He stopped the dramatics and ordered me to get him something to eat.

"What?" I exclaimed. "If I'm all you say, I'm not even fit to wash up your dirty dishes. Get your own lunch, and while you're at it, wash out your mouth."

Of course I wasn't serious. I got him a little lunch. We had bought fruitcake. He ate one slice. The children returned just as Tom finished eating. Jenny was first through the door and by her quick purposeful steps, I knew she was angry.

Straight to me she marched and yelled, "They owe me a nickel. Each one. They cheated me and ran away on me. Make them give me my money."

"Hold it, hold it," I said firmly. "Let me get this right. What– "

"Mrs. Firth," Howie called, as he came close, "it was this way. We went to this place and started singing. When the man came out to pay us, we divided it equally– "

"But at the last place," Billy interrupted, "we didn't get exact change. There was a dime left, so Howie and me split it. We didn't have any pennies."

"You each owe me a nickel," Jenny shouted.

"Give her the goddamn nickel," Tom shouted.

"Shut up," I shouted at the shouters. Then, more quietly, I said, "Jenny, you can't get three nickels out of a dime. Tell me the whole story."

"Mrs. Firth–I know what happened," said Howie.

"Howie, just shut up. I'll ask you when I want to," I said.

"Give her the damn money," Tom ordered. "Billy, get to bed, and Howard, go home."

I stepped to the centre of the room, waved my arms and screamed, "Shut up! Right up. You, Tom, have been yelling since you came in. All right, Howie explain."

"Well you know, when we left here, we started down Dundas and picked out places to sing at–where we thought they'd give us some money." Jenny tried to butt in. We shushed her and Howie continued, "They would open their door and give me the money."

"Why you? Where was Billy?" I asked.

"Billy didn't want to come and take it. I was more in front. I've gone singing at Christmas before, so I know how it's done," Howie explained.

"So you acted as leader. And where was Jenny when you got the money?"

"Hiding under the steps mostly," both boys spoke together in their eagerness to tell me. They laughed scornfully.

"I was not hiding," cried Jenny. "Anyway, I sang so I should get as much as youse. You owe me two nickels."

"Okay. Here's my nickel," acquiesced Howie. He wouldn't have given in to his own little sister so easily. "Now, Billy, you give her one too."

"Just a minute," protested Billy. "Then, if she gets two nickels, she gyps us."

"Come on, Billy," I said, "cough up the nickel. Shame. Trying to gyp a little girl when you know it was her singing that won the money–else they paid you to go away."

"Yes, Mamma, that's right," Jenny spoke up. "You know

what? They can't even sing 'Silent Night'. They didn't know the words and they had to look on the paper, and they wouldn't sing 'Little Town of Bethlehem'. I didn't need no old paper!"

"Can't sing, eh?" I teased. "Fine carollers."

Billy decided to give his little sister a nickel. "Can Howie and me go out for some pop?" he asked quickly.

I looked at Tom. He said, "Just to the restaurant—and don't be long."

The boys left. Tom hunted up a book and went off to our bedroom. I got Jenny a lunch of cookies and milk. She was proud of her earnings.

Later Johnny, Billy and Joyce came home. They wanted to eat the turkey before it grew really cold. Tom was hungry again, and Jenny. So we enjoyed a big lunch of turkey, stuffing, and bread.

Andy Stanley came over. He had his new guitar with him. He could play quite well, and sing. With Andy's contributions and Johnny's record player we had enough country music and songs. I barely thought of old New Brunswick and the good things I had left behind.

We opened our gifts about one a.m.

Christmas day was fine. We did not get up till noon.

After Boxing Day I began to look for another job. First, I applied for unemployment benefits, a thing I'd never done before. I didn't find the clerks even moderately courteous or helpful. They tried to herd the lot of us about like cattle. After learning my business, they thrust some papers at me and told me to go home, fill them out, and mail them back. I wanted to fill the papers in there and just leave them, but that was against the law, I was coldly informed. So home I had to bring the bloody papers. First, though, I enquired about a job. It happened there was a factory hiring a few workers. I was sent for an interview. Luckily, I was hired, but wasn't to commence work until after New Year's. That left me a week to get caught up on a few neglected jobs at home.

I worked diligently and waited happily for the new year that looked promising. One fine day I decided spontaneously to have my hair cut and curled. I'd enter our Centennial with a new look.

The hair cut and permanent cost me the better part of a day

and fifteen dollars. When it was done, a mixture of rain and snow was bombarding the city. I had a block to walk, and my new hairdo got wet even though the lady gave me a small plastic headscarf. Well, next day I was one damn mess. Everybody, and I mean everybody, made fun of me. I had to wait a day before I could see my hairdresser again.

When I was able to see her to complain, she refused to refund my money, even half. The mess, she said, was the result of my getting it wet plus the bit of natural curl I had. She did offer to try again free in a few weeks. I told her no thanks, not in a few years even. I was disgusted, but hell, it would grow out again. Let them laugh.

It wasn't so hard to bear. In public, I kept it hidden under a big woollen kerchief and at work under a heavy hairnet. All the women wore a similar net, so I wasn't conspicuous there. The worst jokers lived with me. Every day, one of them would ask me where I got my "original hairdo" and if it cost much. They wondered aloud if I'd recommend that place to a friend.

Joyce had learned some hairdressing somewhere. She curled it a few times using water as a dampener. Then, she sprayed it heavily. That helped.

Early in the year, Schmidt gave a party for his current tenants and special old ones. He rented a small banquet room on Beverley Street. All except Jenny were invited, but only Joyce and I went.

Gloria's brother, Harold, came to Toronto to stay. He had quit school because of a quarrel with a teacher over words.

"Well we were told to write about something in our own words," Harold explained. "Well dammit I did. You know I'm part French and part English and I'm not good in either language so naturally my writing wasn't the best, but it was my own words. I argued with her about it but she wouldn't listen."

The teacher, he said, had failed him at Christmas and he was sure she'd fail him again in June just over that.

He'd be damned, he said, if he was going to waste another six months in school just to fail. He might go back in the fall, he thought. He was in grade twelve.

He had decided he wouldn't mention his diabetic condition when applying for jobs—but he did confess it. Soon, though, he got a good job. All the time he was there, he was never ill. He worked as well as anyone and made friends. He boarded for a while at Gloria's and then at another sister's. Many a week-end he stayed with us.

Tom began to work from eleven p.m. to seven a.m. One night in late February, while he was at work, I got a call from the police. They had Joyce in a station away out somewhere. They had found her walking along heading north—allegedly trying to hitchhike to New Brunswick. There was nothing they could arrest her for; they found her just walking along in the cold with a bulging suitcase. Curious, they had stopped to talk to her. She told them she was going back to New Brunswick. She had gone a certain distance by streetcar—in fact too far, and was walking back to the right intersection. Was it all right with me, the police inquired. It sure as hell wasn't. She wouldn't be eighteen until March and the winter weather in New Brunswick was a far cry from Toronto weather. I talked to Joyce over the phone. She decided to come home. But now, how to get back? Both she and I were almost penniless. Although Don had a car, he was at work. Well these concerned policemen could arrange transportation home for a troubled teenager. And they did.

"What a stupid fool trick!" I fumed as Joyce came into the house.

"Oh, Mamma, I'm so lonesome," she lamented. "I just got to thinking of the fun we had down there and I got ready and left."

"But, Joyce! What of us worrying until we heard?" I was horrified. Surely this formerly dependable daughter wasn't becoming careless and inconsiderate.

"Oh, Marge Williams was to tell you later that I was staying with a friend." I would have believed her since we had no phone and messages had been relayed from friend to friend previously. "Tomorrow she was to explain where I really was."

Weak through and through, I sat down. "Oh, you kids," I wailed. "What chances you take. Do you think your relatives would like to support you in New Brunswick? They'd be so mad at you quitting school they'd kick you out, except Gramps who can't feed the dependants he has now. And what if some maniac picked you up?"

"Well, I can pretty well tell about people. It's a feeling I get.

Besides, I had your big knife." She was quite self-confident.

"When did you plan this? How long have you been thinking about such a crazy trip?"

"Oh, a week or so. Marge and I planned it together. She helped me."

"Well, now that you're back, I want you to please, please, never be so–so–impulsive and reckless again. Soon it will be spring and I'll give you the fare down. You can be there for Easter. Surely you can save a few dollars from your job by then. You didn't quit that after-school job, did you?"

"No. Marge was to phone in for me that I had left town. They don't know a thing. So, yes, that's what I'll do."

"But you seemed happy. Did anything happen anywhere to hurt you so bad you had to get away?" I asked.

"Well, I don't like some of my teachers. But it was mostly homesickness. And when I had that fight with Mr. Black, I really decided to leave."

"Go on. What was the fight about?"

"Well, we were having a test and I had my head down on my desk. I hadn't written a thing. I was thinking about old Campbellton and Anna and Dora and Marlene and the places we used to go. Well, I could see this girl ahead of me writing away, but I wasn't interested. Then, he said to her, 'You better move your paper. Your friend may be looking.' I knew he meant I was trying to cheat. I got mad. I jumped up. 'I never had to cheat in my life,' I said. I tore up the paper, it was blank, not even my name on it. I threw it on my desk and walked out. He didn't have to treat me like that."

"No, he didn't, Joyce, but you know you've got to take blows like that and not let them break you. Just remember, you'll be free of those bosses and able to give as good as you get soon. It's only for a few years. Your status will change, but don't run away from a few hurts."

"Oh, it didn't hurt much–but I was so lonesome. I don't think I'll ever be able to stay away from home really long."

"Yes, you will. You stayed up here one summer for three months," I reminded her.

"Oh–but I saw Dad and Don nearly every day. That's not how I mean. I mean completely away from all of you," she explained.

We talked more. When I was sure I understood her yearnings and mood and knew she was resigned to stay in school another two or three weeks, I was able to relax and go back to bed. She promised to keep the escapade secret for a while. I just couldn't take another tirade of Tom's right then. Of course Marge would be cautioned too, and I hoped the others involved wouldn't noise it about.

Joyce kept her promise. Johnny was home and though he'd heard some of the story, he was a real nice clam. He wasn't eager to set Tom to thundering and cursing either. It was over, he didn't need to know.

Before I could send Joyce east, a brown pup followed her home. At first Tom wouldn't let her bring it in the house.

"Dogs," he thundered, "are too much trouble in a city like this. It's just a mongrel. Dogs get rabies. They need shots and a license and food. Somebody might be looking for it."

That night, Joyce sneaked it into her room. The next morning, Tom's soft heart was in control.

"What did you do with the pup? We can't leave it outside to freeze. Bring it in. Give it milk. Call the Humane Society and tell them. Maybe someone's looking for it. Some kid crying."

The Humane Society said, "Advertise. Give the description and place found. If no one claims it, you can keep it."

No one claimed it except Jenny. She begged Tom to let it stay. He did. Later, we decided he should have a name. Joyce said "San Salvador", Johnny wanted "King", I said "Fellah". Each of us started calling him by our desired name. He almost went to Johnny, but I was holding a piece of meat under the table that only the pup could see. He came to me.

Fellah became his name even though the others said I cheated. Everybody had been calling him Fellah anyway. It was "Give the poor Fellah a bite." "Come here Fellah." "Lay down there Fellah." So, actually, he'd been given the name automatically.

He seemed to be an intelligent, friendly pup. Jenny loved him. He caused trouble though. He chewed up a good moccasin of Tom's and somebody's gloves. He ruined the front of one drawer on a new dresser by chewing. Tom was furious. He insisted that Joyce pay for it since it belonged to Schmidt and not to us. She couldn't. The row continued another day. I drew a pay and got ready to send Joyce east. Again Tom blew up. He said I was a stupid, contrary bitch, I was spoiling them kids, and he should have left me in the mental hospital. I listened calmly.

He need not try to put all the blame on me, I told him. He did his share of the spoiling as well as certain others, and many people could attest to that.

Eventually Tom ran out of relatives to criticize and accusations to make. The household got to sleep. In the morning Tom was taciturn. Just as Joyce and I were about to leave for the train, Tom passed Joyce a ten-dollar bill.

"Here. Take this," he said gruffly.

Fellah stayed with us. His training fell mostly to me. Jenny fed him and took him for walks.

Letters came from Joyce. She was fine, happy.

In March I was laid off. I asked Canada Manpower to help me find work. Johnny began to talk of quitting school. Tom and I didn't want that but our loud and ferocious arguments concerning my mismanagement of the house and the spoiling of the kids bothered Johnny. I promised him I'd try not to argue so much if he'd just stay in school. Johnny gave in to me for a while.

Manpower could find no suitable jobs for me. I had to reapply for unemployment benefits and wait. My benefit year was still in force. I had not received a cent, but I had trouble collecting. A woman clerk told me I would have to put in another waiting period. Tom had told me that I had put in my waiting period between Christmas and New Year's. I argued with the clerk. She insisted that I had to make a new claim because I had not told them where my book was in January or answered a few letters about it. I insisted that I had told them once where my book was, that that piece of paper had cost me six cents to mail, and I was not their serf. She said I'd have to wait to see the manager, and she did not know when he would be in.

I left the building in anger. I went to Toronto's Central Library and looked up the law on benefit year, duties of applicant, etc. I jotted down a few notes. I returned home furious. I told Tom that they were giving me the runaround. He volunteered to make a trip to 200 Dundas Street with me. He had a little trouble, too.

We insisted on seeing the manager. He wasn't in.

"I'll wait," I said.

A male clerk took over. He tried to explain that my claim of December was no good—I had to serve another waiting period. Tom insisted that the clerk was in error.

The man was agitated. He took all the papers in my file away and we waited. Finally, the manager came in and deigned to speak to us. He, too, tried to cheat me of a week's benefit. We argued. At last, he said it would take another three to six weeks to review my claim.

We came home. Tom was mad at me. I should have answered their letters, he told me. They should read the papers we citizens send in, I told him. We're not obliged to mail information twice if they receive it the first time. I sent information about my case to Action Line. I didn't whitewash myself. A few days later, I began receiving benefit cheques. So, that was that.

Now, our family life became more harmonious. Jenny was happier. I was able to take her more places and we had longer conversations. Don sold his old car and bought a new Renault.

Tom's shift changed again. He went back to the three-to-eleven shift. One morning about six a.m. our door-bell rang. I leapt out of bed, grabbed a coat and dashed out. I yanked open the door expecting to see Joyce. Two policemen stood there. Big brutes they appeared to my bleary eyes.

"You have a dog here?" they asked.

"Yes," I muttered.

"We have a complaint, he's barking in the yard," one growled, "and has been barking all night."

"He has not. He's in the kitchen. We don't leave pups out at night in case it rains," I said firmly, anger pushing sleep away.

"We have a complaint," one said.

"Who's there?" called Tom. "Is it Joyce?"

"It's police," I called back. "About Fellah. Barking!"

"Oh, for— " Tom said and was silent.

"Do you want to see the dog?" I asked.

"No, just keep him from barking," they said and turned to go. I shut the door and went to the kitchen. Fellah was there, under the table. He wagged his tail. I put the kettle on for tea. I was angry and confused. The boys thought it was silly for our police to have to go chasing penned dogs. "Why don't the complainers lay charges?" they wanted to know. "We'll have to get rid of him," Tom announced firmly. "I knew there'd be trouble."

A few days later, a policeman came at noon. Fellah was in the back yard.

"He's not barking," I said.

"He barked when I went by the fence. I checked him," the man said.

"Oh, well. What do you expect? It's instinct for a dog to bark at strangers or when strangers are near his home," I said.

"Who's complaining?" Tom asked.

"I don't know," the officer said.

"You mean people call up and complain without giving their name and you have to check out their complaint?" I asked.

"Yes," he told me.

"I don't believe it," I swore. "It can't be– "

"Oh, shut up!" Tom ordered me.

"I won't," I said. I didn't like his attitude. "What will happen if he barks and you don't know who is complaining? Who'll charge us?"

"Oh, we can lay charges ourselves," said the officer. "You'll have to control him. We have an anti-noise bylaw."

I shut up, but I went on seething.

When he was gone, Tom and I discussed the situation. Johnny joined in. We were sad and angry. With money we could get a license, pay for rabies and other vaccines, buy a muzzle. We had none to spare. Even so, we didn't care to leave a dog muzzled all day. It didn't suit our idea of how tame dogs should be treated.

"We'll just have to get rid of him," I said. "I don't like it, but cities aren't designed for big healthy dogs, and Fellah is going to be a monster. We've got to resign ourselves. People who've had dogs for years finally have to kill them or have them killed to put them out of their misery."

"But Fellah's not in misery," Johnny protested.

"Not yet," I said, "but he will be and so will we. Better to bear it now before we are much too attached to him."

Four days later, Tom took him to the Humane Society to be put to sleep. It was a hard thing to do. "Never again," he said on his return.

The next day, Joyce arrived home unannounced. Campbellton was dying, she said. She had become lonesome for Toronto. She brought two girlfriends, Greta Doucet, seventeen, and May Black, nineteen, from Campbellton and Dalhousie, respectively. The two friends had little money, little experience, but hoped to get jobs. Joyce intended to let them share her room. Her double bed was big enough for all.

Tom and I and Johnny stared at them.

"They can stay here, can't they?" Joyce asked anxiously.

"Of course, now," I said, "but you'll have to help."

"Oh, I will," she said happily.

"We'll get work soon," the girls chorused. Greta had been in Toronto before. She got a good job right away. May didn't have such luck.

May got lost on her first day out. That ended her search, but she didn't go home right away, and we didn't put her out.

Then, one night Johnny heard that a boy we all knew well, Sidney Jones, nineteen, had arrived in Toronto. Johnny went to meet him. Sidney had no money, no job as yet and no place to stay. It was warm weather and many young people were starting to use the parks as bedrooms. Johnny brought Sidney home to share his room. Sidney got work two days later. Now our house was full.

After that one attempt to find a job, May put in most of her time in the house. Well, actually she spent a lot of time out in a big old chair on the front verandah. There she smoked cigarettes and drank coffee while she watched the calm life of our street, and thought deep thoughts.

One day, she got a letter from her mother. After reading it, she announced that she was going home—that night. Joyce and Greta helped her to the train and saw her off.

A few hours later, I heard voices and unusual noises outside. Curious, I went to study the street. There was quite a commotion out there.

Police cars and uniformed men were hustling about. Many people were gathering in groups and whispering, questioning, muttering. Tom was due to arrive any minute, so I remained outside, ostensibly waiting for him but really eager to learn what was happening.

Joyce ran up our verandah steps just as an ambulance whined

to a stop at a house across the street. Joyce was crying quietly.

"Come in the house, Mum," she pleaded. Concerned, I did as she asked.

"What's the matter? Do you know what happened?" I asked. "Joyce dear, what's the trouble?"

"It's Mr. Williams. Marge told me he's hurt bad. He was fighting with Marge's mother and she must have picked up a knife when he came at her. Maybe he'll die." Joyce continued to cry as she explained. "Marge knows they were fighting but she was in her room. Her mother called her to come out, then told her to phone the police. Marge did, then she saw her father in a chair bleeding. He didn't say anything. Marge is scared. Oh, Mum."

I put my arms around Joyce and tried to speak calmly.

"Joyce, dear, don't take it so hard. Marge is your friend. You must brace up if you want to help her. Where is she? Where is her mother?"

"Marge is in a police car. They have her mother in the house. I I guess they have to have a policewoman to arrest Mrs. Williams. Poor Marge." Joyce sobbed.

"Not poor Marge—poor Mrs. Williams. She's the one who really needs help now. Let's go outside. It's too hot to stay in the house. I'm glad Jenny is asleep. A thing like this could give her nightmares."

"There'll be a trial, especially if. . . . Marge'll have to go to court and she's scared. Yes, let's go out. Perhaps I can talk to Marge again. Do you think she'll have to go to a home? She's not sixteen yet."

"No. They'll probably let her stay with an adult relative if they can look after her. They'll make it as easy for her and the rest of the family as they can. Did Marge love her father very much?"

"Well—I don't know. He was real cruel to Rick and he fought a lot with their mother. Even broke some of her ribs one time when he pushed her downstairs," Joyce told me.

"Oh!" I exclaimed. "I knew he was pretty rough on Mrs. Williams. I met her and Doreen at the laundromat one time. Doreen introduced me to her mother and I knew by their actions there was something wrong. Well after we got to talking I found out Mrs. Williams, Gladys, had her ribs taped up. Arthur must have pushed her down the stairs then. Doreen wanted her mother to leave him then. Doreen was moving out herself. She's nineteen, isn't she?"

"Yes. And she did move out. But she came back a month ago." Joyce had stopped crying. Her voice was back to normal. "Anyway," she said, "Mrs. Williams did it in self-defense. Do you think she can prove it?"

"How can we know? But how Arthur treated her and the kids will count. Perhaps this thing has been building up a long time," I answered.

"It has. I've been there and he never said anything to me. But Marge has told me lots. Once he moved a woman in that he said was his real wife. Really, Mum, he did. I believe Marge."

"That'll come out—if anything happens to him. Dad should be coming soon."

Outside more people were gathering in groups. Joyce and I stood on our verandah quietly observing.

"Those people are just curious I bet," Joyce told me. "They probably don't care a bit about the Williamses. Is that what they mean by 'morbid curiosity'?"

"Maybe. Then again it might not be so morbid. After all, it is natural to be interested in other people and what they do, especially the ones in your neighbourhood. I don't suppose any of us would dash out to Don Mills to see the end of a family fight."

Joyce chuckled.

"I'm going to see if Dad is coming," I said.

Usually he came along the opposite side of the street often walking up to the Williams' house before crossing over to our side.

I walked straight across the street and stopped by their front gate. Gathered there, hushed, was a small group. I stopped. Glancing down the street I saw Tom turn the corner and move up the sidewalk. He stopped by my side.

"What's going on?" he asked. "Somebody get hurt?"

"Arthur," I said. "There was a fight. Shh!"

The door of the house opened and a policeman came out. He motioned all of us to move out of the way. We complied.

More police came out carrying Arthur on a stretcher. I didn't look at it but Tom did.

"He's dead," Tom whispered to me.

"Oh, no," I whispered.

"Yes," Tom said. "His face isn't covered and I've seen dead men before."

"Poor Gladys," I murmured. "And the kids. This is bad."

We stood quietly until the ambulance sped away. I glanced around. In a police car farther up the street sat Marge. A policeman was with her. Joyce was standing near the car.

"Let's go home," Tom said. "What happened?"

"I don't know," I said, walking beside him. "Joyce does, I guess. It was just about all over when I took notice something was going on. Joyce and Greta took May down to the station tonight. Then Greta went out somewhere. They're all out somewhere except Joyce and Jenny. Jenny's in bed, and Joyce is up there by that police car. They're talking to Marge. She was the one who called them first. Then I guess she told Joyce before they got here. But me, I didn't hear a thing till a few minutes ago."

In the house I set about getting Tom's lunch. Both he and I felt more than mild concern over the Williams' trouble because we had been getting to know the family and Joyce and Marge were becoming good friends. The girls went to the same school, had similar interests and were in and out of both houses many evenings. I liked Marge and Doreen. I knew Doreen better. She and I had had a few fairly serious mother-daughter-type discussions. I found Doreen mature for her age and I was pleased that Joyce had found two such girlfriends. I wondered where Doreen was tonight, and how hard a blow this would be to her. I wished there was something I could do to help.

Half an hour later the police were still around, I was back on my verandah, and Doreen had come home. I saw her talking with an older brother by their door. I went over to her to see how she was bearing up.

"Oh, I feel awful, Mrs. Firth," Doreen said. "I had just left home when it happened, and so had Henry. If we had only guessed. . . "

"Dear," I said, "these things happen. How is your mother?"

"Not too bad. It was self-defense. Dad died, you know. But Mum can't remember exactly how it happened, only he was coming toward her and she thought he was going to hit her again. She remembers he hit her once and I think she has a broken finger. But Mum has had short black-outs before. They're going to take her to jail but Marge will stay with Joe and his wife on Adelaide. Henry and I are gonna stay here tonight and we'll see Mum tomorrow. Oh. I'd better go. I want to see Mum again." She sounded sad and worried but in control.

When Joyce came in a little later she was less heavy-hearted. She told me Marge was much calmer.

The next day Doreen dropped in to see me. She said her mother had a very good lawyer who assured her that her mother might receive a very light sentence, and might even be acquitted of the manslaughter charge. She said her mother felt the accident was just an accident and not her fault. Gladys had two broken fingers.

Certain female neighbours had a different attitude. I got the impression a few were actually delighted to see Gladys in trouble.

One, Martha, said, "She told me once, she'd fix him. I guess she did. She should get at least two years."

"Really," I said. "Why—do you think she meant to kill him?"

"Well, she could have. Sure they had a fight and she had a right to defend herself but she shouldn't have used a knife. After all! I bet she decided that was her chance to get rid of him and be free, with money."

"Oh, do they have money? Much I mean?"

"For sure. He owned a good restaurant and was a partner in an import business. Besides he had life insurance. I've lived here over fifteen years. Arthur lived here that long but not all of his family. They've only been together here about seven years."

"I see," I said. "I don't think Mrs. Williams planned the crime. Perhaps she didn't realize exactly what she was doing. Sometimes I fear such a thing could happen at our house. A bad temper is a terrible thing. So far we've been lucky."

"Oh," she said, "well I suppose people do kill one another in fights, but you and Tom don't fight that bad."

"We haven't yet. But sometimes I think we might. He's mighty hard to live with at times. Don't be surprised if I leave him."

"Oh, no. What would he do without you?"

"He'd do all right. He's a good man in lots of ways but his

temper flares over nothing. Here I'll be going along doing my best when suddenly he starts screaming and hollering and swearing because he can't find something—wire cutters, hammer, sports section of the newspaper, his pen or glasses. Hell, it's hard on my nerves."

She couldn't suppress a smile. "My husband gets on my nerves too. He picks fights. Really. For no reason he'll strain his brain to find a way to get me mad. Then when he's got a fight going he blames me."

"Haven't you ever felt like killing him?" I asked.

"Well. But only for a second. But no, not really. He's never hit me. I'll give him that. Oh there. I heard him calling. He must need help in the store. We'll see you."

A few nights later Joyce screamed in the night. I ran to her.

"I guess I had a nightmare about Mr. Williams," she said. "I went with Marge to see her father in the funeral parlour. That's what I was dreaming about. Perhaps I shouldn't have gone. I don't like death and all that. It's so final and cold."

"It's cold—but how do you know it's final? I never taught you much religion—just the commandments, Lord's Prayer and a few of Christ's teachings but I wonder myself if there's a life after death, even such a thing as reincarnation."

"Is that true, Mum? I never thought you'd think about the same things I do."

"Why not? I was young once. Lots of questions went through my mind and I've never found the answer to some. One thing I did discover is that we don't need to know all the answers. We can work with what we have. I don't think we need to know if there is life after death. I mean the point I see in religion is that we work for a reward not after death, but here. We live our childhood, if we are helped right, so we'll enjoy our teen years, and live our youth so we'll enjoy our old age."

"That's what I think but now I'm not sure how to live my youth. Maybe I'll do things I'll be sorry for—and if I don't do them maybe I'll be sorry I didn't. I suppose everyone has that problem."

"Probably, but some people don't think about it. They just live mainly for the present and don't worry much either about the past or future. They do whatever seems best for the present.

If they make mistakes they don't fret over them, or even bother to avoid them the next time."

"But I'd like to have a goal that I could work toward—but not spend all my time at it. Like marriage. I think I'd like to get married some day. I want to do other things now. But I don't want to do things that would stop me from having a good marriage or be able to raise my children well. Listen. I'm so glad I have a mother I can talk to. What if I smoked pot and found it bad? What could I say to my children if they wanted to smoke pot and I didn't want them to?"

"The same as me, I guess. You won't be able to stop them yourself. You can only work on their own common sense—but you can't force any one to use his common sense. I can't stop you from doing things that I think you'll be sorry for—I can only try to get you to think carefully before you go ahead and do it. Nobody has certain answers."

"I know. I guess the only thing to do is go ahead and do the things that give you the answers."

"Well, Joyce, we can be pretty sure of some answers because of other people's experiences. We know, for instance, some ways to avoid accidents and sickness."

"Yes, but what about pot? What do you know about it?"

"Nothing. However, you don't need pot anymore than I did, or anymore than great-grandfather needed the airplane. Even if you found out later that pot is a good thing and believed you missed a lot by avoiding it, you've missed other good things like birthday parties and bicycle riding and swimming sessions. You still had fun. People don't have to do everything to have a good, satisfying life. In fact, we can never go everywhere and do everything or get to be friends with everybody. There's just too much to choose from. Look at me. I had to leave my mother and father and sisters and friends in New Brunswick. I hated to leave them but I had to make a choice. I'm just lucky I'm able to make new friends and get fun out of new things. Some people just can't change their way of living, or go to a new place and still enjoy themselves."

"I think it's a good thing we have lots of relatives and friends. What a terrible thing if we lost them all at once in a real horrible thing like an earthquake."

"That would be awful—and it has happened. Some of those draft-dodgers voluntarily give up families, friends and even country all at once. Then they try to start over in a new and sometimes mean country. That takes some kind of grit. I think I'd rather go to jail if I were them."

"I'm glad I don't have that problem. I'm going to work at St. Christopher to try to help kids with problems. Maybe I can't help—but I think I'll try."

"That might be a good idea. Now do you think you'll be able to sleep okay? I want to go back to bed."

"I don't think I'll have any more nightmares. It's just that I never experienced anything like that before. I think I get too involved with my friends. What happens to them is almost like it happens to me. But I'm changing. Maybe I'm growing up."

"You are, dear. Now—goodnight."

After that I felt less anxious about a trauma to Joyce over the Williams thing. Her friendship with Marge, Doreen and Henry's wife grew. Gladys' trial was quiet. She was acquitted. There was just a small note of it in our paper.

6

Greta was on her feet and doing all right. She had seemed content to stay with us. Suddenly she announced she was moving out, getting a room big enough for two because one of her friends was coming up to live.

Fine, we said, we hope you'll keep on doing well.

When Greta had gone I said, "Joyce, don't bring any more animals or friends here without asking us first. You just can't go offering our kitchen and bathroom to everybody you want to help."

"Okay," Joyce replied. She had a job in a small manufacturing plant. I got part-time work there.

Suddenly City Hall began to interfere in our lives. An inspector came around to check the shack for faults, safety hazards, sanitation. There wasn't much wrong but he noticed the TV aerial lying crosswise on the roof. It had fallen during a heavy storm and nobody'd bothered to fix it. He said it had to be repaired or removed, that it was an eyesore, if not dangerous. He wouldn't tell us whether there'd been complaints, or what his salary was. I told him he'd better be careful that he didn't become an eyesore himself.

Tom swore at me for being discourteous to the man. "Hell,"

I said, "I consider him discourteous. What right has he to come in here and tell us to get rid of an eyesore when they have a worse one at City Hall—that silly hunk of metal—the Archer? And why wouldn't he tell me his salary—is he ashamed or guilty?"

"Never mind the Archer," Tom growled. "They've made this law that property owners have to clean up and fix up their houses. You'd better watch your housekeeping."

"Yuh. Well I'd just like to see one of them bastards run down my housekeeping. Just because their own wives have money to hire help doesn't mean they have the right to criticize us poor women. If they want to send in a woman to scrub it up I won't stop her but I'll be damned if they're gonna make me do any better. You're the only one kicking anyway."

Shortly another city official appeared to find fault. There were a few tiles missing from the floors of the bathroom and kitchen. Windowsills had deteriorated and the hardware was missing. There was no wash basin in the bathroom. I couldn't see any need for a wash basin when we had a good bathtub with hot and cold running water.

Neither could Schmidt. He had an argument with an official in my presence. "See," I told Tom, "Schmidt doesn't like to be dictated to either."

"Who's going to pay for repairs and needless wash basins?" asked Tom.

"Yeah. Guess!" I told him.

After a while things quietened down. We thought Schmidt had made some agreement with City Hall.

Some evenings I'd take a stroll around our neighbourhood alone or with Jenny.

Joyce had been urging me to start using our public library. One day I took her advice. I got a card and borrowed an old book. It had excerpts from the works of De Tocqueville, Karl Marx and others. I was fascinated. I kept it overtime to the extent of a two-dollar fine which I couldn't pay. Hell, I knew I'd be fined but there was a lot of reading in that book and I felt a kinship with those authors. Anyway I had also found Billy's used bookstore. It was like discovering the mother-lode. The man had Perry Mason books galore and he charged ten cents a book. I bought a dozen.

At the bookstore I dug out some great books of poetry and readers I had studied in school. It was like a rebirth. They could shove their old library card. If they had anything I wanted to read I'd do it there and not take out the books. There was no fine for reading in the building.

Early in August Joyce came home one night with two hippies. She wanted to know if we'd let them stay overnight. At first Tom refused. The kids sat dejected on the steps of the front verandah with their heads down and their bedrolls beside them. Tom studied them.

"What should we do?" he asked me.

"Help them," I said. "At least a little."

We invited them in for a snack. We talked. They called themselves Brick and Belle. They were nineteen and seventeen respectively and married, they said. We took them at their word. After lunch and some conversation, Tom decided to take a chance on letting them stay the night. A good point in their favour, I thought, was their openness and their acceptance of our attitudes. They didn't promise anything except to act civilly.

Since they arrived on Friday night we let them sleep in next morning. I expected them to leave right after breakfast.

To my surprise, Belle asked if we'd let them stay, providing they could get work to support themselves. Tom and I had a hard time to decide. We just didn't feel it was humane to put those jobless, sick kids out on Toronto's cold streets without a penny. On the other hand, what trouble might we bring on ourselves and our children? I decided to ask the family. Johnny and Joyce said they'd give us a little more money each week. Billy and Jenny said they didn't mind sharing the house with two more people. Over the weekend Tom and I took pains to elicit more facts from Brick and Belle. Each had a loving mother somewhere. Where, we didn't press to learn. They were recuperating from a venereal disease but the doctor was treating them. They wouldn't endanger us. They had smoked marijuana but hadn't tried LSD yet, they said.

"All right," I said. "Now we all know the essential problems, let's try to solve them together. We can help you if you want to change your circumstances."

"Oh, we do," Belle said and Brick agreed.

"Well then, for now you have food, shelter and a chance to rest. The TV is working although we can only get channel six. Our aerial has been down awhile and nobody's bothered to fix it. Monday both of you can go looking for work. You ought to be able to get a day or two through Temp or Manpower."

"We'll do that," they told me. They did. Belle went right to work that same morning. Brick said he had no luck–he was more particular.

But Belle was sicker than we guessed. She became very ill by noon and was excused from work early. She and Brick were both home when I returned from my job. They told me about their day. Belle said she felt pretty bad and went to their room to lie down. A bit later she came to me to see if I had any aspirin. She had a raging headache. She felt worse than she could ever remember.

I asked her if she'd go to the hospital with me. She said yes. She was an outpatient at Women's College Hospital anyway. Don, Johnny and Tom were all away. I had no money. I borrowed a dollar to go by streetcar. Belle was able to walk some.

The receptionist asked for information I couldn't give. At last the doctor came. She said Belle was too ill to be questioned. I was asked more questions. I thought they wanted me to take responsibility for any bills incurred by Belle. I couldn't. My husband wouldn't consider that–it was utterly impossible. They decided they'd go after the welfare people. The child needed care. I let them list Belle as residing with me.

While Belle was in the hospital we all worked except Brick. He did leave the house some mornings but not for long. Tom said he was going to put him out. He did one morning when the two were alone in the house. It was a simple job. Brick left his and Belle's things. I took Belle cigarettes and a couple of magazines. She seemed to sincerely appreciate them. Brick visited her often.

When Belle got out of the hospital she and Brick came to live with us again. Belle found a job within a few days. During the day while she worked Brick stayed away from the house allegedly searching for a job.

I had been wondering if Belle would try to pay us back when she drew her first pay. She gave one week's board–the back one. Tom asked her to pay for the coming week in advance.

She wouldn't. She said she would see later. The two went out. They came back late at night.

Tom told me they had been smoking pot. I couldn't tell. In the morning Tom told Brick and Belle that now that they were no longer destitute he wanted them to move out right away or pay board in advance. They moved out.

My washer and toaster broke down, both the same day. We had no money for repairs or new appliances. Added to that we discovered that besides our few mice we had another pest to battle–cockroaches.

I was horrified. Gloria had had her house fumigated a year before and that was expensive.

"Oh, we don't need to fumigate yet," Tom said, "There's hardly any and you can keep them down by spraying cupboards, cracks and baseboards."

Well that didn't sound too bad. Mrs. Stanley had had her battles with them. She gave me pointers on the kind of spray to buy and where to put it. Both of us had helped fight bedbugs in our childhood. I began to look at the problem philosophically.

At the end of September I was laid off. I filed for unemployment benefits and looked for work. There were no jobs for me. Friends told me I could draw unemployment benefits as I had stamps. No waiting period was required this time.

Fine, I thought. Now I could look into Jenny's complaints about school. It was math again. I went to the school. Jenny was using a new math book. Her old math book with the exercises right in it had been put away. Why, I wanted to know. I had examined it and liked it. It had been set aside for later, I was told. Could I bring her new math book home to help her, I asked? Yes, but it probably won't do much good, I was told. That did it. My husband, I snarled, was one of the finest mathematicians in the world and it had been one of my best subjects in school.

I was displeased with that switch in math books. Jenny had gotten used to another one. It was expensive and designed to carry them through three or four grades. I was determined to find out more about their policies.

I wrote a long letter to a famous MP in Ottawa. I wanted to know about that book, and how to stop Jenny from being pushed around or subjected to derogatory comments every day from fellow pupils. Soon I was invited to the school for a discussion with the school inspector. He answered my questions fairly satisfactorily. About the book, well a mistake had been made in some office and the wrong book was ordered or delivered last year–it had been put away but would be used again. He agreed that such mistakes cost us taxpayers a lot of money and caused confusion and other troubles. As for Jenny being pushed around, etc., she should tell the teacher. She was unable to because of her fear of the teacher and repercussions, I said–surely it was up to the staff to encourage pupils to bring their troubles to them–not discourage them by a cold, remote attitude. If, I warned, Jenny turns out like the rest of us, she may become too aggressive. I returned home feeling Jenny would have an easier time. She did, and perhaps some of the other kids did too.

Brick and Belle dropped in for a chat. Brick had done a week's work somewhere after they left us. Belle had worked until recently but was presently unemployed and ineligible for unemployment benefits because she hadn't enough stamps.

"I'm back with my mum," Belle said.

"Your mother lives in Toronto?" I asked.

"Oh, yes. I have a little girl too. She's eighteen months old now. Mom's been looking after her. They kicked me out of school for that."

"So, why didn't you let your mother know you were in the hospital?" I asked Belle.

"Oh, Mrs. Firth, I just couldn't. I was sort of ashamed and scared. I just couldn't face her after I got sick," Belle explained.

"I see," I said. "But you did get your nerve up. I'm glad you're with your mother and little girl."

"So am I," said Belle fervently.

"And you, Brick," I asked, "do you have relatives here in Toronto?"

"No. My mother lives in Winnipeg," Brick said.

"Do you write to her?" I asked.

"Sometimes. Not since we stayed here though. I think I will though," he said.

"Well if you care to, tell me if you think your mother is a good parent or not," I said.

"Mine is good," Belle said, "except she doesn't understand

everything and sometimes expects too much."

"Mine's the same," Brick said. "She was scared I'd turn out like my father."

"It was stay in school, do your homework, don't go here, don't go there, don't do that, all the time with Mum," Belle went on. "She just wanted me to suit her."

"Well, but—don't you want your mother to suit you too? Have you considered that? Have you really tried to see how similar people are in what they want from others?"

"Well, not too hard. I didn't think much about it," Belle said.

"But look. That's the trouble with lots of you kids. You're so concerned with your side of it, and how society tries to brainwash you that you don't realize you're trying to brainwash the establishment and force it into your mould. The only difference is in what each generation sees as good."

They looked at me quietly, not speaking. I offered them some tea or coffee. They accepted. They left soon after.

A few days later I was down at the unemployment office looking for a job. I spotted a sign advising people to inquire about the Government adult retraining plan. I inquired and was gruffly told I didn't qualify because I hadn't been working steadily for three years.

When I returned home I wrote a nasty letter to Ottawa about their stupid schemes. Soon I received a fat pamphlet explaining the plan. It didn't sound so harsh. I thought I could qualify and so, I was sure, could Belle. For Belle it would be wonderful, I thought, since it paid a living allowance while one took a course.

I wrote to Ottawa describing my circumstances. A letter came back informing me that an appointment would be made with a counsellor at 200 Jarvis Street to discuss my case.

When next Belle and Brick dropped in I told them about the plan and showed them the newsletter. If they were brushed off at Jarvis, I advised, write to Ottawa. They said they would. They were both sure they qualified for retraining. They did have to write to Ottawa and in the end were found to qualify. Belle was jubilant when she came to tell me about it.

"You see now, Belle," I said, "that's the way to fight the establishment—you defeated the part that tried to step on you."

"Oh, boy, did we ever. And did they deserve to be slapped

down! And Mrs. Firth I intend to pay you back when I get working," Belle said happily.

"No, Belle, I don't want that," I told both of them. "Pass it on. If you see someone who needs help give it to them."

Sure enough I got my appointment. I had the interview and my name was put on a "waiting list". The city didn't have the staff or facilities to train us all at once. All right, I'd wait. I couldn't do anything else.

While I waited I used my time and talents to straighten up my house and family affairs. The kids were getting along fairly well at school, and work, and socially. But my appliances were giving me trouble. The iron decided to join the TV, toaster and washer. It stopped steaming. Johnny, Don and Tom all took it apart in turn and finally it worked dry. Tom fashioned a toaster from strips of steel and wire. It sat over two burners on the electric stove. We enjoyed toast again.

Peace was not yet to be. City Hall kept after Schmidt and he would complain to Tom and Tom would growl to me. What worried Tom was that we might be badgered or forced into moving. What bothered me was the stupid dictatorship from City Hall. I knew other and far worse homeowners who were not being forced to upgrade their properties even though they were rented out.

The newspapers carried stories about tenants complaining that they were powerless to get their landlords to obey City Hall and Queen's Park. I felt Schmidt, and my family, were being discriminated against.

I yearned to fight back. Was there something that I as a Toronto citizen could complain about other than the annoying inspections? For some weeks Jenny and Mabel Stanley had been talking disparagingly about the posters of near-naked females plastered on the Victory Theatre. They didn't think such pictures should be displayed. I wrote a letter to the Mayor about it giving the names and ages of the children.

After a while I received an answering letter. As I understood it, a commission of some kind had looked at the posters and felt they were not obscene.

I went to the library and studied the laws on obscenity. I then wrote another letter suggesting that although the commission "felt" the posters were not obscene, they might in fact be obscene under the law. The possible harmful effects of these pictures on developing children might, in turn, be visited upon society. I couldn't prove that–but neither could they disprove it. They didn't answer that letter.

Sometime in November my unemployment cheques stopped. I was told that my claim had run out but I could qualify for seasonal benefits in December. I didn't know what "seasonal benefits" were.

Mr. Stanley and other people explained. They also told me that I should still be getting regular benefits because it wasn't a year since I had filed my first claim and I still had stamps unused. I was puzzled. Surely the Unemployment Commission knew its business. I was urged to make an inquiry. I did and discovered I had more than the required stamps for seasonal benefits. I argued. A lady clerk told me I should be on regular benefits. A male clerk told me I would get seasonal. I asked what happened to my extra stamps. "Oh, we're saving them," I was told.

I thought that might be the rule. My neighbours howled. Someone was crazy, they said. Another trip to the library. When I understood what "benefit year" and "seasonal benefit" and the rest of it meant I wrote to Ottawa. I'd had enough of the local runaround.

Again I was laughed at by Tom and friends and neighbours. For sure I'd never get regular benefits–they must know their business; after all they had education. I sizzled. I had no job and no income and no great family troubles. What to do with my time? Certainly not clean house as Tom suggested. I'd done that in the summer.

I counted the days I'd been waiting for rehabilitation training. It was long enough, I reckoned. Time to bother the powers-that-be. I did by phoning and visiting, and the response, to my mind, was indifferent and discourteous. Actually I suspected they didn't want me, a trouble-maker, in their plan at all. There was a connection with the Unemployment Commission. I was told that sometime in the new year I'd be assessed and placed in a student group. I waited some more.

Christmas came closer. I began drawing seasonal benefits.

Then a letter came saying I couldn't draw any more because my claim was being re-examined and another from Ottawa saying they'd asked for the re-examination.

"You stubborn bitch," Tom laughed, "causing all that trouble, making them poor clerks work and costing us tax-payers money—for nothing. Well, we'll see."

Brick and Belle called to say they were doing all right. They were studying and receiving their living allowances regularly. They had some good teachers but one miserable one. Because of the good ones they figured they could tolerate the snide remarks and obvious distaste of the bad. It wouldn't be forever, thank God and Ottawa.

As the Christmas season drew closer it seemed a lot of our young people got the urge to make a change, to travel. Joyce disappeared one day. She did it sort of sneaky because she had to use her board money for the fare. She left me a note saying not to worry but listed no destination. Tom was fit to be tied—but soon calmed down.

His attention was soon diverted to our teenaged nephew who suddenly arrived from the east to spend his school holidays in Toronto. Earl had been here as a young boy and thought he'd enjoy another visit. His friend and a former school-mate of Don's, Larry Miller, made the trip with him. Larry had a job waiting and relatives to stay with.

With Joyce away we were able to provide for Earl quite easily. We were pleased to have him. Larry was a welcome evening visitor. They brought news and flavour from old New Brunswick. Larry was a little older than Don but still under twenty-one. He drank but never brought beer or liquor to our place. Don drank a bit too, but he spent most evenings with a girlfriend. To take his place Andy, Harold and Howie, one at a time or all together, would walk in.

Our home became a "Christly madhouse", Tom complained. "How do you expect a man to get any rest around here?"

He could if he shut the bedroom door and the boys confined their bull-sessions to Johnny's room upstairs. But when they began to wrestle or troop in a bunch to the kitchen for coffee, Tom objected strenuously. The kitchen was off our bedroom and was a comfortable place to sit around, drink coffee and talk. I called it our community hall.

Within a week I received a letter from Joyce. She was fine, she wrote, in Edmonton. She had been able to rent a room and get work right away. She'd even been able to save a few dollars for food until she'd have a pay cheque. Tom dashed out and wired her ten dollars. "Poor little fool," he said, "I don't want her cold or hungry."

What's one more inmate in a madhouse? Johnny met and liked a seventeen-year-old American boy from Florida who was in Toronto staying with his grandparents. At Johnny's urging he came over to meet some friendly Canadians. Glenn Connors was his name. He must have liked our company because he visited us three or four times. He told us he hadn't studied much about our country in school but he was enjoying his visit. He was to return home for New Year's Day.

There were serious and silly discussions, continual music with the record player going and the boys singing, and card games played for nickels and dimes. Those kids put their hearts into things. They played as hard to win a dollar pot as grown men sometimes do when a million is the stake. I reckon it wasn't the money involved—but the half-serious competition with friends.

It wasn't all joy and light though. One evening the boys were all home, even Don. They got talking about life—and the Vietnam War.

"Boy, I'm glad I'm too young to go," I heard Howie comment, "but then Canada isn't in it, not really."

"Yes, but we can go. Just cross the border and the Americans'll take you, eh, Glenn?" Don said. "So Howie, don't let that stop you."

"Go yourself, Don," Howie retorted, "you're old enough. Or are you too chicken?"

"Well—you can think what you want but I don't see any good reason to go. It's better to be a mercenary in Nigeria—if you want to fight."

"Yuh, that's something," Johnny said, "killing other guys for money, the mercenary bastards. I think I'll go and kill them for free, myself."

"Oh you," Don said, "you dream too much. You've got to

face facts. That's the way people are. To survive you've got to strike first and hard."

Larry spoke, "Glenn, what do you think about it? I suppose you'll soon have to go."

"Well," Glenn answered slowly, while the record player sounded *Folsom Prison Blues*, "I don't have to go. There are other things."

"Yuh, like coming to Canada," Billy said, perhaps a bit sarcastically from the safe age of fourteen.

"You shut up!" Johnny cried. "You don't even know what you're talking about. You won't be so ready to go out to get your own head shot off—in a few years."

"Well if you guys would fight now it'd be all over by then," Billy laughed.

"Yuh—well why should we do all the fighting while guys like you live it up?" Harold asked. "We're not that much older."

"Anyhow my father went to war before so I could be free," Sidney said, "and a hell of a lot of good that did him—or me. Even when he was dying with cancer no one helped except you people and George Patterson. But I would go if Canada got in it. What the hell's the difference if you die one way or another?"

"The difference might be what you die for. Who in hell wants to fight somebody else's war?" Earle said.

"We are," Glenn reminded them. "Everybody expects America to keep the world free alone. We're fighting your fight too."

"So. If them Vietnamese bastards asked you to fight did you have to? Let them settle it themselves. Christ, we're in for trouble with them French Quebeckers," Johnny said.

"Haw—haw!" Don laughed. "Boy—we'll see poor old Billy and Howie run then. When our civil war starts."

The conversation brought sad memories to me of 1943 when I had two brothers overseas. I felt the tears start to form.

"Boys, that's enough," I interrupted. "We've had too many wars. But now it's near Christmas and no time to pick at one another. You won't have much time together. Get out the cards. I'll make fresh coffee. Andy and you, Sidney, sing for us. Now come on. Give us that one Sidney—'God Rest Ye Merry, Gentlemen' or 'Good King Wenceslaus'."

I began to heat water. Sidney picked up his guitar. Nobody

wanted to play cards. Don was going out and Larry asked for a ride uptown. Our earlier air of convivial gaiety had been replaced by one of unpleasant depression. I had my pills to help relieve my tension but the kids had no such thing—not even alcohol as older men did.

7

Christmas Eve we were surprised to receive a visit from Sandra Berube. She told us she was home from training school for Christmas because of good behaviour but had to go back in a few days. She had turned sixteen and looked very well. She was surprised to find Joyce away. I invited her to stay awhile. Harold and Andy were upstairs with Johnny, Earle and Sidney. As usual they were involved in a music session.

Sandra and I talked in the kitchen. I confined the conversation to simple amenities.

Billy came in from visiting a friend on Spadina. He knew Sandra's mother and two brothers. At once he wanted to know what reform school was like.

"Well, it isn't so bad," Sandra said, "but you're not so free. Nobody likes it. We're pretty well bossed around but some of them are nice."

"Do you have to study like in school?" Billy asked.

"Oh, yes. It's almost the same. I'm learning more there than at school."

"Really. I wouldn't want to go to one of them places."

"I didn't want to go either."

"Well what really happened, Sandra? Tell me," Billy said.

"Why should I tell you? What does it matter?" Sandra asked.

I answered for Billy. "Because Sandra, you've got to face it. Now you're over sixteen they'll publish your name if you get caught breaking the law. You know that. Billy reads *Tab* and *Hush* once in awhile. You don't have to tell what happened but it's recorded anyway. Still, if you can talk about it it might help you to choose what kind of life you really want—after."

"Oh, I can talk about it," Sandra laughed. "We used to read *Tab* and *Hush*. There were stories about some of us—not me, but Viola, and Laura, and Marie. The papers didn't tell the whole thing either. There's things we know the papers don't publish."

Sidney came for coffee. He had heard Sandra's last sentence. "Well, why don't you tell us?" he asked.

"Oh, well it wasn't so much," she said. "You know, down on Queen near the big tavern? Well Helen Star, that's what she calls herself, said it was a good place to pick up johns. So Nancy and I went down one night, just to see. We weren't very good—no experience—but we tried. Well—what the hell—thousands are doing it and the men are just as bad as we are. But they get off. It's all right to buy but wrong to sell. Crazy. Anyway a good-looking guy came over after a while. He looked young and good for a few bucks. Nancy said she'd go with him, anywhere. He said he had a friend—the friend had a car. He'd need a girl for his friend. We fell for the shit. Nancy and I went with him to the car and got in. Hell, they were undercover detectives. What could we do? We'd been drinking too—but Nancy didn't get sent up. Her mother said they were leaving Toronto anyway so the judge let Nancy go with them. I don't blame my mother. I'dda just got in trouble again."

"But, Sandra—why?" I asked. "Oh, I know you don't like school and all that, and your father's away and your mother works and your brother tries to boss you—but there are other ways to be free and independent."

"Oh, I don't really know why, I don't really think about why—but it is sort of fun travelling around with fancy-dressed men in big cars to real plushy places. Besides, they don't shit all over us like lots of people. They treat us real nice—like we're worth something," Sandra said.

"Yes, they probably do—while they use you kids. But what'll

it be like if you ever want to get married, to have children?" I spoke seriously, trying to get Sandra to look at a possible future.

"Oh, I don't think I want to get married. What is marriage? Fighting all the time—and too many kids. Why don't married women protect themselves more, or the husbands?" Sandra asked.

"Well, it's your life," Sidney said, "but I don't think there's much in it. Unless you get rich fast so you can retire young. Were you and Nancy working alone or was there a gang?"

Sidney had been on his own since the age of fifteen. With his father dead and mother married again he decided to quit school and travel a bit. He had worked his way across the country from the east to west and back by the time he came to board with us.

"We helped each other," Sandra told Sidney. "We didn't have a gang, really. We'd just get together in the evening and sort of let things happen. We'd walk around and if a guy came along and asked us for a date and we liked him we'd get in the car. We knew the places to go where johns would look for dates."

"Well, it's a free country," Sidney said, "but it shows how your mothers brought you up."

"It's not my mother's fault," Sandra flared. "What about my father? What about the damn men? They're as bad as we are. If they didn't buy, girls couldn't sell. I bet you've picked up girls like us before for a one-night stand."

Sidney looked coldly at her. "You're wrong," he said. "I don't happen to believe girls are things to be bought and sold. If a man wants sex there's always marriage."

"Well, I don't see all the bloody difference between selling it plain and covering it up with a piece of paper. Marriage, I hear, is a form of prostitution. Look what a wife gets for putting out to her husband. Most of them sell it just like us but they pretend they don't."

Before the boys could say something, I did. "Sandra, in a sense you may be right. But a husband buys more than sex and he gives more than money. He buys help and labour and care and he gives the same, as well as companionship in good times and bad. Sure, sex is involved, but it isn't the main thing and as a by-product there are kids that most women want. A husband helps with the kids too, and he also gets something from them if he takes pride in them and likes young people. If you get pregnant will a john give a damn, will he help you out of it, or through the long wait?"

"No. But marriage is still a business," Sandra insisted. "I know women who marry for security. They don't care about their husbands or do all that stuff you're talking about. I don't mean you, Mrs. Firth."

"You can mean me, Sandra. If you can't speak your mind, I'm not much of a friend. Now Tom and I fight—but that, too, is something we get from marriage—a place to blow off steam. Fighting is a kind of therapy, too—it can be healthy if people are honest. Sometimes people simply can't see what they're doing to others. A fight can help the other party understand, or it can make him respect your feelings. But women who make a business of selling sex have to take more shit than us wives. No woman can ever hope to get as much out of prostitution as out of marriage. A lifetime with one man if he's half-decent is a lot better than many scattered minutes with a lot of men, I reckon."

"Yeah, sure, if he's half-decent. I don't know one happy married person, unless it's you. Shit, I have friends married only a year and they wish they'd stayed single."

"Oh, well," Billy said, "you're too young anyway, Sandra. I know how old you are—but you try to act older, dressing up and using all that make-up and bleaching your hair. Why don't you just be yourself?"

"Who are you to talk, Billy? I bet you've had a drink, and smoke and gamble. Why do you? Where'd you learn it? It's just because I'm a girl that people get mad. Us girls are always put down and made into slaves. We're born slaves, that's what."

"Well, anyway," I said, "people have been down before and made it to the top. Your life isn't ruined Sandra, but you can waste it if you just live for the present. And the same goes for all of us. Now I'm going up to listen to some songs. Coming?"

Sandra was on curfew. She had to go home then. I wished I could help her but I felt incapable.

When Sandra had gone all the boys decided to go out for a while. Jenny and I sat down by the kitchen table to read. We had a tree up. It was pretty good. I had lugged it home from her school for Jenny. We had a few lights from the year before but no one had got them working yet.

In the summer I had been able to buy for fifty cents the Centennial Edition of *The Treasury of Poems.* I had read just a tiny bit of it. This Christmas Eve I felt like reading it so that's the book I chose.

Before I sat down to read I thought a small drink of wine would be nice. A neighbour had given us a bottle only that morning and I'd placed it well back in the cupboard under the sink. I went to get it. It was gone.

I couldn't believe it. I bent right down and felt all around. I contorted myself and craned my neck. Nothing was in that cubbyhole except my scrub pail. An ugly suspicion crossed my mind. One of the boys might have stolen it. No, my instincts protested, they wouldn't. Sandra? She hadn't had a chance. Perhaps the boys hid it—to see if I'd get mad.

Oh, well! I settled for a cup of strong tea with plenty of canned milk. Happily reading, smoking and sipping tea I never noticed the time until I heard Tom's key in the lock. As he came in yelling "Merry Christmas", I looked up.

"Is it that late?" I asked.

"Sure is. Jenny, are you still up?" Tom said.

"Of course," Jenny said. "Is it Christmas? Really Christmas? Can I open my presents?"

"Sure, honey," I said, "go ahead."

Johnny came cheerily back in.

"Oh, you're home, Dad," he called. "Well, Merry Christmas all. Well, break out the wine." Suddenly I remembered.

"Tom," I accused, "you hid it, didn't you?"

"Hid what? The wine? Oh, I didn't hide it. I just put it away so they wouldn't drink it all on me," Tom said.

"They, who? You mean the kids or my friends? Do you think I wouldn't save you one lousy drink? Goddam but you have an evil mind," I said.

"Okay, okay. The damn thing isn't hid. It's in the bedroom in the clothes-closet down under the old boots in the box.

"Well, for— " I muttered. Not hid, hummm.

Tom took off his outer clothes and draped them on a chair.

Jenny began to shout in delight. Johnny got out glasses and we drank. Even Jenny had a taste. She twisted her face in displeasure.

"How can you drink that?" she asked.

"Oh, we're foolish," I said. "Now stop some of your noise. Why don't you take that doll to my room?"

Jenny gathered up her few but good gifts and went away.

"Well I work again tomorrow. Hey, where are the lights for her tree? Why aren't the lights up or did you throw them out?" Tom said.

I brought out the lights. I had two sets. Johnny and I disentangled the bulbs. We plugged them in. Not one bulb lit up.

"They're burnt out," Tom said.

"Oh, not all of them," Johnny told him. "One or two. I'll find them."

He started to look. The sets were the cheap kind—when one bulb went out the others followed suit. Johnny would remove a bulb from set A and replace it with one from set B. If it didn't work he would keep on until all Bs had been tried. If still unsuccessful he'd have to replace A's first bulb and repeat the process with another. It could be a time-consuming job.

"Why don't you make a tester?" Tom asked. "Here, I'll make it."

Tom took Set A and cut off the plug and a bulb socket. He joined the two by splicing the wires. I watched in fascination. When he had the wires spliced he wrapped the naked wire with plastic tape, then he inserted a bulb and plugged it into our wall outlet. Zip-zap, a little flash of light, and one coloured bulb lay dead on the table.

"You can't do it that way," Johnny said. "The current is too strong for one bulb. It'll burn out every time."

"How can it blow out?" Tom demanded angrily, testing another bulb. It burnt out too and I grabbed at the rest.

"Tom," I said, "I see what he means. I don't know much about voltage and amps and resistance but if these sets are designed so that a dozen or so light up together then one alone must be too weak to stand the same current that heats my iron. These are my lights and I'll be damned if you're going to blow them all out just through stubbornness."

"I tell you I know what I'm doin'! How in hell do you think

I got my license?" Tom roared. He was referring to his stationary engineer's license, not an electrician's.

"I don't know how you got it but I do know you're tryin' to ruin all my bulbs," I roared back. "Gimme that bloody tester."

"Oh, fer– no brains. I tell you, no brains," growled Tom.

"No brains, Lord. Talk about pots and kettles calling names," I laughed. "You remember last Christmas and who broke whose case of beer?"

Tom subsided. He busied himself with the wine. Johnny went on quietly screwing the little bulbs in and out of sockets on set B. I made an effort to sing "The First Noel" and was joined by Jenny who had returned to the kitchen to listen to the shouting. " . . . was to certain poor shepherds in fields . . . "

Bright lights flashed in our faces. Johnny had achieved success. The set of little coloured bulbs lay glowing beautifully on the table-top.

"He did it," exclaimed Tom. "What a boy!"

"Don't you mean, what a brainless boy?" I teased. Tom and I began to laugh together, at one another, and at life's little comedies.

Later Earle, Sidney and Billy returned together. They were surprised and pleased to see the lights on the tree. Don arrived a little later. Everybody except Jenny and Billy drank a toast to the New Year. Billy didn't like the "stuff" either.

The bit of Christmas Day we got up to see passed quietly. Tom went to work and came home just as I finished boiling my pudding.

"Oh, you made a bugger in the bag," he greeted me. "Good. Let's have some. I'm hungry."

We all sat down to eat. It was really good. That was 11:30 p.m. Soon we were all in bed.

Boxing Day was quiet too. Too quiet. The kids began to look for mischief.

On December 28 I returned home from the corner store to find my kitchen full of smoke and an acrid smell permeating the air.

"Johnny made a bomb, Mama," Jenny cried, "a bomb–but it blew up too soon."

"Oh, God. Johnny," I screamed, "what are you trying to do,

drive us crazy?"

"Oh, Maw. It wasn't that dangerous. I just lit the fuse too soon. It was mostly smoke. You worry too much."

I fought to calm myself. "Johnny," I said, trying to speak quietly, "dangerous or not–this is no place to play around with chemicals and do your experiments. Now, I can't stop you but you should have more care for Dad and me. We're a family and the members should have consideration for one another."

"Okay, okay. I'll not do it anymore if it makes you so nervous."

"Don't be sarcastic. You'll be old like us some day, probably. You mightn't be so damn calm then either. Now get this smoke cleared up–'cause Dad'll soon be home. He's liable to have a heart attack."

The next day I caught Billy melting wax in a small frying pan on the stove. Wax got on the burner and burned. Again the kitchen stank. Billy was "only trying to see if he could combine wax and water."

I began to wish for school to open in a hurry.

The next evening around ten I received a telegram from Joyce. She was in difficulty; would I please send her fifteen dollars right away? The wire gave me quite a jolt. I had no money. Tom and the boys were all out except Billy who could not help. My only hope lay in Mrs. Stanley.

Luckily she had her rent money and was able to lend me twenty dollars for a few days. She knew Joyce and liked her. She was glad to be able to help, she said. I rushed down to the station and wired the money to Joyce.

"She's coming home!" Tom said when he returned from work and read the telegram. "Sure. She's quit over something," he continued. "Probably a fight with her boss and she hadn't enough for her fare. You'll see. She'll be here in a few days."

I hoped Tom was right but I was afraid Joyce was in some kind of legal trouble. The newspapers carried daily reports of kids in trouble and often illegal drugs were involved. I kept those fears to myself.

About six a.m. I was awakened by the ringing of the doorbell. As I hurried to see who was there I heard Joyce's cheerful cry, "Let me in. I'm back!"

I opened the door to her. She strode in, laden with suitcases and bulging shopping bags which she deposited in the hallway. Into the kitchen she walked with an air appropriate to one who has pulled off a successful coup.

Before I could properly welcome her the rest of our household came crowding into the kitchen eager to hear of the adventures and troubles of our prodigal. A few apologies were expected too.

Well she had wanted to see Donnie—that was the main reason she'd left. She certainly had not gone like a thief in the night—it was broad daylight. Sure she'd gotten a good job—only her widowed employer, Mrs. Jones, had reverted to her old state of alcoholism after a disappointment—and since Joyce boarded with her it became very bad. Well Joyce couldn't stand that. She'd wired for money because she'd seen enough of Edmonton and she'd saved only thirty dollars and her boss, drunk-sick, refused to pay the wages due. Joyce couldn't wait to lay charges and collect. Yes she'd been scared—the woman talked of putting a gun to someone's head—but the strange, cold city hadn't got to her. In fact she'd thought of going right on to Vancouver. Oh, she'd have made out fine. Anyway when Mrs. Jones sobered up she'd probably send along the twenty dollars owing. Certainly she had every intention of getting a job and paying us all back: the twenty dollars back board, the fifteen dollars wired plus costs, and the five dollars borrowed from Tom away back in July.

Yes, she'd brought most of the "borrowed" items back. Of course she hadn't stolen them. The items consisted of Don's wide leather belt with the large buckle, my snow-boots that were cut too low for the snow out there, the corduroy jacket Tom liked to wear to the races—she hadn't worn it at all, a new can of Johnny's Rightguard, my old and only pair of scissors for which we'd all been searching, two of my best towels, Don's girlfriend's sweater, and a pair of Sidney's jeans he'd thought he lost at the laundromat.

No, she didn't expect her old room back—she was willing to sleep on the floor, at least for a while as long as there weren't any cockroaches, the first room she'd had had been full of them. At least at Mrs. Jones's she'd had a clean room and the woman had been very nice until that drunk. No, she did not regret her trip. She'd learned a lot and had a lot of fun. We were not to worry, she'd pay us all back.

Joyce had come home by bus. She'd have preferred the train but it cost too much. As it was she had only enough for one meal after she'd bought her ticket. She'd not starved because she'd been befriended by a French-Canadian girl who boarded the bus in Calgary. She was on her way home to Montreal. The girls travelled together. They had a jolly time discussing their many great experiences.

I was glad to have Joyce home again. I looked upon her return as an omen that the year ahead would be good to my family.

School reopened.

Joyce had little trouble getting a job as a clerk in a large grocery store. In no time it seemed our lives were back in the old routine.

Our friends and neighbours were having family and job troubles. Andy Stanley told us he was going to leave home and live with his father's sister. He couldn't study at home or even relax much because Bill was always picking on Olga. We were all sorry for Andy. He said he would continue school if he could get a part-time job.

He saved most of the money he made at odd jobs he did after school and one day he dropped in, said good-bye to us, and left Toronto. Later I heard his father say that it was good; that Andy was old enough to support himself. He was not yet seventeen years old.

Late in January I received a neatly-typed letter from Ottawa. After a long, careful account of my work and unemployment history, it stated that a recheck of my current claim showed that a mistake had been made, that I should not have been so abruptly taken off regular benefits in November, 1967. I was advised that my claim was being adjusted and I'd receive the money owing shortly.

Who can describe the feelings that swept me at the news? Even Tom seemed uplifted at the victory. "You beat them," he said. "You showed them bastards they can't put it over on us."

Yet while I was glad the mistake was theirs, not mine, and it was to be corrected, I was sad and angry that at least partly because of it I'd been unable to send a Christmas gift to my parents or Nell and her little ones. How many such mistakes, I wondered, did they make on less fortunate people, mistakes that were never corrected because the victims didn't know their rights?

Now it was time to get after the rehabilitation people again. I began phoning them. At first I was told the counsellors were all busy, wait and they'd call me. After a few days of that I began to pester them at their offices. I was really out to fight.

Eventually in February I was properly interviewed and allowed to join their program. We weren't allowed to begin retraining right away. First we had to go through an assessment period—this would take from three to six weeks, they told me.

When I reported to a city-owned building I was put to work assembling mattress handles. I was familiar with similar work and found it easy.

In one big room about twenty other people were going through their assessment period. Most of them were young and handicapped in some way. Another woman about my age started work there the same day as I, doing the same thing. Both of us tried to work well and steadily but we noticed the youngsters were doing a lot of playing. They were peeling labels off long rolls of tape and sticking them on various spray cans. They would take a can and spray it into the air, making silly comments. Nobody told them to stop or quieten down. One supervisor even joined them, laughing and joking. The other woman and I slowed our work pace and began to talk.

A supervisor came over and asked us to stop talking. I said, "I'm willing but you'd better make that rule apply to everyone." She moved the other woman away.

At coffee-break I found we had to pay for coffee and milk. After break I noticed those kids were not required to put the garbage in any receptacle. The spoiled labels and empty rolls of tape were allowed to unwind in long, hazardous strips on the floor. To get out of the room I had to wade through their mess. I began to think that I didn't belong here and no good could come to me from it.

I decided to ask the supervisor if I could have another talk with the counsellor who'd placed me there for assessment. She said no, I couldn't.

"In that case," I said, "I'll talk all I want as long as I'm here."

Five minutes later she came to me and told me I could see the man at three that afternoon.

At noon I punched out and went home. I told Tom about the place. He asked if there was a fire escape.

"I didn't see one and there were no signs. The washroom is dirty, the floors are dirty and there's no nurse or proper first-aid station."

"Complain to the Department of Labour," Tom advised. I did, by phone.

That afternoon, I saw the counsellor. There was simply nothing he could do for me, he said. That's the way the plan was set up. There were other courses but I couldn't get into them because of my disability—the disability being the nervous breakdowns I'd had and the fact that I was still under a doctor's care.

All right, I thought, that's the way it is but I'm not quitting just yet. However, I didn't intend to slave there three to six weeks, five days a week for no pay whatsoever, not even a free cup of coffee.

The next morning I reported to the centre, punched my card and sat down to wait. Shortly before eight the supervisor came in and announced that we weren't to do our regular chores yet, we were required to do some cleaning. He was not joking.

Well then I learned about our Department of Labour. They cared so little about working people less able than themselves that they wanted us to clean ourselves a spot to work in. I was disgusted and enraged. Clean that cruddy hole for nothing? Not me.

While the male supervisor bribed and coerced the others to clean up I went to the female supervisor and demanded a signed statement showing the hours I'd been "employed" there and the fact that I was receiving no pay.

It took two hours to get it and then they wouldn't give it to me until I'd been able to contact Tom at home and he'd come down to see what the matter was. My former counsellor arrived just after Tom and he tried to tell Tom we didn't get pay because we were not regular employees.

"Don't you sell those things to the public?" Tom asked.

"Well we have contractors," the man said.

"Then you're breaking the Labour Law," Tom said. "They're entitled to the wage required by the Department of Labour."

My little fight didn't end there though. I sent long, explanatory and bitter letters to leading newspapers, heads of businesses and government people. I even scrounged up the money for a couple of telegrams. I found out about many of our country's leaders. I even sought help from our Civil Rights Commissions—they said they couldn't help me. And some labour unions—same attitude—they washed their hands.

Meanwhile I tried to have another go at the assessment deal—no dice. They wouldn't have me. Apparently I had caused a bit of a ruckus. Anyway the counsellors had me go to a psychiatrist in an effort, it appeared to me, to prove that I was unfit for retraining, or at least a person prone to make mountains of molehills. I had seen the psychiatrist when I had been sick the previous summer. He found me no worse than before. Then I found out about some of our doctors. To my astonishment I was informed that some medical doctors and psychiatrists had okayed that place and the program. When I inquired about what kind of people would okay a program that forced handicapped people to labour for nothing, I received no direct answer.

The doctor did listen carefully to my story and complaints. Then he shook his head and asked, "How do you get into these—er—things?"

"I just seem to walk into them," I answered.

Well even with the psychiatrist's second okay I didn't get back into their program. I'd have to be put back on their waiting list they said.

It dawned on me that I was defeated. Without money to hire a lawyer to fight for me I couldn't win. I'd never collect for those few hours of work nor could I stop the blatant exploitation of those other unfortunate people.

Naturally I wasn't allowed to quietly forget my defeat—not right away. Gloria heard about it. My penchant for battles was a kind of joke to her and most members of both our families. As soon as she could she came down to ask about my trouble. As was our custom we made ourselves comfortable in the kitchen at the ends of the table with coffee and cigarettes for our talk.

"Johnny told me how you started the retraining you were telling me about and how you quit the first day. Why do you get into these fights? What good does it do?" Gloria asked.

"I can't tell you exactly why. I have my reasons of course, but a psychiatrist might be able to figure it out better, though they're not interested. The good it does is emotional. I hate to see people picked on, tramped on and taken advantage of. I can't say why about that either but I hate myself if I just close my eyes and let such rot go on, especially when I'm right in there."

"But that thing's run by the Government. You must have known you couldn't beat the Government."

"I do now but I didn't when I started. I didn't think the Government knew what them money-grabbing bastards were doing to the handicapped people. I couldn't believe our Government would let it go on. We have laws to make employers pay a certain wage."

"Didn't you get any money at all?"

"Not for the work we did. We got our unemployment benefit or welfare. Some were on welfare and some on pogey. But we're entitled to that without slaving for some damn crooked company and its cohorts."

"But that was only for a time wasn't it? Wouldn't they have started paying you later on?"

"Well that I don't know. They said they can't say—they can't even say if you're gonna go past the assessment period. They won't tell you anything you need to know like how much they want you to do in an hour or a day. It's a real slimey place. I'm not gonna work six weeks or so for nothing and still get nothing after. How'd you like to do that?"

"I'd do it if I had to. You've got to take shit on every job."

"Ah Gloria, you'll never understand. I can take shit. I've taken it before but then I was working for something. There it looked like I might just get shit and more shit and in the end that's all I'd have; a pot full of the stuff."

"Well what have you got now for Christ's sake?" Gloria laughed.

"I've got the knowledge that I tried to stop the corruption.

I've tried to tell you before that sometimes a person just has to stand up and fight for the sake of ego and pride. It's a matter of principle. Can't you see?"

"I guess so. But I still don't understand. I can't see any real good it does—this fighting over principles."

"That's because you never did that. You've got principles, sure, everyone has but you've just never been in a situation where you had to forsake them or fight. If it does happen you'll understand. Otherwise you'll never know. It isn't easy to understand until you've experienced it."

"I understand but I don't see where you think it's getting you."

"Gloria you don't see that because you don't understand. I don't know if it's because you can't understand or simply because you're too stubborn to admit other people prefer to live different from you. This protesting or fighting I do is not to get me anywhere except into a state of mind. It gives me a sense of honour or something. I don't know why but I can't just look on and let bullies walk all over weaker people. I never could. Perhaps it's because of my upbringing but when I see poor, weak people getting the dirty end of a deal it riles me—I can't just turn my head and pass by because I'll feel ashamed and guilty."

"But Sophia, you can't change the world. You're only one person."

"Oh for gawd's sake. I'm not trying to change the world alone. I'm merely trying to help clean it up a little and if I can't do that at least I feel I'm not increasing man's inhumanity to man. Oh, you'll never see so there's no point in talking it over and over. It doesn't matter if you see or anyone else sees. I'm the one with the problem—so it's what I see that matters. Honest to God, I don't see why sometimes I bother trying to explain to you, unless it's because I see in you a possible ally. Listen, will you try to explain something for my benefit for a change? Explain why you're always helping them fellows at work, that Arthur Bruce from old N.B. and the one you call Eddie, and that poor girl who gets picked on by nearly everybody. Yes, smartie, you explain your motives now."

"Well I, uh, I guess I like them and—well they ask me."

"Now Gloria, you're lying again. They don't always ask you—

you offer your help and advice freely. Why in hell do you help me? I don't ask. You jump right in and start trying to assist before you even know if I want your help or will even accept it. It's no good to lie. You're cut from the same cloth as me and you know it. It's just I'm older by eight years and I've seen more. But you're learning. Why in a few more years you'll be just like me."

"Oh Christ no! Dress like you? And tangle with everybody? No. No. Never. I'll–I'll go back to New Brunswick with Bob first and hide in the hills."

At the picture of such a situation we both began to laugh.

8

Just about that time as I was glancing through one of our large dailies, my interest was captured by a story about an unusual kind of international organization. It was called Mensa and the prime requirement for membership was an IQ score higher than ninety-eight percent of the population could make.

This club offered to supply and check free an unsupervised test for one to do at home. I was intrigued but dubious. Could I score that high on a tough test? After deep thought I decided to try.

I wrote to the given address. Within a few weeks I received the test and more information about Mensa. Tom was home. He got the mail first, to my annoyance.

"What in hell are you up to now?" he asked, and nothing would satisfy him but a look at my letter.

After reading the enclosed brochure I handed it over. He read it and began to jeer.

I jeered back. In time he grew tired of teasing me and went off to read. I took my test papers and secluded myself in the girls' room to write in peace before the children would come noisily in from work and school.

Luckily I got it done and mailed before they arrived to join their father in teasing.

With the test done and away in the mail I settled myself to wait for a report, impatiently. I might not, I knew, be able to join so exclusive a club but it was a good chance to learn more about myself. But I had little time for solitary pursuits.

One Saturday afternoon Billy and Howie went skating together while Jenny, Nancy and Brucie went to a movie. I thought that would keep them all out of mischief and went happily about my housework.

About six p.m. just after Jenny had returned and we were having supper, Billy arrived home in the care of two policemen, one a special juvenile worker.

Billy entered the house first and called me aside.

"You're not gonna like this. I'm in trouble. I was stealing papers from an honour box and I got caught. That's why the police are here. They want to talk to you or Dad," he said, rushing the words together.

"Oh," I said, "well, I'll see what they have to say."

I invited the uniformed men in. They told me Billy had been observed acting suspiciously. They had taken him to a police station and questioned him. At last Billy had confessed to stealing papers from an honour box and selling them, in company with Howie.

"Confessed?" I asked, eager to believe the story wasn't true.

Yes, well he had been seen with the papers, not actually taking them, I was told.

"But confessed?" I asked. "How come he confessed? And how come I wasn't told when you arrested him?"

The gist of it was, Billy had not been arrested. He'd just been questioned. There had been a number of complaints about the loss of papers from honour boxes recently. Billy and Howie had been seen walking down the street, each with five or six papers under an arm. At the approach of the officer Howie had moved swiftly, not quite running, in the opposite direction. Billy had made no suspicious moves but continued ahead. He was asked where he got the papers. He said he had a paper route and was selling them etc., etc. The detective asked Billy to get in the car. Billy did and asked if charges could be laid against the police for false arrest.

"But," I said, "If you couldn't prove he had stolen those

papers I don't think it was right for you to take him to the station and keep him there without telling me."

"Aw, Maw, I did it. I told them," Billy said before the officers could speak. I realized Billy was upset enough.

"All right," I said. To the officers I directed a question. "Well now what are you going to do?"

"We want to help him. My name is Hailey," said one, stepping forward. He looked around at Johnny and Jenny. "Can we talk–er–in– ?"

"Yes," I said. "Upstairs in Billy's room. This way."

I led the way upstairs. Mr. Hailey thought it would be better if Billy weren't present.

"Okay," I agreed. "But first I must ask Billy a few questions."

I had Billy go with me to Johnny's room. There he told me how it happened. Then I returned to Billy's room.

"Well," I opened, "Billy admits he did wrong–and the family will deal with that. But I don't really think there's much you can do to him."

Billy came in and listened. "I'm not condoning his deed but I don't think it's so bad. And according to law I believe you can't do much since you didn't see the crime."

"But Mrs. Firth– " he began.

"Aw now, why do you have to talk like that?" Billy interrupted.

"Because I believe a person is innocent until proven guilty," I said.

"Well I am guilty, I admitted it."

"Yes. After they questioned you. And for how long? And did you have a friend or a lawyer? Sure you admit it and I believe it but I'm not sure if you were treated right."

"Oh you!" Billy yelled and left grumpily.

"Well, how did you plan to help him?" I asked, turning to Mr. Hailey. "What can you do now? Charge him?"

"No, we don't think we'll have to charge him. We want to stop this sort of thing and help these kids before they get in deeper. That's my job. I'll leave my name and number. You can call and ask for me if you have any trouble with him, or he can call if he has any trouble," he said.

"Well that's good. And did Billy tell on Howie or did you catch him?"

"Oh well, he gave us the name, finally. We'll see Mrs. Dubé too. We really want to help these boys. If they do one thing and get away with it they often try something else."

"I know–but Billy'll not get off with it. He knows he did it and now we know and he's got the job of living it down which may be worse than reform school."

"Oh, he wouldn't go to reform school. It's his first offence," the man protested.

"I didn't say he'd go there," I said. "But anyway I am glad he was caught now before he did something worse. Still I feel I should have been notified sooner. However, I'm glad I can call if there's any more trouble."

"Well thank you, Mrs. Firth. Billy is a basically good boy, I'm sure. He probably won't do anything like that again. I think you'll be able to deal with him but feel free to call on me. I'll be glad to help. Now–if you'll excuse me." He looked at the watch on his wrist.

I said, "All right then. Thanks anyway for bringing him home."

I wasn't so thankful when I found out after the police had gone that they'd kept Billy almost four hours at the station, questioning and accusing before he confessed and gave the other boy's name.

When the police had gone I gave Billy supper. As he ate he answered Johnny's probing questions about the case. I let the boys talk and phoned Gloria.

To my surprise the police had been there and gone. Howie had told her about it just before they came. She was very upset.

"I told those police to take that damn little thief and put him in jail. I could kill him. It's not as if he needed the money. Goddamn, I work and slave and he goes and does that. I knew him and Billy would get into trouble running around together," she screamed over the phone.

"But Gloria, for sense's sake shut up. They haven't killed anyone. It's only a boy's trick. It's not such a bad thing," I said.

"Not a bad thing! I suppose you think it's good then? Sophia they should both be in jail."

"Oh Gloria, you're worse than Tom's gonna be and he's all I can stand. Call me when you're sober," I said and hung up the phone.

Shortly before Tom was due to arrive I swallowed two tranquilizers. I was braced when he came in but I waited until he'd eaten before I told him. There are two things I've learned in my twenty-three years of marriage: one, Tom is always hungry when he gets home and two, it's dangerous to give him bad news on an empty stomach.

He ate quietly. Johnny was in the kitchen with me. Jenny and Billy were in their rooms. The rest of the household were out. It was midnight. While I waited for the best moment I spoke of things mundane.

Tom finished eating and pushed his plate away. He doesn't smoke but chews snuff. Soon he had a good chew going and began to ask Johnny for news of his day.

Now was the time.

"Tom," I said, "there's a little something I have to tell you. Billy was– "

"What's Billy been up to now?" he yelped without letting me finish. "If that little son of a whore has cost me more money I'll break his neck."

"Oh shut up, you goddamn evil-minded clown. He hasn't cost you money. How come you worry first about that and not whether he's hurt or not?"

"Well is he hurt?"

"Yes, he's hurt–but he did it himself, mainly. I helped I guess," I said.

"Hurt? Where? How? Hit by a car? Where is he?" Tom was worried, as I knew he would be. When he discovered the kind of hurt I meant he'd direct most of his wrath at me which I preferred to having him railing for an hour at Billy.

"Oh he's not hurt like that. He's hurt his reputation and conscience," I said giving Tom a chance to guess.

"What did he do? Break another window or steal something?"

"He stole."

"Stole what?"

"Newspapers, four or five from an honour box."

"The little son of a whore, bastard, I'll break his arm."

"No you won't. Even for killing at his age the law doesn't require a broken arm. Now you might as well calm down or you won't hear any more."

"Where is he? How'd you know? The police come? Yes, I

know they caught him. Damn his lousy soul. Always causing me trouble."

"Oh yes, causing you trouble. For God's sake what trouble is that to you? You didn't see the police or listen to them."

"But what about the next time?"

"Oh next time. There might never be a next time. Millions of boys do a little stealing some time."

"Not me. I never stole. And I can't stand a thief."

"Me neither," I said, lying right in my teeth. "Tom, is it true that when a juvenile is picked up they've got to notify the parents if he identifies himself?"

"You're goddamn right. How long did they keep him before you knew?" Tom roared.

"Billy," I called loudly. "Get down here!"

Billy came reluctantly.

"You little– " Tom began.

"Never mind that," I yelled. "I want to find out something. Billy when did they pick you up?"

"Oh, around two o'clock." Billy said.

"There, Tom," I said. "See them damn police? Two o'clock and they brought him home about six. Four hours. That's not right, I know it."

"You're goddamn right it's not right. The c.s. bastards. Keeping a kid without letting his mother know." Tom was shouting. I relaxed a bit. The worst was over. He had more than one thing to direct his anger at. He continued, "Of course it's his own fault. Still–they've no right to do that. Billy did they hit you or threaten you? What all did they do?"

Billy looked at his enraged father. It appeared to me that the boy didn't know exactly what to say. The wrong word, we both knew, and Tom would ignore any wrongs done by the police, and the full brunt of his wrath would be back on Billy's head. There was, I thought, a strong temptation to exaggerate or lie a little. I wanted Billy to be man enough to take it, on the other hand I wanted Tom to be man enough to forgive.

"Billy," I said, "don't lie. I know some police can be pretty rough but don't tell lies on them. Just tell Dad what they did to you."

"Well," Billy said, "they took me in and put me in a room and talked to me. They asked questions about my name and age and where I lived and where I got the papers."

"And what did you tell them?" I said before Tom could start again.

"Well at first I lied. I told them I lived on College. I made up a name and address."

"You see. Lying too," Tom said less angrily.

"Well, Father dear, he had a good teacher," I said. "Who's the champion liar around here?"

"Never mind," Tom said. "Go on, what else?"

"Well I think they believed me at first. The first guy went out and another came in. They kept saying to me, 'We know you're lying.' One big guy sat down to bug me. He said, 'I have a boy at home about your age and I thought he was a pretty good liar, but boy, you make him look sick!' "

Johnny and I laughed.

"You made him look sick, eh Billy?" Johnny said encouragingly. "Tell us more."

"Well," Billy started entertainingly. Tom was silent, resigned now and nearly his normal self. He seemed as eager as Johnny to learn how Billy had conducted himself while in custody. The crime was bad enough; breaking down immediately and acting the baby would only have compounded it. If Billy had taken one dose of his medicine and was prepared to take the rest it would be in his favour, I knew. Billy knew it too, but before he could tell more, Don arrived.

Billy had to start from the beginning. When he was halfway through, Joyce came in. He had to start again. By the time the whole family had heard the tale I was tired and bored with it. And there was still Gloria to hear.

She came down the next evening, Sunday. Tom was home. It was his day off. In fact it was everybody's day off. Sidney was home too, having returned from a visit to a friend in Port Credit. Johnny had told him the story.

Gloria had received two police visits. One from the Informer Squad and the other from Mr. Hailey. By the time Mr. Hailey arrived to offer his help she'd gotten over her initial shock and rage and gone over to her son's side.

"Boy, I told him," she told us. "You should have heard me. I told him about the crooks in the Government and business. Even in the church and the police force. I said, half the grownups are thieves and crooks. Everybody's out to gyp the rest. What in hell can we expect from the kids? Even the doctors charge ten dollars for a five minute office visit, I said."

"Was Howie there? What did he say?" I asked.

"Howie was there. Everybody was there, even Bob. They were listening. Goddamn but I was mad. I'd been thinking it all over about how much crookedness there is and how the papers are always full of crime, and TV too. Damn the lousy TV. Sometimes I wish we had none. You're lucky Sophia."

"Never mind that Gloria. Tell me what Bob said. I mean after all the police had gone," I said.

"Oh he didn't say much. He just told Howie that if he got in jail he'd have to stay there. He wouldn't bail him out or pay his fine."

"That's what I say," said Tom fiercely. "If they're going to steal let them take their goddamn punishment. By Gawd Billy'll go straight to reform school if he ever does it again."

"Ah come on Tom," I said, "you know you'd run down there and bail him right out and you'd go without snuff to pay his fine. Don't deny it. I know you."

"Yuh, you know me like hell. I don't go for stealin'."

"Well neither do I. Neither does anyone here—that is, big stealing. But what's a little snitching in a boy's life? You know lots of grown men who do it every day and brag about it. Can you deny that?" I asked.

"Well, but . . . . "

"No well and no but. You know it's true. Steal a million and what happens? They all begin to bow down to you."

"Yes," Gloria said, "steal a million and they'll give you a medal. Steal a penny and you'll get ten years."

"That is if you're caught," Don said.

"What do you know?" Gloria asked. "I suppose you've done a little stealing yourself."

"I plead the fifth amendment," Don laughed.

"Well I don't," I said. "I did a little. I helped steal a hen one time."

"Did you really, Mother?" Johnny asked, teasing.

"Yes, I did," I said. "I'm ashamed of it now. But I did it so I've got to face it. I'm just as bad a thief as Billy and Howie. But then so is everybody here except Jenny and maybe Gloria."

"What do you mean? Are you calling me a thief?" Don asked still laughing.

"I sure as hell am. I know about the case of pop you and Sidney and Bart Miller and Tony Lindo and the rest stole that time in New Brunswick."

Sidney and Don looked at each other. The rest looked at them.

"Did you guys steal a case of pop?" Johnny asked, incredulously. "A whole case? When and where?"

"Tell them," I said to the boys, "or I will. This is our night for confessions. When you're done it'll be Tom's turn and Johnny's."

"Come on," Gloria coaxed, "tell us. This I want to hear."

Don and Sidney remained silent. The front door opened and Howie came in to join us.

"Here's my thief," Gloria announced.

"Oh shit," I said, "you mean here's just another thief come to join the den of thieves. Come right in Howie. You'll want to hear this. You're not the only thief under this roof tonight. Okay, the gang's almost all here, boys. Who'll start? Will it be Don, or would you like to be first, Tom?"

"What? I never stole anything," Tom said emphatically. "I might lie a little but I don't steal."

"Well I'll confess," Sidney said. "You know where they make the pop in Campbellton and you know how sometimes they just park a big truck in front loaded with cases of pop. Well one summer night about five years ago, Don and me and Tony and Bart and Harry Doucet and Greg Beste decided to steal a case of pop. Not just a bottle or two. That was no fun. We wanted a whole case."

"Why didn't you steal the whole truck?" Gloria asked laughing.

"Well that was too much," Sidney said. "Will you keep quiet while I tell it? Well Don was the scout. And Bart the lookout. They said the coast was clear so we sneaked up. But just as we got to the truck a man came out of the factory and walked around. So Tony and me and Greg had to hide under the truck.

I mean we could have run away but that was no fun. So we waited under there while he walked around. Two or three times these goddamn big feet went right close to my head. I was scared we'd get caught. I expected every minute he'd look under the truck and flash a big light in my eyes but he didn't. At last he went away and Don came up and said okay so we got up and grabbed a case and got to hell out of there. When we were almost clear that stupid Tony opened a bottle, then he dropped it. We lined'er then. But after a while we thought about fingerprints and Don went back for the evidence. So we got away and had our pop."

"And didn't get caught," Gloria said.

"Yes," I said, "and none of us would know if I hadn't caught Don and Bart taking pop from under the loose board in our shed. Don knew I knew he had some nefarious reason for hiding it so he told me the story. A year or so later I told Bart's mother. Well of course she was fit to be tied but then Bart's father told us of things he'd done that weren't so angelic, so she decided perhaps Bart might eventually turn out all right. Actually, we both agreed that one misstep by a man or boy is to be expected and is forgivable, and such is Howie's and Billy's petty crime."

"Bart is married now, isn't he?" asked Gloria.

"That's right. He's married and has two children. He's had a steady job for three or four years and is paying for his house. I guess his boss would never dream that when he was sixteen he was part of a pop-stealing gang of young hoodlums. Then again, since the boss was also once a boy maybe he'd dream even worse things," I told her.

"Well I guess poor Howie and Billy have had some poor examples set," Gloria said, "But what did Tom do? You said we were all thieves."

"Oh, well, Tom. He only helped steal a cake when he was young and working in a cake factory. At least that's what he says. Now I can't prove it but he told it and what the hell; to tell such a thing to us innocent children is as bad as doing it and keeping mum."

"Tell us, Tom," Gloria cried excitedly. "How'd you come to steal a cake and was it a big one?"

"Big one? I'll say," said Tom. "One man couldn't eat it. It

was laying out there on a table one night when me and Gerry Hanley were working late, so I just took it. We cut it up and put it in our lockers. They looked for that son of a whore of a cake for weeks."

"And the funny part is, Tom is not a cake or cookie man. He hardly ever eats sweets," I said.

"No damn wonder," Johnny laughed. "He sickened himself. I bet the other guy doesn't eat much cake now either. Oh boy, what a bunch of crooks I know."

"You're not all that bloody innocent yourself, Mr. Johnny Firth," I said severely. "Remember how you used to steal my cigarettes and smoke them in hiding?"

"Did I do that?" Johnny asked rolling his eyes heavenward.

"You told me you did. Of course you were only nine or ten but it's still stealing and you knew it or you wouldn't have hid. So now whitewash yourself if you can."

"Ha, ha, Johnny," cried Howie and Billy in unison. "So we're all thieves then. Now who's left to confess? Oh yes, you." They pointed to Gloria.

"Well I know I was bad," Gloria said, "but I can't remember stealing."

"Oh no? Well I can remember you telling me about it," I said sternly. "What do you call taking all the eggs, throwing them against the barn wall and telling your grandmother it was your brothers? I guess you broke more than one commandment there, old girl. Now do you remember?"

"Well yes, I remember all right, but I didn't call that stealing."

"What did you call it?"

"Nothing. I've just never thought what to call it—unless a venial sin."

"Call it what you want. I call it stealing. That doesn't matter. What matters here and what I'm trying to do is let those boys see that we have all risen above our childish crimes or sins. All they've done so far is prove they're of the same breed as us. Now if they run true to form they'll go on to better things and live this bit of mischief down. In time they'll be able to look back and wonder why they were so foolish."

9

One bright day I received a letter from the Unemployment Commission and another from Mensa.

I opened the one from the UIC first. It had money; nearly 170 dollars, in four cheques. I waved them in the air for the delighted family to see, and laughed.

"Well, you did it. You made them cough up!" Tom said. "But it's Saturday. Where are you gonna cash them?"

"Oh, don't worry. I'll cash one—somewhere. You'll see. Now let me see how I did on that test," I said.

The Mensa letter didn't state a specific score, it just noted my test showed it might be worth my while to take another test—under supervision. For a small fee I could join a group preparing for such a test. The fee insured that I'd be advised of the results of my test.

"You're not going to take it, are you?" asked Tom sarcastically.

"Why not? Why should I stop now? I might as well go the whole route," I said.

Jenny changed the subject before a loud argument could start.

"Buy me something, Mummy. Buy me a pair of slacks, a pair of shoes and a dress," she said.

"Oh, Jenny honey. I'm not buying all that today. Slacks and maybe a pair of sneakers. That's all," I said.

Tom and I went out. Tom said he knew a store manager who'd cash the cheques. He was wrong. The man said he couldn't spare enough cash even for one forty-dollar cheque let alone four of them. I thought he suspected I'd forged the damn things. Tom was disgusted. I took him to a ladies' dress store whose woman manager knew me. I picked out twenty dollars worth of clothes for Jenny, Joyce and myself. She wasn't too eager to cash one of those cheques but she did want to sell her merchandise. She cashed one. I was happy. After a long miserable wait I was affluent again.

A few days later I made the arrangements for the Mensa test. I did it quietly; I was growing tired of the razzing. What I regarded as a little lark my family treated as a major project—and Expo was over.

I had begun to feel quite miserable in January suffering abdominal cramps often, especially during menstruation; frequently my head would ache for no reason I could name, and I began to get up a lot at night. When the kids were all back in school and life was running smoothly I went to a doctor for a thorough checkup. He found I had tumours of the womb and my bladder was out of place. He told me I'd not feel much better until I had an operation. I was shocked and scared.

Tom was no help. "Well you'll just have to have the operation. What's there to be scared of? When are you going?"

"Well, not right away, that's for sure. Next year maybe," I said.

"Oh, well. Perhaps it shouldn't be put off."

"It'll have to be. I just can't face it yet. You might not understand or even believe it but I'm scared as hell. Anyway he didn't say an operation was absolutely necessary. I'll have to get used to the idea."

I told the kids and my friends. Most advised me to get it over with. One woman sympathized with me. She said she was terrified of having a tooth pulled and had been suffering for over a year from frequent toothaches. Her husband laughed at her fears.

"He doesn't understand," she said, "but that doesn't make

me any braver. I just can't get up nerve enough to go to a dentist."

I couldn't get my nerve up either, not even to seriously contemplate an operation. I thrust the idea to the back of my mind and concentrated on pleasanter things.

The prearranged date came for my supervised IQ test. I told the family I was going out for a while. They insisted on knowing where. I tried to be evasive but they persisted. I don't like lying anyway, so finally I told them. Hoots of derision broke on my ears.

"You're having a good laugh now," I told them, "but wait. I've enjoyed a last laugh before and watched people eat crow. I'm not like some people I know; scared to try anything new for fear of failure. If I fail, so what? I'll be the same old me. If I pass—well I'll have found a way out of this damn rut—a way I can afford. You've all got your outside interests and clubs. What have I got? Where do I go? Who do I see? Well it doesn't matter so much if I pass or not. This is just the first step toward a more interesting life for me. Jenny's nearly nine years old and I don't have to stick around here so much. But where can I go or what can I do without lots of money? In all these years I've never been to a movie, never been to Bingo though Gloria goes every week, never gone to the races, haven't even been to the CNE. So laugh all you want. That don't bother me."

It did though. I hoped fervently I would succeed in scoring high enough on the test to get into Mensa. Fail and I'd never live it down, not with Tom. He was the worst scoffer and would, I knew, tell all and sundry how I'd spent good money just to find out how stupid I was. How he and George would laugh. My courage faltered. Could my ego survive another failure, I wondered. Oh well, I assured my quaking heart, they won't be able to prove they can do any better. I determined to go through with it and dropped all thought of turning back.

The test was being conducted in the basement of a church. There were about twenty of us taking it. I was almost late. The others were seated and waiting. I chose a seat at the back of the group as I had been wont to do in school, sat down and glanced around. Suddenly the tension left me and I became completely relaxed. This was going to be fun and it didn't matter one iota what my critics thought.

Home again, I was pleased to find the family had changed

their attitude. Now they were sympathetic and curious.

"What was the test like? Was it hard? Did you pass?"

"The test was simple. I think I passed but I don't know. I got hung up on a math problem and forgot where I was. I think now I should have skipped and gone to another because speed is a factor in determining IQ. I think I scored high on the vocabulary section so maybe a low on math won't hurt. Anyway I can take the same test again—so I'm not worried."

"Tell us some of the problems. Tell me the math one," Tom said.

"Well. I'm not supposed to tell the problems. That would spoil the test for other people. Maybe some of you will want to try it sometime and it wouldn't be fair if you'd already worked out the answers. I'll tell you what some of the problems were like though. There was a large word section where you had one key word and were required to choose the next nearest one from a group of five or six. That I found real easy and so would most of you Then there was a page of pictures and I had to decide if I was viewing the left or right side of things—things like the sole of a foot or side of a window. That was easy too."

"The math. What about the math?"

"Oh simple problems too. Fractions and percents. Take the test yourself if you want to know about it. It's the same thing as those in Don's book of IQ tests to be done at home for personal pleasure. The main thing is to get a lot done. The more you get done in the specified time the faster it proves you can think and so the higher your IQ. Some of you could pass I'm sure. You could even score higher'n me. I'm not the smartest person in the world. I don't pretend to be. I just know I can think faster and get more right answers than lots of people. Now I'll know where I stand among the morons, average joes and geniuses. Are you scared to find out where you stand?"

"I'm not scared," Tom scoffed. "What do I want to take a test like that for?"

"Well you're all willing to have your physical height measured. Aren't you curious about your mental height? Or brain power? Anyway I'll know mine so I'll be ahead of you there."

"How soon will you know? How long does it take to find out your score?"

"Oh about a month. If I could afford it I could have myself tested right here in the city and know in a couple of days. Remember how I had Archie tested in Campbellton to see how retarded he was? Well it didn't take long."

"Archie, who's Archie?" Jenny asked.

"Don't you remember Uncle Archie? My brother. The big guy who lived with Gramps."

"Oh, yuh. Him. He played cards with us and he couldn't even play cards right, or read. He used to haul Ken's toboggan up the hill for us to slide on. I remember him. I just forgot his name."

"I remember Uncle Archie," Billy said. "Boy was he strong. He used to help me carry my papers. He didn't mind the snow and wasn't afraid of dogs. I'd like to see him again."

"Well take a trip down this summer. Save your money and maybe we'll all go," I said. "We'll see the old swimming hole, the mountain, the beach and all our friends. Yes, that's a good idea. Let's all go east this summer, Tom."

"Not me. I won't be able to go. We're going on strike. I told you that already. What's wrong with you? Can't you remember anything?" Tom said.

"Oh well, the strike mightn't last long. A week, two weeks," I said.

"A week, like hell. The company's stocked up. They'll never give in. I told the union it's the wrong time. They can't win but the stupid sons of whores won't listen. Foreigners–puyaw! I might have to look for another job myself. I don't want the strike."

"I don't think I could make the trip both ways anyhow. I'm not up to such a long trip yet."

"Aw c'mon, Maw, you can make the trip. I'll get a good job soon's school's over and I'll pay your way," Johnny said.

"No thanks," I said. "Save your money for school next year. I don't want the trip. Anyway some of them might get up to Toronto themselves. No, I'll find enough to do to keep me busy this summer. I may look for a job."

"Are you finished drawing unemployment?"

"Yes. But Ottawa owes me one hundred dollars refund on income tax. Damn them, they've no right to keep it without paying interest. Well they have the legal right yes—but not the moral right."

"Now, Maw. Don't start on the poor Government again. You know they need your money to pay those guys their salaries," Don laughingly teased.

"Oh, piss on you. Have you paid them all you owe yet? See the difference. They take too much off a poor old lady like me but a young buck like you rolling in dough gets away with owing them money. It's not fair."

"Well, when I'm Prime Minister, I'll even it up," Johnny said.

"Humph. Prime Minister," Tom scoffed. "Listen to him. You won't even get to be a labourer. You can't get out of bed in the morning."

"Oh, Tom, don't be such a drip. Christ, anybody can get out of bed if they've something to get out for."

"Yuh, to get clear of the wet blankets after someone's dumped a bucket of cold water on them, for instance," Sidney said.

"Well that's a pretty good reason—or to get the bastard that did it," Johnny said.

"Aren't you gonna get supper?" Tom asked. "You've done nothing all day but go for that foolish test. You should be able to get supper."

"What? You expect me to get supper and me all dressed up. I thought you'd get it and wash up the dishes while I visited Gloria," I said.

"No. I'm not getting it. I'll get my own but the rest can get theirs if you're too lazy," Tom said.

"Do you call that dressed up, Maw? Why other women dress like that to scrub floors," Don said.

"Oh, I just said that to see if Tom would offer to get supper. But I suppose I'm lucky to get a few hours to myself. Other slaves don't get so much."

I chased them all out of the kitchen while I got supper. When it was over and the dishes cleaned up I settled down with my book of poetry. Our TV hadn't been fixed yet. It wasn't missed much except by Jenny.

The spring days flew by. I spent an hour or two each day on my front verandah or in the yard soaking up the sun. Other women were doing the same thing. Sometimes I'd walk around a bit and talk with them. One in particular I talked with daily. She ran a variety store on our corner. Quite often she took her poodle out for exercise. She was married with no children but took an avid interest in mine. We spent a lot of money at her store. She kept me posted all year on the changes taking place on our street.

Darlene's family had sold their place and moved to the country. Darlene kept in touch with Jenny by letters. The couple who bought the Mann's house were young Americans. They had a baby. "He's a draft-dodger," the lady with the poodle, Martha, told me.

"How do you know?" I asked.

"Everybody says so," she answered.

"Well, I don't believe what everybody says. I'm one body and I don't say so. Besides everybody's been wrong before."

"Oh, well." She changed her subject. "Did you know we're getting class on our street? Professors are moving in."

"Professors of what?"

"Professors of the University of Toronto."

"I mean what kind of professors. What do they teach?"

"Oh, they teach at the university. It's close."

"Ah, but what subjects do they teach–law, history, philosophy, economics?"

"Oh, I don't know. Maybe law. It doesn't matter, it's still class."

That evening I kidded the family about getting classy. "You'll have to smarten up. Watch your language. Become gentlemen."

"Hah! That'll be the day. What's a professor? Just a guy who teaches," Johnny said.

"Didn't you know that fella in the house next to Martha is a university professor?" Tom asked.

"No. You mean that guy who wants her to get rid of her fence? No wonder she wouldn't take my advice and tell him to jump in the lake. I offered to do it for her but she wouldn't let me."

"Would you really tell our 'class' to go jump in the lake?" Johnny could hardly speak for laughing. "Oh this street won't be big enough for our hippie mother and that professor."

"Well Tom, I suppose you know all his history by now and his ancestors back two or three generations. What does he teach?"

"He teaches economics."

"Oh, maybe that's why he left the ice on his sidewalk all winter."

"Oh, he was away then. But Martha was taking care of it."

"Some care. Hell, she couldn't get anyone to clear it for the wages he paid. I'd of done it myself for a decent wage."

"I bet you wouldn't," Sidney said, "I heard he's queer as a three-dollar bill. He don't like women."

"Well there goes our class," I said. "I guess it's up to us and the Russians next door to jazz up the street."

"They're not Russians. You mean the woman who gives you the rhubarb? They're Greeks," Tom informed me.

"Greeks! Russians! What odds. Some neighbours say she is picturesque. They don't say that about me and I dress just as well as she does. She always wears a turban-like kerchief on her head."

"Oh, she keeps her old country style."

"Well I keep my old Gaspé style. And you guys all laugh. Martha doesn't say much but she hints pretty good telling me where she gets good dresses cheap and smart shoes. Wait'll she talks class to me again."

"You better keep your big mouth shut," Tom warned me. "You'll be in trouble if you don't. It's all right to talk here but . . . "

"Oh it's all right to talk to Martha. Boy, you should hear the stuff she tells me. So help me I'll bet she's already heard about her 'class'. Yes and I bet she wouldn't mention it because I put her down about the draft-dodger."

"You mean the guy in Mann's house? Well that's what he is," Tom said. "Why else would he move here?"

"Oh you believe every rumour, too. You and Martha make a damn good pair. You like to know everybody's history but try hard to keep your own hid. You and me can both look back and find draft-dodgers in our ancestors, and queers are there too probably."

"Maybe so but never mind that," Tom said. "Did Martha tell you we've a bootlegger, too?"

"No. What bootlegger?"

"Oh the one at the corner, across from Martha. She didn't think I knew but I'm not deaf and I'm not blind. There's a madame living farther up, too. Did she tell you that?"

"No. And I didn't ask. And poor Martha thinks one professor is gonna give our street class. Bro–ther!"

"Well Maw, this is the slums! Didn't you realize that yet?" Don asked. "We've got streetwalkers, too. You better watch yourself at night. Hasn't anyone propositioned you yet?"

"There's no poor man that hard up for a woman around here. That's another reason I don't dress up much. I've heard Jeannie talking about being accosted and followed for three or four blacks and she's sixty at least. I thought she made up all her stories–but maybe not."

"She doesn't have to make them up," Tom said, "but she probably does. You haven't seen anything of this city yet."

"There's not much more I want to see either except those brilliant people. Surely they'll be a cut above what I've seen so far."

"What have you seen, Maw?" Johnny asked. "Where do you see it? On this street?"

"Oh I see lots. I'm not interested in their damned old cement and steel structures. It's the people I notice. When I go back I'll not even remember what the city looked like but I'll be able to tell them about the people."

"You're like me," Joyce said. "How do you find the people, Mum?"

"Just like Maritimers, underneath. It's true. But they remind me of lonely Maritimers. I've heard people say Toronto is cold but those people are cold themselves. I think people are afraid to show signs of friendship for fear of a rebuff. Why the other day up by the drugstore while we waited for a streetcar a little Chinese boy's nose started to bleed. His mother was loaded down with bundles and was having a hard time finding a cloth or tissue to swab the blood. A lot of people turned to look but none offered help. I did. I took some clean tissues from my purse and gave them to Jenny to give her. She accepted them with a smile and thank you and was able to save his clothes from getting badly stained. She didn't repulse our offer of help. But that's only one side. I get a lot of help. I find many people real glad to help—if you ask. Most streetcar drivers and police are real friendly too. I see them helping people all the time. Once I saw a streetcar driver help a drunk—on to the streetcar and help him off. Maybe he knew him—I don't know. That's the things I notice."

"I'd have done the same," Joyce said. "If I had the tissues. If I see kids fighting or doing wrong things I tell them they shouldn't. I don't get mad or anything. I just say 'It's your city too—so let's keep it nice.' Most of them stop. Oh, a few say it's none of my business or go fuck yourself. Or some other rude things."

"Your big mouths'll get both of you in trouble," Tom said. "If they wanted your help they'd ask."

"No, they wouldn't, Tom. Did Oscar ask you to bring him in here to get warmed up?" I asked.

"Well, that's different. I could see he was freezing."

"Yes. Well I can see when people want to talk too. I can see when they are friendly—I can after I ask them a simple question. I don't run up and ask them how old they are or where they were born or if they're divorced or queer or bootlegging. I just ask where a certain building or street is and if they offer to help we soon get talking. Nobody's ever refused to help me yet on the street or in the laundromat or bus station. Even at work I find most people willing to help."

"Well that's because it makes most people feel superior to help someone who acts so dumb," Johnny said. "They've probably never seen a character like you and are curious to find out more."

It became time for Tom's union to make new agreements with the company. The men voted to refuse the new contract. They went on strike. Tom had to do picket duty but he was home much of the time growling, fretting, and criticizing my work methods. Often I'd tell him to get to hell out of the house or shut up. If he refused I'd take a walk to the library or park, or just around the streets.

Strike pay was low. The kids were able to help a little more but I had to economize. I could no longer do all my wash at the coin-laundry. I started using the old washer again. There were two fine steel sinks in the basement. I bleached the whites in the sinks, stirring them about in the solution with an old broom handle. One day for something to do Tom took an empty plastic bleach container, punched holes in it and fastened it to my wooden handle.

"There," he announced proudly. "Now you have a real old-fashioned washer. You just agitate the clothes around with it. The same principles as your washer."

It worked fine, better than the old washboard method I used in New Brunswick. The electric washer began to malfunction. I didn't tell Tom. I just quit fighting it and sloshed my laundry up, down and around in the sinks. The boys paid for the drying at the laundromat.

Tom stopped his yakking and nagging. I guess he didn't like my walking out on him so often. He looked around for something to pass his time.

One night he, Don and Johnny got into a long discussion about chemistry. Their conversation ranged over a great territory, from air pollution to wine and beer making. The latter subject I understood.

Next day Tom set up his brewery. The Greek lady had given me some rhubarb. Tom said he was sure his mother had made wine or cider from that plant but he couldn't remember her method. He decided to see if he could make rhubarb beer. I encouraged him in his project. (Johnny had bought some chemistry apparatus.)

Now the atmosphere in our home changed for the better. Tom became very cheerful and treated us to snatches of songs and jokes. The rest of the family, except me, found some activity to hold their interest and keep their spirits up.

Jenny had skipping, hop scotch, tag, ball playing and marbles for the weekends and after school. She didn't lack playmates, outdoors.

Billy began to take an avid interest in chess and found a sufficient number of opponents to keep him busy in his spare time.

Joyce busied herself taking underprivileged youngsters to points of interest in the city, supervising games for them, and helping them develop creative skills.

Don put his car in the nearby garage he rented and started

some repairs on it. Sidney got his car back from Harold and did the same. Johnny helped them, as did Harold and Larry. They all knew something about motors—and wanted to learn more. That was the main reason they did the work themselves.

I became, for a short time, errand girl for the boys and Tom—and cleaner-upper too. All the work wasn't done in the garages, or in the basement. My kitchen was a busy workshop with Tom brewing and Don cleaning little car-motor gadgets.

One night Sidney and Johnny brought Sidney's transmission down the street on an improvised travois and deposited it in our basement without waking Tom or me. I heard about it from Martha whom they had awakened with their racket around one a.m.

The boys heard about it from Tom when he discovered what they were up to. He found out when Jenny asked how the oil got all over the basement floor.

Hobbyless me went back to sitting in my front yard watching the life of the street, or standing around with Martha discussing it.

One day while I was thus engaged with Martha the letter arrived from Mensa. Tom opened it before I returned home to serve lunch to Jenny who was coming from school.

"You got an answer. You failed," Tom said, grinning, as I entered the kitchen.

With heavy heart I picked up the letter and read: "We are pleased . . . " I glared at Tom.

"You damn liar!" I cried. "Why did you lie? Did you think I'd start to bawl?"

"Oh, just for fun. I'm glad you passed. Now what are you going to do, genius?" Tom asked happily.

"Why I'm going to join the club and meet the other geniuses, naturally."

"Well you'll not get any money from me for that racket."

"Thanks, but I won't need your old money. I'll borrow it from a better friend. If those crooks in Ottawa would send my hundred dollar tax refund I'd have lots of money."

"You're a fool to spend money to join a racket."

"Maybe I am, but you're squandering money on your blasted old beer so I'll spend mine on a blasted old club. I've a right to some fun too."

When the children heard of my success they made a great to-do. Their teasing took a new turn. Instead of teasing me about stupidity or odd habits they began to tease me about having more brains than I knew what to do with. Joyce told a few of my neighbours and Gloria.

Don loaned me the money for my membership fee for Mensa. I mailed it in and shortly received a copy of the club's monthly magazine and a schedule of forthcoming meetings. One scheduled meeting was two weeks away.

I determined to go. As usual Tom opposed my plans. Day by day he grew more hateful and belligerent. Finally the conflict between us flared into physical violence.

It began with Tom complaining of my "poor housekeeping, extravagance and crazy tricks". In time he tired of pounding inanimate objects and struck me. I retaliated and he tried to choke me. I defended myself. Don was home and he quickly entered the fray pushing us apart. The battle was short. Tom came out of it minus a tooth, I had superficial cuts and bruises on my face, arms, and neck.

I took a few minutes to catch my breath and reorganize myself, then I walked to Old City Hall to lay a charge of assault against Tom. The officials there wouldn't let me do that. They told me it was a rule of our Attorney-General's. I became furious at such a trespass of my rights. They referred me to a government employed family counsellor. I found him to be a very busy man and I was unable to consult him for a few days.

When I kept my appointment I told him as much of my family troubles as I deemed necessary for my purpose, which was simply to get objective advice to help Tom understand that marriage is not a one-sided association and that his methods would not gain his desire. Even if he succeeded in beating me into submission, my type of obedience would not satisfy him.

Tom received orders to visit the counsellor. He went unwillingly. It was either that or face charges. He returned in a chastened frame of mind. He said the counsellor had agreed that I was crazy.

"Oh, did he, eh? I don't believe you. No man in his position would commit himself like that," I said. "But anyway, how did he advise you to treat your crazy wife?"

"Oh," Tom spoke sheepishly, "he says I daren't lay a hand on you, and it's impossible for you to steal my money because it belongs to you too."

Tom looked dumbfounded. I had to laugh.

"Yes, but did he give you any pointers on how to save trouble if you get mad? That's what I want to know."

"He said to take a walk around the block and cool down."

"Do you mean you had to be told that that's a better idea than trying to murder me or fracture my skull?"

"I guess I'll take my first walk," Tom said.

10

One evening Jenny became very angry at me and decided to leave home. She had had a bad day all around and by 10:30 p.m. she was very cranky and uncooperative. Finally I gave her a firm but not really hard slap on the rear and sent her to bed.

As she started up the stairs she called, "I'm leaving. I'm going to live at the orphanage."

"Good night," I answered, amused, and went out to the kitchen.

For a while Jenny could be heard moving around in her room. It was her usual practice to check on her dolls and tidy up a bit before she put the light out. After a half hour had passed I called to her.

"Aren't you going to bed?" I asked.

"No," she answered. "I'm leaving. I'm just about packed."

"What!" I asked. "Leaving tonight?"

"Yes," she said, and started downstairs with a full suitcase. I watched her descend in silence. Leaving the suitcase in the hall near the front door, she returned to her room for more stuff.

I went back to the kitchen to consider the ways and means of dealing with her unhappiness. Finally I decided to pretend to offer her assistance in her plan yet try to make it clear I was doing so because I cared about her.

When she had four cardboard boxes piled by her suitcase, I said mildly, "Do you know what an orphanage is like, Jenny?"

"I know it'll be better than here," she said, anger still high in her.

"Well maybe in some ways, but you know you'll probably have to share a room. I was just wondering if there'll be space for all your stuff and whether you'll have to let other kids share your toys."

"I'll share. They'll be my friends," Jenny said. "I don't want to stay with you bosses any more."

"Oh well, I was just wondering, that's all. I suppose you'll get all nice bosses at the orphanage. Will you let me come to see you?"

"Maybe. That depends."

"You know you could leave some of your stuff here just for tonight if you want. You don't know for sure yet if there's room for you."

"There'll be room. But perhaps I'll just take my suitcase. Well I guess I'll be going." Jenny was still angry.

"Well wait a minute. If you're so determined to leave perhaps Don will give you a drive, okay?"

"I guess so. Yuh, I'll take a drive."

I left Jenny standing by her boxes and went to confer with Don.

"Jenny's hell-bound and determined to leave," I said. "I want her to discover what it's like to feel all alone or nearly alone in unfamiliar territory, so would you drive her somehwere and see if she'll really leave? Don't, though, let her leave. You can handle her and get her to come back without force. Will you do it?"

Back with Jenny I said, "Don'll be ready in a minute. Do you want him to wait to see if the orphanage takes you all right?"

"No. Well—maybe, but I think they'll have room. I'm not going to tell them who I am. I'll make up a name."

Don came then.

"Are you taking all this? There'll be no room for it. Well, come on. I'm ready," he said.

Don started out the door. Jenny picked up her suitcase and followed him.

"Good-bye dear," I called. "Good luck."

Jenny didn't answer. When the two were gone I was alone in the house. Then I began to have misgivings. Maybe I had done a foolish thing. What if Jenny actually left the car and went off by herself? Oh no, Don wouldn't let her do that. But what if she took it into her head to leave some other day without telling anyone? Many kids of her age ran away. Some never came back alive. What could I do to make Jenny give up all ideas of running away ever? Was she getting enough attention at home? Oh hell. Stop worrying. No matter what I did, I'd always wonder whether it was right or wrong or if there was a better course.

Before Don returned Joyce and Johnny came in.

"Is everyone out but you?" Johnny asked.

"Yes," I answered.

"Well where'd Jenny go? Up to Gloria's?" Joyce asked.

"Jenny has gone to see if she can get into an orphanage. Don took her and her suitcase. That's her stuff in the hall," I told Joyce and Johnny.

Johnny stared at me a moment.

"You're nuts, Mother," he said. "Absolutely nuts."

Joyce laughed. "No Johnny. Jenny'll come back. That'll just do her good."

"What do you know? You're nuts too," Johnny said. "For Christsake."

"Maybe I am nuts," I said. "But I want her to want to come back. I want her to realize she wants us."

"What if she doesn't want to come back, though? Have you considered that?" Johnny asked.

"Oh Johnny. Don't be so stupid," Joyce cried. "Jenny's only eight. She'll come back."

"Oh sure. You know it all. You're both nuts and you don't know how to raise kids!" Johnny cried.

"Maybe not but I figure it's not all my responsibility to keep the kids home. I want Jenny to feel she's here partly because she wants to be here, not just because I am big and powerful and her jailer."

"I know what you're trying to do. You're trying to make her choose and she's too young for that," Johnny argued.

"Well if she's old enough to consider leaving home she's old enough to consider staying. Now she knows what we are like but what does she know about foster homes or orphanages?"

"Not very much but you could tell her."

"Sure I could tell her, but how can she understand what it's like to feel motherless? It takes a damn good imagination to feel things we haven't experienced. I've tried to put her in an unfamiliar situation where she'll have to decide against unknown but possible unpleasantness elsewhere."

"Yeah, you're so goddamn smart. You're making her test herself and how do you think she'll feel when she fails and has to come back? Eh? This could hurt so bad she'll never get over it."

"What?" I was aghast at Johnny's reasoning. "It can't hurt her to come back. It's the natural thing to do."

"Not necessarily. There's her ego. She might feel pretty shitty about not being brave enough to leave home. You could break her."

"Oh Johnny, no. When we accept our needs and weaknesses we grow up. There's no shame in being weak when we can't help it. Jenny admits she's scared of the dark. Why can't she admit she's scared of leaving home?"

"Oh it's no use talking to you. You've got this goddamn crazy psychology and you won't change."

Don arrived then. He entered the house carrying Jenny's suitcase. Jenny was behind him.

"She wouldn't get out of the car," Don told us laughing.

"That was no orphanage," Jenny countered. "He wouldn't take me to the orphanage. I'm going tomorrow."

"Okay, Jenny. Anyway I'm glad you're back," I said.

"What happened?" Joyce asked. "Where'd you take her, Don?"

"Oh I took her down to the orphanage and stopped."

"Oh," Jenny cried, "you took me down to Bay Street or somewhere and said the orphanage was behind that other building. I know it wasn't. You were laughing. That's how I know. Anyway I'm going to bed."

Jenny flounced away. The rest of us got busy with other things. When Tom came home he wanted to know why the boxes were in the hall. I told him. He laughed.

"Do you think she'll really run away?" he asked.

"Not now," I said. "I'll talk to her more in the morning."

In the morning Jenny came to me as soon as she got up. She gave me a strong, happy hug.

"I'm glad I came back. I want to stay here now," she said.

"Oh I want you to stay darling," I said. "There'll be rough spots but we'll talk them out. We all love you."

"I know, and I love all of you," Jenny said. "What's for breakfast?"

Now Joyce suffered an upheaval in her life. She was working her heart out trying to help many black children develop the characteristics and talents to make a success of their lives. The death of Martin Luther King wiped out a lot of her work. Overnight it seemed the kids reverted to their old, cynical, defeatist ways. The assassination of King was taken as an affront and a direct blow to them. Joyce was very grieved over it too, but she saw it as another reason for her and her fellow youth leaders to work even harder, to give more of themselves.

Not all of them agreed with her. Some of the black leaders thought King had been wrong in advocating peaceful changes. Violence was a last resort and now they had to turn to that, they said. They'd have to take their rights by force because Whitey would never accord them any. Live in peace with Whitey? Ha! Look what it got the greatest of modern men!

Joyce cried. Jenny cried. I cried, but not for long.

"This is a real cry-in, kids," I said wiping away my tears. "We'll start a fad."

"Maybe that's what this sick world needs," Joyce sobbed, "a cry-in."

"Well crying is supposed to be good for a person. But think of it, a world wide cry-in. Heavens what a flood, and for a while most things would be stopped. Wouldn't that be awful Jenny—no school because the teachers were all crying their heads off?"

Jenny laughed. "Yeah. But that'll never happen. Don't worry."

"Now that we've had our cry, Joyce," I said, "do you feel like talking a bit? Perhaps we can help each other."

"Well you might be able to help me, but I don't think I can help you much. I can't even help myself." Her face crumpled as she finished speaking.

"Oh Joyce, grow up. You can at least help Jenny. You must

have heard that helping a less able or less fortunate person can help us by keeping our minds off our own problems or making our problems seem trivial compared to theirs."

"I guess so. But I want to help make a better world for Jenny and other kids. It's awful for them to have to grow up in this sick, hateful environment."

"Well, Joyce, you are helping to make a better world. You are helping other kids and perhaps grown-ups to learn and act better."

"But I'm not doing much. I think I'm not doing enough."

"That's one of your problems—trying to do too much. You've got to learn to be satisfied with what you *can* do. Every human being has limits, his time and energy will only go so far. Even the best doctors can help only so many patients and no more. I had to learn that. I used to overwork myself but I take care not to do it now. In order to help others you must first learn self-control, you must learn to keep up your own courage when theirs fails. Yes, and also learn not to let yourself be driven by others. And leave other people free to learn. Sure I'd like to be able to teach you all I know and save you pain too, but I can't. I have to let you grow and learn for yourself. There are certain things you have to experience for yourself. It's the same with those underpriviledged kids. They have to experience certain things—we can't teach them, only living can. Maybe I'm talking too much."

"No, it's okay, I understand. But I wish things were different. That war in Vietnam is awful. All those little kids getting burned."

"Well it was hard in my time too. There was World War II when I was a teenager. I cried sometimes but I learned to shut my mind to things I couldn't change. And that's what you have to do. Some people say we are apathetic because we don't take part in peace marches or sit-ins or demonstrations. It's not all apathy, Joyce. It's just that we either see no good in such things, or just can't take part for physical, mental or emotional reasons—but many of us cheer you on. We're with you because you believe in what you do."

"I thought peace marches were good once. Now I don't know. It seems the world is getting worse instead of better. I think I'll never get married nor have any kids. Life is too horrible."

My mind made a backward leap to 1945. I remembered talking in a similar vein after "they" dropped the atomic bomb. I think I felt then as my daughter felt in 1968.

Don went on vacation. He and his girlfriend Pearl left for British Columbia in the car.

I got a job in a chocolate factory. The first week I worked packaging wrapped chocolate bars. The second week I was shifted to another department. There I was required to take large pans of fresh chocolate bars and candy from one conveyer belt and place them on another. The pans were dirty, and often the unprotected products fell on the floor where people walked. Some of the girls picked the chocolates up and sent them on to be wrapped. I let them lie where they fell. It was not the fault of the girls that the bars fell off the belts. I made up my mind to report the filthy practice to our Board of Health. A supervisor came over and ordered me to pick up the fallen bars and place them in the pans. I did.

I would have quit right then but I wanted to stay there long enough to see if the Board of Health would look into the complaints I intended to make. That evening I wrote them a letter.

The rest of the week was more of the same. Once a young man lost a container of chocolates off a skid as he hauled it through the swinging doors. About twenty pounds of unprotected candies scattered over the well-trodden floor. Hurriedly he grabbed them up, returned them to the carton and went on. Once I saw some girls sneeze right over the cooling chocolate bars. They did not cover their mouths. I hoped the Department of Health had received my letter by then.

Payday came. The plant closed for the weekend.

Tom started his vacation. He asked me if I wanted to go to the horse races with him. To his surprise I said I did.

At the tracks Tom found me a seat in the grandstand and gave me a program of the races.

"Pick a horse," he said. "Any horse." I glanced down the page for race one.

"This fellah," I told Tom, pointing to a name.

"You can't bet on him. He's scratched," Tom growled.

"I don't care," I said. "He mightn't be hurt bad. I like him and I want to bet on him."

"You dumb dunce. Scratched means he's out of the race."

"Why? Did he get hurt?"

"Oh they don't announce why a horse is scratched. Just pick another. Hurry up."

"Okay. This one. I'll put my money on him."

"Good," said Tom. "Now pick one in the next race. There, that page." I glanced over the names of the horses in race number two.

"Here. Try him," I told Tom, pointing out a name I liked.

"Him? Hunh," Tom said. "Oh well, it's your first time. Give me two dollars."

"Is that all it costs?" I asked. "For two horses?"

"For a double," Tom explained and walked away. I shrugged mentally. Tom must know what he was doing–with my money. Oh well, at that rate I'd be able to do a lot of betting.

The minutes ticked off. Tom drew my attention to the mobile gate where the horses were getting into position.

"They'll be off in a minute if there isn't a recall," he said.

"What's a recall?" I asked.

"Oh that's when they have to do it over," Tom said. "Watch the horses." I watched.

"No recall," said Tom. "Look, they're off."

A loudspeaker was blaring information to the crowd about which horse was where. I couldn't follow it.

"See your horse," Tom laughed. "He's last."

"Oh he is," I said and started to shout, "C'mon– "

"Shut up," said Tom.

I shut up.

Tom grabbed my arm and shouted in my ear. "Look at your horse now. See him coming up. He's made it to fourth. He's gaining."

"Oh shut up," I said. "Who cares?"

Tom shut up and moved away. The race ended with my horse the winner. I looked around for Tom. He came up to me grinning.

"Well your horse won," he said.

"I know," I answered. "Where do I go to get the money?"

"There's no money yet. Your second horse has got to win too."

My spirits sank. I could have cried.

"But—but— didn't I give you two dollars to bet and didn't he win? How come I don't get any money? How do these races work anyway?"

"Well I didn't bet him to win. I bet him for a double. You didn't say you wanted to bet him to win."

"What the hell! I don't know what a double is. Why would I pick a horse if I didn't want to bet on him? Oh, go away. You don't want me to have any fun." I turned and walked angrily away from Tom. I found a seat among some old ladies. They had pencils and pens and were marking programs and newspaper clippings. I wanted to ask questions of the old ladies but I thought they might not want to be bothered. They were very busy with their pencils and papers. I remained silent and smoked a cigarette. I was of a mind to go home.

After a while I lost my anger and cheered up. It wasn't all Tom's fault. Maybe he wasn't aware of just how ignorant I was. I should have asked him more about the races before we left home. I decided I'd ask him for help with the rest of the races. I began to look around for him. As my eyes searched the crowd for his familiar figure he came up behind me.

"Oh here you are," he said. "The next race'll soon be starting. After it, I'll take you to the beer room. There might be a fellow in there I want to meet you."

"Okay" I said. "Where's the ladies' washroom?"

"This way," said Tom. "Follow me." We threaded our way slowly through the crowd.

In the washroom some women were fixing their hair and re-making up their faces. All the seats were taken. I stood around and smoked. I liked the quietness there.

When I returned to the grandstand the second race was over. Tom was waiting near the ladies' door. He was very happy. My horse had won again.

"You picked the double," he said gaily.

"Oh, well now do I get some money?" I asked sarcastically.

"Yup. I'm waiting to see how much. Oh there, it's on the board now. Twenty-five dollars. I thought it'd be more than that. Well c'mon. Let's go cash the ticket."

I went along eagerly. Twenty-five dollars for two was great in my opinion.

In the beer room Tom found a few gambling friends. Tom introduced us and began bragging about my having won the double.

"She's never been to a track before in her life," he crowed, "and look at that. Picks the double the first time. What luck."

"Beginner's luck," a friend commented. "But good for you."

After that I lost fifteen dollars. One of my picks got three lengths ahead and broke. Another interfered with another horse. He came in first but was disqualified. The other choices were just slow, except the one I liked in the last race. He won easily, but I had no money on him. I had put my bet on one Tom favoured. That one came third. Even so I was ahead money when we arrived home. I was quite happy.

The following week I was transferred back to packaging at the chocolate factory. In a couple of days I was back moving trays of sweets from belt to belt.

To my joy I found the pans were being cleaned up slowly but I was surprised that we were still using dirty plastic trays. I had expected the Department of Health to close the plant until all the utensils were cleaned or replaced with new ones. They did not, and some of the girls continued to reclaim dropped bars from the floor and send them along the belts to be wrapped, labelled, and sent to stores to be sold to a trusting public.

I was bitterly disappointed in our Board of Health. I was also disgusted with it and that company. I purposely got myself fired by telling off a foreman, collected all money owing, and got a more satisfactory job.

Johnny and Sidney worked for the same man who had a small woodworking factory not far from where we lived. One day Johnny stopped work for a few minutes to speak to Sidney about the car. The boss called Johnny into his office and started a long spiel about hiring people to work, not to talk. Johnny quit.

"I told him I was doing a man's work but he wasn't paying me a man's wages. He damn well knows I was doing as much as the other men there," Johnny told me when he came home.

"Did you really, Johnny?" I asked.

"You're damn right I did," Johnny said vehemently. "Don't think I'm scared of him."

"Then what did he say?"

"He said, 'Do you want to work here or not?' So I said, 'No, I don't.' I picked up my stuff and came home."

"Did he give you your pay?"

"No. I didn't stop for it. I'll get it payday. I'll get my unemployment insurance too. They're not supposed to be taking money off me for that. That's another thing I don't like." With that Johnny left the room.

Tom was not pleased about Johnny quitting but Johnny got another job, just as good, within a week.

"Well maybe he did right, then," Tom philosophized.

Mrs. Stanley left her husband. She left at night and came to our house for sanctuary. She said that Bill was drunk and fighting with her. She showed me large bruises on her arms and legs.

"He's acting worse year by year," she said. Just for the kids' sake she had been staying with him, now for the kids' sake she had to leave. It would not help them if Bill crippled her. She was afraid he would follow her to my place. She did not want to cause me trouble. She went to another friend's house for the rest of the night.

Next day she phoned her son Andy. He had bought a car. He drove up and took his mother and the other kids to St. Thomas.

Jenny soon missed her games with the Stanley girls, Mabel and Ruth. She began to whine about having nowhere to go and nothing to do. Johnny tried to make her a swing on the big old tree in the back yard. The rope was too short. He tied one end securely and let it hang from a strong branch. It became Jenny's vine as she played "Jane". Other kids liked the game too. More and more they came to play with Jenny. Soon they became too confident and daring. I thought it best to impose a few rules on their Jane and Tarzan games. Jenny protested. I threatened to take the rope down. Jenny agreed to let me be boss.

Don and Pearl came home; they had had a wonderful time. Don had a souvenir for each of us and Pearl also had one for Jenny. Don had grown to dislike his foreman so much that he quit his job and took a different type of work at a lower wage.

He got a phone put in, in his name. He said he would make the payments but if any of the family offered help it would be welcome. Long distance calls had, of course, to be paid by the caller.

School opened. Joyce wanted to try it again. I told her I would help her if she would buckle down and study. She said she would. Her boss let her work evenings and on Saturday. She was able to buy her own clothes and school necessities. She could no longer pay board but we did not miss it much.

Don bought an extra car, an old one. He tore down part of the back fence and put it in the yard. He intended to work on it and get it into better running shape.

Johnny got his yellow belt in karate. He persuaded Sidney to join the club.

School had been open almost a month. I was pleased and surprised at the children's lack of complaints. All seemed to be doing well enough, even Billy. He had buckled right down and was doing his homework without protest, and without my urging.

His teasing of Jenny was getting worse, I thought. He didn't tease her all the time. Generally he was very good to her, taking her places, buying her little gifts and teaching her games. He was very patient in teaching her chess, checkers, and a few card games. Jenny was quick to learn but she had a strong temper.

She didn't like to be teased but we all teased her at times, just as we teased one another. Billy seemed to tease her more than the rest and she'd get so angry she'd try to hit him, sometimes by throwing hard objects.

One September evening as the sun shone brightly outside Billy and Jenny sat down for a game of chess. Billy beat his young sister easily. She was angry. Billy began to tease her about being a poor sport. Jenny became angrier. Billy kept on teasing.

In a blind rage Jenny ran full tilt at her brother. Billy warded off the intended blow. Jenny fell, hit her arm, and began to scream. I checked her arm. It wasn't even bruised. Billy teased her more. Jenny screamed louder.

Johnny had been in his room trying to study. He'd heard the battle. He came crashing downstairs. Within a minute he and Billy were fighting. Billy ran out the door. Johnny ran after him. Billy got away and Johnny came back in.

Jenny had stopped crying. She was no longer angry. I began to set the table for supper.

Johnny went out on the front verandah. Billy was lying in wait. He threw a pop bottle. It hit Johnny on the hip.

Billy took off. Johnny didn't bother to try to catch him that time. He came into the house mouthing threats.

I thought it would get really bad if Billy came in right then. Billy must have shared my thought. He stayed outside.

He didn't report for work either.

I began to suspect he'd run away. When Tom returned and we all went to bed Billy still hadn't come home. Next day he didn't show up at school. He didn't come home and nobody we knew had seen him by nightfall.

We were sure he'd run away—or something had happened to him. We preferred not to think about the latter possibility.

We speculated about whether he'd set out to hitchhike to New Brunswick. He had pay coming to him and hadn't stopped to collect it.

I forced myself not to worry. Fortunately I had help. Gloria phoned to ask if we could take in a friend of hers, Norman Bell, for a short time. He was twenty-five and had come up from New Brunswick four years before. He worked with Gloria. I had met him and Don knew him pretty well. Norman had fallen getting off a bus and injured his leg on the curb. It was pretty sore and stiff and he was finding it hard to get up to his room on the third floor of his boarding house. He had little money, no medical insurance and hadn't been to a doctor yet.

Of course we had room.

We had Billy's empty bed and an extra single bed in Johnny's room.

About six p.m. Harold brought Norman over directly from work. We shared supper and reminisced about the Maritimes. Tom was out. He wouldn't be back until the morning.

I found Norman a personable young man. He said he'd thought at first he hadn't hurt his leg very bad. Hardly a bruise showed but now it had begun to swell and was getting very painful. He played the guitar and sang well. It had been a long time since he'd touched a guitar. Sidney brought his to the kitchen. Norman played and sang for us and we all enjoyed it.

Before I went to bed I bathed Norman's injured leg in warm, salted water. Then we wrapped it in an elastic bandage of Johnny's. Norman went to work next morning before Tom got home.

I took the day off from my work. Tom came home, asked about the kids and Norman. I told him.

"No word from Billy?" he asked.

"Not yet. But I expect he's all right."

About four p.m. the phone rang. It was Billy calling from Nagogami, 600 miles west. The operator asked would I accept the charges. Yes, I would.

"I'm all right," Billy told me, his voice sounding as clear as if he were calling from Gloria's.

"Do you need any money?" I asked.

"No. I helped a guy do some work. He paid me. I've got over five dollars left."

"Well what are you going to do?"

"I'm coming back as soon as I get a drive."

"I can send you the money. Where will I send it?"

"Don't send money. I'm all right. I'll get back myself."

"All right. When will you be here?"

"Oh, Saturday, I guess. If I'm lucky. I just called because I thought you and Dad would be worried."

"Thanks," I said and started to cry. It was good to know Billy was safe, and wonderful that he cared about his parents. "I'm glad you're coming back. I'll tell Dad. You're sure you're all right?"

"Yes, I'm all right. I'll make it. I've gotta go now. Good-bye."

"Good-bye." I let Billy hang up first.

Tom was at work. I couldn't reach him easily but he had said he would call me if he got a chance.

The kids came home from school. They were glad to hear that Billy was all right and heading back. I wasn't sure of the name of the place he had called from then. It was in my mind he'd gone east instead of west. If I had remained calm I could have got more information from Billy. But we didn't care as much about where he was, since he was coming home, as about how he was.

Around seven p.m. Gloria's brother Harold arrived with Norman. Harold had borrowed his brother-in-law's car. Norman had worked that day and gone to see his doctor after. His condition was much more serious than any of us had realized.

He had phlebitis and thrombosis. He was to go right to bed and stay there, getting up only if absolutely necessary, for a few minutes. The doctor had prescribed three or four kinds of medicine, one a tranquilizer. He would have hospitalized Norman but there were no beds.

Norman was blond, slightly built, about five-five. He had been drinking a lot and neglecting his health. We couldn't say he had a dependence on alcohol but he loved beer.

I was very worried. Norman was seriously ill. I was working during the day and Tom worked part of the night. I feared another nervous breakdown for myself and was seeing a doctor regularly and taking tranquilizers.

I knew we were not in good shape to look after a man that ill, but there was nothing I could do but put Norman to bed right away.

We made him as comfortable as we could in Johnny's room. His injured leg had to be elevated. Johnny raised the mattress end sufficiently by placing many books under it.

"Well you'll have an educated foot, at least," Harold joked.

I made Norman a light meal. Harold and Johnny kept him company while he ate. He hardly touched the food. The light switch was on the wall too high for Norman to reach. When Norman was ready to sleep the boys put out the light and left the room.

Tom phoned. He was glad to hear our youngest son was safe and coming home. He hadn't time to ask about Norman. Anyway I preferred to keep that news until he was home.

I was still up when Tom arrived. He was astounded to hear how sick Norman was.

"He should be in a hospital. Those things are dangerous. He could die tonight. He's in bad shape," Tom said. "But we can't move him now. Anyway I'm off for two days. Then Sunday you'll be off. That's three days we can give him good care. Monday Johnny can leave school early. Four days. Then Don should have a couple of days off. We can take him his meals. But what about a bedpan? Never mind. I'll think of something."

Before Tom went to bed he talked to Norman. Norman vetoed the idea of a bedpan. "I'll go to the washroom. If I die, I die, that's all. I should have gone to the doctor sooner. I'm sorry to bother you. But there are no beds in the hospital. But I guess I'll be okay here. Of course I'll pay you when I can."

"Never mind the pay. We'll make out, but I'm worried. Still, you're young. It can't be so dangerous or he'd have got a hospital bed somehow."

"I guess it's not too dangerous if I keep quiet. But God, I worked all day. Of course driving the truck isn't like standing all day or walking. I think I'll be okay. I hope so anyway."

That was Thursday. Early Sunday morning Billy arrived home. He was too weary to talk much. We didn't pressure him for details of his adventure. He went to bed and slept soundly for twenty-four hours.

When he awoke he was able to eat a good meal and tell us something of his travels. He'd soon got a lift out of the city. Then a woman driver gave him a ride a couple of hundred miles. After she let him off he waited a short time then got a ride with a youngish truck driver right to Nagogami. The driver had bought Billy some meals and paid him well for his help unloading the truck.

Billy had slept in a Husky station at the end of his journey. People he met were friendly and helpful. A young man about Johnny's age took him hunting for about an hour. He let Billy fire a few shots at some grouse. He didn't hit any.

I ran Billy some water for a good bath and laid out clean clothes. The ones he'd been wearing were terribly dirty. When I put them to soak in my basement sink they gave off a noticeable odor of skunk.

Billy explained. He wasn't travelling through cities all the time. Often there were no houses or people for miles. Sometimes the road passed near forests. They saw a few animals on or near the road as they passed, sometimes a deer, sometimes a rabbit. Once they thought they'd hit a skunk, then they decided they hadn't, but perhaps they had after all.

"Well," I said, "if you didn't hit him perhaps he hit you."

The trip seemed to me to have had a maturing effect on Billy.

He studied harder and seemed more appreciative of our home comforts, few as they were.

Norman's invalidism wasn't upsetting our household too much. He had books to read, the record player, and a radio. Though alone most of the day he never lacked for company in the evening. Besides Gloria, Bob and the children who often came down and brought cigarettes, fruit or candy, other friends came when they heard how ill he was. He was a good patient, asking for as little service as possible. He steadily improved.

Gloria made a long distance call to his parents to let them know Norman was sick and had a new address. Then she wrote a letter giving more details. Toward the end of the second week his mother and two sisters arrived to see Norman. Norman was surprised but delighted. Gloria and Bob managed to find room for them the three nights they stayed.

The day they left Norman determined to get out of bed for a while. He had started to sit on the side of it but hadn't been moving around much.

Gloria phoned the doctor for him. The doctor allowed Norman up for a little while but cautioned him to take it easy.

Since we were all to be away that afternoon Norman's mother took him to Gloria's. The Dubés had known the Bells in New Brunswick. Just before train time they brought Norman back and saw that he was once more snug in bed. Johnny and I had returned by then.

Norman began to get out of bed and stay up longer each day. He increased his activities gradually and continued taking his medicine. At the end of the third week he started coming to the kitchen for meals.

He began to talk of getting back to his job. He went to see his doctor who told him to take it easy for another week. At our insistence Norman did.

Johnny received word from his school about commencement exercises. A letter informed him that he had been awarded the highest prize for chemistry in grade eleven. We were all very proud and happy.

Johnny would not go to school for the commencement exercises because he could not afford a suit. He got the prize later—chemistry books.

I turned my attention to preparing for a good Christmas. Schmidt had been promising for nearly three years to paint my kitchen. It was his idea, not mine. He had also been promising to fix the oven.

Since Olga had moved I could not use her facilities. Martha offered me the use of her oven for a day, but I refused it. I decided it was time Schmidt or Tom provided me with my own oven.

I began to harp on the subject. Daily I nagged Tom about it to his intense displeasure. Schmidt came for his rent once a week but I saw him other times as well. Each time I saw him I nagged him about the oven and the painting and a few other things as well, like the toilet backing up and the traps in the basement, and our lack of storm windows.

Schmidt had a few complaints too. He didn't like the boys' cars in the backyard and part of the fence being down.

He promised to have the kitchen painted and to get me a new stove before Christmas.

His electric stove in the other part of the house had a good oven. He brought the stove over one Saturday. I cleaned it well before they installed it in place of our old one. Tom put the old one out in our backyard.

I was happy. The painting could wait.

One late November evening I arrived home from work to find an old man happily painting my kitchen.

The stove was out from the wall unusable. Every cupboard door, top and bottom, was hanging open freshly painted. The floor, the chairs, and the table were all covered with newspapers and the ceiling, the doors and most of the walls were wet with new paint.

Tom was at work. The kids were home from school, hungry. Don, Sidney, and Norman were due to arrive for supper.

I wasn't up to attempting to prepare a meal in that kitchen. I checked my purse. Twenty dollars was all I could find.

"Well, kids, we'll have to eat out tonight. I'll give you each two dollars for a meal. That'll have to do. Jenny and I'll go to Gloria's. We'll buy some food and stay there. I'm not coming back here until all that paint is dry. I'll borrow the money for a hotel room if I have to."

"Good," they said. "Give us the money."

Don and Sidney arrived. Norman didn't show up.

"What's going on?" Don inquired. "Where are we supposed to eat?"

"At a restaurant," I said. "Here's two dollars. I'll treat you all to a two-dollar supper, except Jenny. I'll take her to Gloria's. That's all I can do. I don't know why in hell Schmidt had him start painting so late or try to do it all in one day. Wait'll I see that Tom or Schmidt!"

I didn't have many two-dollar bills. Johnny went out to change a ten and a five. I gave Joyce and Billy their supper money. Don refused to accept his. I insisted because he was paying in advance for room and board and had already bought his own lunch that day as had Sidney and Johnny.

Don, Joyce, and Billy left to find something to eat. I gathered up a few extra pieces of clothing for Jenny. Sidney drove us to Gloria's. Johnny came along as the two boys had decided to go to a restaurant together. I gave them five dollars.

Gloria's family was finishing supper when Jenny and I barged in. She listened with amusement to my story. She didn't want me to send out for food, so I gave Brucie and Nancy each fifty cents. They had to wash the dishes so I called the money a tip.

About an hour later Tom called me at Gloria's.

"I thought you might be there. What happened? Where is everybody? I called the house and Henry answered. He didn't know where you'd all gone. He thought you were mad."

"Henry's right. I'm good and mad. What kind of a trick is that? How'd you expect us to eat supper in that place? Why didn't he paint earlier?"

"Is Henry still painting? Well, Schmidt told me not to get him drunk."

"So you got him drunk. That means he didn't start painting until after two o'clock. Well you can just keep Henry and his paint. I'll not be home until that kitchen's dry and maybe not then. Good-bye."

I hung up.

Tom called back.

Brucie answered the phone.

"It's for you again, Mrs. Firth. It's Tom," he said.

I took the phone.

"What are you so mad about?" Tom asked.

"Are you so dumb? What woman wouldn't be mad, coming home to find her kids hungry and she can't use her kitchen or stove? On top of that the damn place was cold."

"Schmidt must have turned the furnace down again. He says we're using too much oil."

"Well you tell him to get us storm windows and fix the doors. You better have it warm and dry before you expect me back."

"It's good paint. It'll dry in a couple of hours okay. I've got to go now. Good-bye."

Tom hung up.

"Do you mean to say you're not going home tonight?" Gloria asked as I returned to her kitchen.

"Not if the paint isn't dry. I'll go to George's if I can't get a hotel room. I'd be gone now except I want to work tomorrow."

To pass the evening Gloria and I talked, played cards, read the newspaper and watched TV. Brucie, Nancy and Jenny played well together. Brucie had a new game, a Christmas present he'd opened really early. Nancy had a new game too, one she'd gotten for her birthday the previous month.

At 11:45 Tom called again. He was home. The house was very warm and the paint was dry, he assured me. Was I still mad, he wanted to know.

Well I wasn't but I warned him that if he was lying again I wouldn't stay after I got there.

Jenny and I came home. The paint was dry enough. I could use the kitchen. Henry had put the stove back in place. Tom had done the rest of the replacing and made fresh tea. I grumped a bit, but actually I was relieved to be home again rather than imposing on my relatives or sleeping in a strange hotel. However I didn't tell Tom that.

11

After the painting episode I enjoyed a short period of serenity. The kids and boarders were busy with social activities away from the house. Most evenings the house was quiet for three or four hours, with just Jenny and me at home. We spent the time reading, playing card games and chess, and writing letters, or baking. The Christmas spirit gripped us.

One Friday night Don failed to return after an evening out. It wasn't an unusual thing but this particular evening it was surprising because he had planned to take Tom shopping early next morning.

I was working Saturday mornings now. At coffee break I was called to the telephone.

It was Tom.

"Sophia?" he asked.

"Yes, what's happened?"

"It's happened. Don's in jail. He called."

"No. Is it bad? An accident?"

"No. He was drunk, I guess. They picked him up last night. He'll be home soon. He's got a lawyer. They're letting him out on his own recognition."

"Well, it can't be too serious then, I might as well stay at work. Okay, see you." I hung up. Tom could do his growling to the kids, and he would be growling, I knew from long experience.

I got off at one p.m. Don was home. He was to have a hearing in the new year. The charge was being in possession of a motor vehicle while impaired.

"Tell me about it, Don," I said.

"Well, I had a few drinks at Pearl's," he said. "Then a big lunch. When I started home I felt pretty good but I wasn't drunk. As I drove I got sick, so I pulled off the road and parked. Then I took a walk in a field and it all came up. Gawd, I was sick. When I got back to the car I still felt pretty bad so I sat down on the running board. These two OPPs came along and stopped. They came over to investigate. They asked if I'd been drinking and I said yes. Hell, I'm twenty-one now so they couldn't get me for that, and I wasn't driving at the time so they couldn't get me for that either. Anyway they took me to the station and had the car towed in. I've got to get Sidney to take me out to get it.

"I was so sick I didn't care. I tried to call here but nobody answered. I guess I dialed the wrong number. I didn't even mind their damn bunk. Next morning they handcuffed me to another guy who said he was in for stealing or shoplifting or something, and took us down to see a judge. The lawyer says I'll probably get off. All I'm worried about is my license, but I suppose I can get along without a car for a while."

"Well you shouldn't try to drive after you've been drinking. It's stupid. I'm glad they picked you up. It might have saved an accident."

"Oh, I wasn't that drunk. I could drive all right."

"You think you could. That's the trouble with alcohol. I've heard it makes people think they can act or drive better than they can when they're sober. I don't know. I've never been drunk. I can't swallow enough of the stuff. I hope you don't lose your license, but now the deed is done you'll have to take the consequences. You can get used to being a pedestrian again."

"Well I may have to," Don agreed. "I won't like it but there's not much I can do about it now."

A week later Norman got into a bit of trouble and spent the greater portion of a night in jail. He failed to get help until the next day because he couldn't remember our number and Gloria didn't answer her phone. Next day he was able to contact Gloria at work. She sent down some money, he paid his fine and costs, and went to work.

Christmas was rushing closer.

One evening after I came home from work Jenny dragged me to Christmas Fairyland. We walked around and looked at the interesting displays. There was a sale of prize packages. I let her buy two. One was a nice little round hatbox-type purse. There was a Cinderella shoe display. You slipped your foot into it and if it were set on your size a light flashed and you received a coupon for shoes or boots. Jenny tried it. No light came on. We walked around some more. I had been tired to begin with. I feared I might exhaust myself and be unable to work next day.

"We'll have to go home now, Jenny," I said. "Perhaps you can come back another time."

"Aw Mum, do we have to go? Oh well, okay."

We started to leave the grounds. We neared the Cinderella shoe.

"Can I try it again?" Jenny asked, darting aside before I could answer. I caught up to her just as she slipped her foot into the glass slipper and the light came on.

"Look! Look! Mum!" Jenny screamed in happy excitement. "I won. I get a pair of shoes. Don't I get a pair of shoes?"

"You lucky little girl," the attendant said. "Merry Christmas! You get a five-dollar coupon good at any of our stores until February."

Jenny was so excited it was contagious. I was suddenly glad I'd given in to her pleas to take her to Christmas Fairyland that particular night.

Jenny had to wait until the next night to spend her coupon.

Don took time to drive her around but the store wasn't where I thought it was and we had to return home without Jenny's shoes. Don had to go out on other business.

Jenny was very unhappy. Johnny told me where a store was located. Sidney drove Jenny and me there. He couldn't wait to drive us home. I told him that was all right.

Jenny wanted winter boots. They didn't have her size in the style she wanted. She refused to wait until another day to go to another store. She settled for a nice-looking pair of snow boots that she could barely get her feet into. The price was eight dollars including the coupon. Jenny wore them home. She insisted they were big enough.

The next day Sidney called a scrap dealer to come for his car, Don's and Johnny's. They were towed away before nightfall. There was a new law that cars had to pass a roadworthy test. The boys said they couldn't afford to upgrade their old cars, that it was wiser to scrap them.

Tom repaired Schmidt's fence and the yammering about it ceased.

The night before Christmas Eve, Harold called to see us. He had bought a new Volkswagen. He had rented an apartment and moved out of his sister's house. "I couldn't stand the fighting," he said. "And the kids. They're not brought up at all. They wouldn't leave my stuff alone."

Harold gave us two boxes of chocolates.

"You can eat these all right. They're clean. I think. Howie told me all about your chocolate company, Mrs. Firth. I don't blame you for quitting. I wish I could quit and get another job myself."

"Why?" Johnny asked. "Is your company filthy too? Or is it you want better pay?"

"Well, I see cockroaches every day. And a few mice. Once we caught a little mouse and I was going to keep him for a pet but he died. I only work in the warehouse so I can't see what goes on in the factory. But it isn't that. It's some of the guys at work. I don't like their attitude. They don't give a damn about the company or their jobs—just their pay cheques. They smoke where they shouldn't and do their work—well—like it doesn't matter unless the boss is watching. I'd like to get out of there but what can a fellow do? I can't just walk into a place and get a job anytime. I'm stuck."

"That's the trouble where I worked. The women are stuck. Most need the money, not really to keep from starving but to make a better life; to buy things for their families. I tried to get a few interested in a union but it was no-go. The typical attitude was, why should we pay into a union? We have jobs and the pay is not too bad. Why should we worry about someone else? Let them do their own worrying."

"We have no union either," said Harold. "I'd like to have one. But some of those guys are so ignorant a union wouldn't help them."

"It might," I said. "Don't forget you workers are in the position of being alone. If you had a union and felt the other members cared about you and you all had some say together in running the company you might be very surprised how the people would change."

"You may be right. Some of us have talked about it but—well, some are married and there's too much taken off their pay now. Union dues are high. What do Don and Tom pay a year?"

"Oh, sixty or seventy dollars—but look what they get. They can't be fired for no good reason—like some boss not liking them. That's one kind of dirt a union protects them from. And then their dues are tax-free. So a union gives some benefits. A good union can help a man feel more like a decent human being and not some miserable dog who has no say about his job or wages or working conditions. Sure I know labour unions are blamed for a lot of things we don't like, but when a company doesn't care about its employees how can it expect the employees to care about it? And if the public doesn't care about its producers, usually the producers don't care about the public. Those women who were sending dirty chocolates out to the public probably wouldn't let their children eat a cookie or candy that fell on their own floor."

"Not likely," Sidney said. "But they probably let them buy dirty food and don't even know about it. I worked in a tomato ketchup factory and after what I saw I don't eat ketchup any more."

"What did you see, Sidney?" Johnny cried. "C'mon, tell us."

"I don't want to spoil your appetite. If I told you you'd never eat it again," Sidney averred.

"That's the way it is," Harold said. "You can pay high prices but you never know what you're getting. When I was a kid I just thought all bought food, ice cream, candy, bread, butter and stuff came from shiny clean factories where clean, careful, honest people worked. Now I know better and it fair turns my stomach."

"Sad, ain't it? Well, kids, let's open Harold's chocolates," I said, opening one box. "Here, who'll sample them first?"

"Not me."

"No thanks."

"Eat them yourself. I don't feel like candy right now."

"I'll have some, Mummy," Jenny said. "I'll take this one and this one and there, that one. Hmn. They look good. See? There's no dirt on these. Look. I can't see no dirt."

Don entered the room then.

"What's the big conference about this time?" he asked. I told him.

"Oh," he laughed. "You know we've all got to eat a peck of dirt before we die. I'm starting my fifth."

"Well," Sidney told him, "I'd like to stretch mine out and live longer. Eat yours as fast as you want, though. Don't mind me."

Jenny came back for more chocolates. I let her take two. "That's all, Jenny," I said. "I'm going to make a midnight snack for everybody now."

Actually it was only ten p.m. The boys, Don, Johnny, Sidney and Norman trooped upstairs. Billy was out, supposedly with Howie, skating or playing pool. Pool had taken the place of chess in Billy's life.

The doorbell rang. I answered it. To my joy it was Andy Stanley.

"Come in! Come in! Santa Claus!" I cried. "You're a little early aren't you?"

Jenny came running to see.

"Oh, it's only Andy," she cried in disappointment.

"Who's there?" Johnny called from the top of the stairs. "Is that Andy? Oh, boy!" He bounded down.

"Hi, Andy! How are you, old buddy?" Johnny cried.

"I'm fine, old buddy. How's the world treating you?" Andy said. The two boys clasped hands. I retreated to my kitchen.

"Bring Andy out here, when you're done hugging and kissing, Johnny," I said. "I want to hear the news of his mother."

"Okay, Mother. Come on, Andy. Let's go fill the old gossip in. Then we'll go upstairs and sing. I can't sing but I'm a real good listener."

Andy told me his mother was fine and doing part-time work.

The kids were all fine and doing well in school. He was still in school but had a part-time job. He was earning a little money singing with a group of young people at parties in hotels and places. He enjoyed that immensely. I was happy for him. Soon Johnny took him up to join the merry group in Sidney's room.

I prepared sandwiches and laid out a large plate for them. I put sugar, coffee and teabags on the table, laid out cups—no saucers—spoons and knives on the table, then I went up to hear a few songs.

Andy was starring as our singer. Everybody wanted to hear "Give my Love to Rose". Andy could sing that to bring tears to my eyes. He did. Then he did "Jimmy Brown" and stirred everybody deeply. After that we ate lunch and talked. Then more songs until Tom arrived at 11:30.

Christmas Day Tom was going to work at two so I cooked vegetables and heated the remainder of the turkey and made sauce for the pudding.

At twelve I called everybody for dinner. We ate in relays. When all had eaten Johnny decided to make a long distance call to my sister Lois in New Brunswick. Joyce, Jenny and I talked too. Next Sidney called his mother back home. I talked to her too. Then Norman made two more calls to New Brunswick.

Tom got out the remainder of his liquor. There was enough for a stiff drink for himself, Don and Norman. The rest of us declined his offer to share.

When Tom had taken his lunch and gone, Norman went back to bed and I went upstairs to play a record.

I left Joyce washing the dishes and Don, Johnny, Sidney and Billy talking in the kitchen.

I hadn't set up the record player when Joyce came dashing up the stairs screaming that Don and Johnny were fighting.

I ran down. The boys had stopped, almost. Don was by the back door, Johnny by the cellar door and Sidney between them trying to calm both brothers who were bitterly criticizing each other's abilities and attitudes.

My table was on its side, the radio and a few other things on the floor, chairs upset.

"What's going on? This is no place to fight and no day either," I said reaching to upright the table. Sidney moved to assist me.

"I didn't start it," Johnny said vehemently. "He needn't think he can push me around."

"No, but you think you can push Billy around," Don called derisively across the room.

"I didn't lay a hand on Billy," Johnny cried.

"You threatened to!" Don said.

"Yes, and I'll keep the threat if he doesn't leave Jenny alone," Johnny vowed. "You're not big enough to stop me."

"Come on outdoors and we'll see," challenged Don turning and starting out to the backyard.

Johnny marched across the room and out. Sidney followed him. I followed Sidney, running.

When I got outside Sidney was trying to separate Johnny and Don. He was very cool. The yard was extremely slippery with a few bits of junk protruding from the ice patches. I realized two things at once: that the yard was a dangerous place for fighting but at the same time, since the antagonists couldn't keep their footing, they might feel as foolish as they looked, slipping and sliding around as they made ferocious jabs at one another and, I hoped, would thus be easily persuaded to stop the battle.

"Come on now, Don and Johnny, this is no good," I said, "it's even dangerous."

Johnny paid me no heed. He made a run at his brother and swung his left fist wickedly towards Don's jaw. Luckily one foot slipped and he was forced to pull his punch as he strove to keep upright. Don made a run then at Johnny but Sidney was trying to impede him. Between Sidney's pulling and the ice under his leather-soled shoes Don had a hard time keeping his balance and moving. His blow fell short. Meanwhile Johnny was doing a lot of sliding too, and was using one hand to pull himself along the fence as he tried to reach Don.

"It's damn silly of both of you," I said. "Don, you're older. Stop it! You know Johnny can't fight for long. He can have a reaction. Johnny, stop! Somebody might get hurt bad! This is no way to settle things." I reached out to pull at Johnny while Sidney pulled at Don. "What started this? What happened anyway?" I asked. "Come on. Stop these crazy goings-on! Don, listen! You have better sense. What good is this fighting out here? It's just spoiling my Christmas."

As I talked I tried to reach the icy space separating the warriors. It happened I slipped and nearly fell flat on my face. Both boys stopped their forward struggle.

"Come on in the house," I pleaded. "It's too dangerous to fight out here. You can settle it another time in a better place. Out there in the lane is better than this junk-yard. C'mon Don, Johnny. You boys have better sense than to fight here."

Don gave in. "All right," he said, "I'm going in. Fuck, if I got beat it'd be the ice, not you anyway."

Don moved past the silent Johnny to the house. I followed him, greatly relieved.

"Come on, Johnny. Don't let a little fight spoil Christmas," I said.

In the house Don righted an overturned chair and sat down at the end of the table. I picked up the radio which was still plugged in, put it on the table and turned it on. The alarm clock, too, I picked up, checked, saw it wasn't damaged, and placed on the table.

Sidney and Johnny entered the house as I finished straightening up. Johnny and I sat down. Sidney remained standing.

"Well, how about coffee?" I said, moving to get the water ready.

"I don't want coffee," Johnny said.

"You, Sidney?" I asked.

"No thanks. Well yes, maybe," Sidney said.

"Now boys," I said, turning from the stove and sitting down again. "Keep your tempers down and tell me what that was all about."

"I don't know," Don said. "Johnny just got mad at nothing."

"I didn't get mad at nothing," Johnny said. "You started pushing me around and I don't stand for that. You might have been able to do it one time but not anymore."

"I didn't push you," Don said. "I just warned you to lay off Billy."

"And I warned him to lay off Jenny," Johnny said. "And you did push me. I was standing by the fridge and you got up and came over and pushed my shoulder."

"Oh that. I just laid my hand on your shoulder. That wasn't a push. That was just a touch."

"Well, I thought you meant to fight," Johnny said, "and I was ready."

"All right," I interjected. "I understand now. I've got to do something about Billy."

The kettle began to boil. I arose to make some coffee.

"You better," Johnny siad. "Someone better make him leave Jenny alone or I will. I'm not putting up with her screaming all the goddam time."

"Well, I'm not either," I said. "I can't. We'll just have to do something."

"Something? Yuh something, probably just talk as usual. You should realize by now talking to Billy isn't enough. What he needs is a good licking and that mightn't do any good, he's so hard-headed."

"A good licking might help some, at least for a time," I said. "But it might not make him see the harm he does everybody by teasing Jenny so much—that's why I talk. Remember I have a responsibility to him too. If I could beat him myself I would— "

"Well why doesn't Dad beat him, then?"

"Because it hurts Dad more than Billy, that's why. Dad just doesn't seem able to be a disciplinarian or even a boss. He never learned that. Oh, he can strike out after he gets so mad he doesn't care, and that's dangerous. Then he worries that he injured the kid and he frets at me and that is just as bad as Jenny screaming at Billy."

"Oh, sure it hurts Dad more than Billy. Well, I'll do it then," Johnny swore.

"But that mightn't do much good either, not in the long run. No, the only solutions I see is take him to a psychiatrist or psychologist and if that doesn't work place him in reform school."

"Psychiatrist? Why a psychiatrist? They can only tell you what you already know about Billy."

"Oh, it's not to tell me but to tell Billy. A psychiatrist should be able to help Billy see how he harms himself, how he alienates his relatives. You know damn well he gets his teasing ways honestly. There was no worse tease than Tom. You should hear what my mother has to say about your father—she hasn't a good word for him, all because of his teasing. There's another side to it too. Even though Jenny gets very angry at Billy and screams and kicks she likes some of the attention. She does or she wouldn't ask him to play chess and checkers and cards with him. Do you know how many times Billy took Jenny to the show this year and looked after her? Five or six, and you never took her once."

"Well, I can't do things like that. I hardly go to a show myself, so you can't expect me to sit there all afternoon just to watch over my little sister."

"I don't. I don't expect Billy to either. It just happens that he'll do it once in awhile when he wants to see a show. I only mentioned that to remind you that Billy does some very good things for Jenny too. I'm not trying to excuse his mean teasing. He goes too far, but some teasing from Billy helps her to learn to defend herself from other kids who tease her. Jenny, too, has to learn to control her temper and how can she learn if she has no chance to practice? I'll have to talk to her as well as Billy."

"That's true. Jenny is a spoilt brat. So is Billy. Well if something isn't done I'm moving out."

"So move out," Don said, "who's stopping you?"

"I am," I spoke quickly before Johnny could answer, "or I'm trying to. I'd like Johnny to stay in school awhile and I figure he'll soon quit if he moves out. I think I can keep it peaceful enough for another few months. It's not a madhouse here all the time, you know."

"But most of the time, eh, Maw?" Don teased.

"So why don't you move out yourself, Don?" Johnny asked.

"I've no reason to move out," Don said. "I can take the madhouse. Billy shares my room and he knows better'n to bother me."

"Yeah, because he knows you'll beat him and Mum and Dad won't do a thing about it. Perhaps that's why he picks on Jenny—because you pick on him."

"I don't pick on him," Don was laughing now. He seemed not a bit annoyed. "He's got his junk scattered all over my room and I have to kick it out of the way to find mine. That's all."

"Your room? It's his, too."

"Well he doesn't pay board. I pay board so I have more

rights. Isn't that right, Sidney?"

"Don't bring me in on this argument," Sidney said. "I don't know a thing about it."

"Well, we all get on each other's nerves at times," I said. "All I know is some people can stand kids' racket, yelling and crying more than others. I could stand it when you were young better than I can now. I really could. Poor Dad was the one who was always threatening to leave. Now he lies awake nights wondering where you big fellows are or whether you're lying around somewhere injured or dead."

Johnny became silent. He seemed normal again.

Don said, "Dad should realize by now there's no point in worrying. It won't prevent or cure anything."

"Oh, he knows that. But it isn't easy to turn your mind off or switch instantly from one mood to another. Not for us old folk anyway. It seems to me the older we get the longer it takes to do lots of things. For instance it takes me longer to cool down now after I get mad and it takes me longer to shake myself out of a blue mood—but on the other hand it takes me longer to get mad, too."

"Well, you are getting old, Ma. There's no doubt about that," Don laughed.

"That's what I've been trying to tell you. We're all getting older. For you fellows it's good because you are becoming freer, more independent. For Dad and me it's the opposite. We're on the decline." I stopped talking. To my mind there came the vision of my parents so far away sitting in their bleak living-room talking, perhaps about me and my family. Tears started to well to my eyes.

"Are you starting to cry, Ma?" Don asked.

"No, no. I just thought of Grandpa and Grandmother away off there in old N.B., Grandpa in his wheelchair and Nell's kids running around probably fighting every few minutes."

"You're lonesome. You should have gone home for Christmas."

"Oh, no. I couldn't face the cold and the snow this year. I wouldn't mind seeing them but I just can't face the trip yet. Besides, if I took a holiday who'd keep you guys from killing each other?"

12

December 31, 1968, Johnny celebrated his eighteenth birthday. That evening Alice Dubé threw a New Year's Eve party.

Johnny was invited. It was to be a quiet but happy time with dancing and singing and refreshments but no alcoholic beverages allowed, and of course no drugs.

Johnny went to the party early. He talked Sidney into accompanying him. Sidney was welcome, in the way friends are, to drop in but Alice had thought he might consider himself too old at twenty for her party.

Around eleven, Norman arrived home somewhat intoxicated. He asked me where the boys were.

"Don is out at Pearl's, I think," I said. "Tom is at work but will be home soon. Sidney and Johnny are up at Gloria's. Alice is having her party tonight."

"Oh, that's right. She told me she was having a New Year's party. Well I think I'll go up for a bit—I'll be their chap—chaperone," Norman said. His voice was a bit thick and his gait uneven but he seemed quite clear-headed.

Norman left. Tom came home, then Joyce. Jenny had been waiting for her. She came downstairs to pick at a little food. Billy came in. He had been to Alice's party earlier but had left with Howie to go skating about nine. It wasn't much of a party he told us.

About 12:30 we five went to bed. The rest were still out. I went to sleep quickly and so did Tom.

At 1:30 the ringing phone woke us. Tom got to it first.

"Hello. Who? I'm Thomas Firth," he said. "Who? Johnny? John Firth? Where? You have him at 14 Station?" To me he screamed, "They've got Johnny in jail. He's drunk."

I was scrambling into my clothes. "Take it easy Tom," I called. "Tell them to get a doctor right away. He can't be drunk! There was to be no liquor. It's a coma. He needs a doctor."

Into the phone Tom continued. "Hello. Listen. That boy's a diabetic. Had it since he was nine. Get a doctor. What? How do you know he's drunk? He needs a doctor."

"Let me talk, Tom," I yelled. "Here, give me the phone. You get dressed."

Tom gave me the phone.

"Hello," I said. "Do you have Johnny Firth there? How is he acting?"

"He's acting drunk. I've explained to your husband."

"Yes, but now I want to explain to you. Even if he is drunk he needs a doctor. He may be acting like that because he needs sugar or insulin or something. Is he able to talk?"

"Yes."

"Has he eaten? Did you give him sugar?"

"No."

"Did you get a doctor? You better get a doctor."

"May I speak to Mr. Firth again, please?"

"Here, Tom. They want to talk to you again." I passed him the phone.

"Hello," Tom said. "Yes, okay. Yes. How much? Yes I have the money. All right. I'll be right up. Okay. Goodbye." Tom hung up.

"Goddammit," he roared at me. "A man can never get any rest around here. Bastards. Why doesn't Johnny leave that Christly liquor alone? He'll get himself killed one of these days."

"Oh calm down, eh?" I said. Joyce came down asking questions. "Oh—don't bother me now," I told her. "Dad's got to go to the police station for Johnny. They said he's drunk. Here's your goddamn shoe. What's all the rush? He'll be okay."

"Why in hell doesn't that kid carry his card?" Tom bellowed, throwing on his coat. "Where is my cap? I had it– "

"Here's your lousy cap," I told him, "and Johnny always carries his card, unless he lost his wallet. Oh, go on. Even if he didn't have one tonight the police know now and it's their duty to get a doctor." As I spoke, Tom was moving toward the front door. Billy leaned over the upstairs railing to ask about the racket.

"Never mind. You get back to bed," Tom screamed at him. "I've got enough trouble." Tom went out and roughly hauled the door closed behind him.

Billy came down the stairs to join Joyce and me in the kitchen.

"Is Johnny in jail? What happened to him?" he asked.

"Yes, he's in jail," I said. "I'm not sure what happened but they've picked him up anyway. Maybe it's a good thing. Something's wrong with him. Dad's gone to see. He'll get a doctor, by God."

"He's probably drunk," Billy said.

"How do you know?" Joyce yelled.

"Oh shut up, both of you," I commanded. "There's enough racket and I don't want Jenny up. I'm going to make tea. Do either of you want any?"

"I do," Joyce said quietly.

"I'll have a glass of milk," Billy whispered. "Then I'm going back to bed."

I started the water to heat, got Billy a glass of milk, then sat down but jumped up quickly.

"Oh, I better call Alice," I said. "If the police find out where Johnny was they're likely to raid the place. That'd probably scare Alice. Gloria too if she and Bob are home, and Bob'll be mad."

I phoned Gloria's.

"Alice," I cautioned, "listen. The police have Johnny. You better end your party just in case, or quieten it down. There's no liquor or bottles around are there?"

"No. No. They've got Johnny? What for?"

"For drunkenness, they said. But Tom has gone to see about it. Don't worry."

"Johnny!" Alice seemed incredulous. "But Norman? Is he there?"

"No. Maybe they've got him, too. Okay, my kettle's boiling. 'Bye now." I hung up.

Suddenly we were startled by voices and shuffling at the front door. It was Sidney helping Norman in.

"So you made it, Norman?" I laughed.

"Oh, yes. With Sidney's help," he said, staggering about. "You're a good pal, Sidney. Thanks."

"Well Johnny didn't," I said. "They got him. Sidney, do you know if Johnny was drinking?"

"Well–uh," Sidney said. "Watch it Norman, you'll fall." I sensed Sidney was wary of telling tales on Johnny or Alice or the other kids.

"Oh, don't worry Sidney," I said. "It doesn't matter. The police only found him drunk. They didn't see him drinking."

"Well he may have had some," Sidney said. "I didn't. But he seemed all right. We were all leaving to come home. The last I saw, Johnny was on the verandah and I went in to get his jacket and Norman. When we came out he was gone."

"Gone. Without a word? Where's his jacket then?"

"Up at Gloria's. No, he never called out or let me know he was leaving at all. I thought he was going to wait but he didn't."

"Well, there's something wrong for sure. No wonder they thought he was drunk. Running around the streets in this weather in his shirtsleeves this late at night. Oh, the poor cops!"

"Poor cops! Ha!" Norman laughed. "They couldn't get me because I had Sidney. So they settled for Johnny. Poor kid."

"Poor cops. They have nice warm cars," Sidney joked. "Poor me, you mean. Lugging a drunk along the street. And you flagging the cops down for a lift. Boy you're lucky."

"Yuh, that's right. I did flag one, didn't I?" Norman laughed. "Oh, they'd have picked me up sure if you hadn't said you could take care of me. But Johnny? I didn't think he was drunk."

"Me, either," Sidney said. "But I couldn't look after both of you. I wonder why he disappeared. I was only in the house a minute. Where'd they pick him up, Mrs. Firth?"

"I don't know. I hardly remember anything they said, I was so worked up. Being roused from a sound sleep and all. Them poor police'll be wondering what kind of people live at 79 Huron. First Don, then Norman, now Johnny. Maybe they've got an alert out for you boys."

"Well, I'm going to bed. I'm beat," Norman said. He hauled himself up the stairs. Sidney went into the hall to make sure Norman finished ascending safely.

Don arrived. We told him of Johnny's escapade. I fixed him a lunch while we waited. Our vigil wasn't long.

Johnny came in ahead of Tom. He was quite happy and exuberant but he didn't appear drunk to me. I made him some very sweet coffee.

Questions and comments were flung at Johnny from all sides. He made a general reply.

"Oh, I had a little trouble, that's all. But I wasn't drunk. It was an insulin reaction, I think. Oh, maybe the rum had a little to do with it but I threw up in their car and that helped. I don't know what happened exactly. When Sidney went back into Gloria's I stayed on the verandah but suddenly I got awful hot. I caught a streetcar at Queen right away but hell I got off at Bathurst. I thought it was Spadina but when I reached the street I saw this patrol car and a motorcycle cop behind it and I realized it wasn't the right stop. So I started across the street and they came over and stopped me. Two of them came up, one on each side of me and started talking. They said, 'You better come with us,' so I said, 'Okay.' I didn't feel like arguing. I could feel myself getting sicker. We got in the car, me in the back seat, and they drove off. Then I got really sick and I told them but they didn't stop. When we got to the station I was a little better but still dizzy and nauseated. I couldn't be bothered sorting my identification so I gave them my wallet. I went outdoors a couple of times and did pushups on the floor. They asked me if I'd been drinking. I said, 'Sure, I've been drinking.' I didn't say where or what. After about ten minutes they put me in a cell. I sat down on the cot, then I fell asleep and Dad came."

"You were doing pushups, Johnny? In the police station? At one a.m.? No wonder they decided you were drunk," I said. "How come they let you go outdoors?"

"Oh there was someone watching me all the time. I wasn't on the street."

Tom had been busy taking off his heavy boots and putting away his cap and coat in the hall. Now he entered the kitchen.

"You shouldn't have been drunk at all," he said. "But once they had you they should've got a doctor. They can't tell what's the matter just by looking. How'd you get the liquor anyway?"

"Oh this guy Jeffrey knows Alice and Gloria. He called at the party late. He had a bottle of rum. Four or five of us took a slug or two. That was just before I left. I never figured it would make me drunk. I bet I wouldn't've registered more'n one-hundredth percent actually."

"They should have given you a breathalizer test. They made a mistake by not doing it. We've got them there. We'll beat that rap. I'll plead not guilty and let them prove it," Tom said.

"Well what are the charges anyway?" Don asked. "Drinking under age and being drunk?"

"Yes," Tom answered in a growly tone, "and being drunk in a public place."

"Oh well, what's the penalty for that?" I asked.

"Don't worry about a penalty," Johnny laughed. "They can't prove a thing. It's only their opinion. Isn't there some law about a guy not having to convict himself?"

"Oh, the Fifth Amendment, but that's in the States," I said.

"We've got one like that here," Don said. "The Evidence Act, or something."

"They can convict him on any goddamn thing at all," Tom said. "You know damn well there's no justice in this country."

I laughed. "Hah! Awhile ago you said he could beat the rap. Now you tell a different story."

"Well I meant he could if there was justice. They hung Coffin didn't they?"

"Well it's his first offence. He'll probably get just a suspended sentence," Don told us.

"Unless he goes down there and shoots off his mouth. Then he'll get contempt," Tom sneered.

At that a yell from Johnny. "I don't shoot off my mouth. That's your trouble, not mine. But I'm not scared to face any judge and defend myself. I won't even get a lawyer."

"Yeah!" Tom yelled right back. "You'll defend yourself all right. Right into jail."

"No I won't!" Johnny's voice was very loud. "What have they got on me, huh? Yeah, tell me that."

"Pipe down!" I ordered. "What's there to get mad about? Can't we ever discuss anything in a civilized way?"

"I'm not mad," Johnny said in a much quieter tone. "He's the one who's mad. But it's my problem so you can all just stay out of it."

"Well who wouldn't be mad, having to get out of bed at one a.m. to get someone out of jail?" Tom roared.

"Oh you didn't have to come and get me. I could have stayed," Johnny growled at his father.

"Okay now. Just get your tempers down," I said quietly. "Johnny, Tom has a right to be mad, except he should have expected things like that when he got married. Anyway, you went to that party, you took a drink or two and here we all are roaring like rogue elephants over nothing."

"It's not nothing," Tom said. "My twenty-five dollars is gone. That's something."

"Oh, twenty-five dollars. I'll pay you back, with interest too," Johnny sneered.

"Oh shut up, eh?" I cried in disgust. "Such a damn big fuss over a little thing like an eighteen-year-old taking a drink of liquor. He's practically supporting himself and paying taxes. He's got most of the responsibility of an adult and none of the privileges. This episode will be laughable twenty years from now. So what's there to get all raging and yelling about? Johnny are you sure you don't want anything more to eat? You'll be all right?"

"Yes, I'll be all right," Johnny assured me.

"Okay then. I'm going to bed," I said. I left the room.

Shortly Tom retired too. Interest in Johnny's trouble petered out. Soon everybody was in bed. I wasn't long getting back to sleep.

Within a few days Johnny made a court appearance. Tom went with him. Johnny pleaded not guilty. His trial was set for the middle of the month. We set ourselves to wait.

The date for Don's trial arrived. He, too, was pleading not guilty. His case was remanded until February. More waiting. We were pretty tense.

I tried but failed to find a job. There was nothing for which I was qualified listed with Canada Manpower centre either. I began receiving benefit cheques.

Early in February Don's case was remanded again. He did not appear worried. He had resigned himself to an expected loss of his driver's licence for awhile. It would not affect his job much but it would restrict his social life a great deal—and mine a bit since he drove me quite a few places.

I came down with another cold. It just hung on and on. Added to that misery we suffered a loss of hot water.

Schmidt had taken out our gas-heated water tank and installed an electrically-heated one and had connected it up in such a way that our water was heated from his side of the building. There were no tenants living in that section and though he was there once in awhile himself we seldom saw him other than on rent day.

When we lost our hot water there was no way we could contact Schmidt. We resorted to heating water for baths and scrubbing on the stove in pots. The scrubbing, you can bet, was neglected. The clothes were done at a laundromat.

Every day we growled about the lack of hot water while we waited for Schmidt to appear. Tom kept trying to find Schmidt but all efforts failed.

After a week Schmidt showed up. He had the water bill with him. Tom adamantly refused to pay it. There was a rip-roaring argument. Finally Schmidt agreed to put in a gas-heated water tank.

Then the basement flooded. Again Schmidt was unavailable. We had heard that he had family troubles--his youngest son had committed suicide in January.

Tom called in city inspectors. They tested the water that was about three inches deep on the basement floor and not receding. The water had come in through sewage pipes but it was not sewage water.

Schmidt appeared. He was very angry. So were we. We argued. We contended that it was Schmidt's responsibility to get rid of the water. He did not want to lay out money to pay qualified men to clear his pipes. In the end he decided to do it himself. He brought in plungers and snakes. Tom used the tools to try to clear the trap in the basement floor to let the water run out. He got nowhere.

Then because the city was going to do the job and charge Schmidt he went to work himself. After a day and night of hard labour he got the pipes clear and the basement cleaned up.

I thought by then we had had our quota of trouble, but no. My iron stopped heating. Don took it apart. He said it was worn out, not worth repairing, and threw it in the garbage. At that Joyce was very angry. She took good care of her clothes and used an iron two or three times a week.

"I'll get a new one." Don promised. "It doesn't cost a fortune." Well maybe he was right but his car broke down and he spent my iron money on it. Joyce began to do her ironing at her friend's. The rest of us wore our clothes unironed. Most of the boys' pants and shirts were permanent press anyway and a few wrinkles never bothered Tom or me so we took it in our stride.

Around that time Joyce asked me to fill in for her as baby-sitter a few nights a week for the young Americans. I did though Tom protested. He had a grievance against the husband because he had refused to lend Tom his circular saw earlier. I had no grievance, as I pointed out to Tom, and Joyce had told me they had a lot of very good books. It looked like a real good deal to me; I could read Plato and Marx while I earned fifty cents an hour.

"Go on, then. Do what you like," Tom told me grumpily.

So I began baby-sitting. The baby was an eighteen-month-old boy. He could walk and climb and make signs of greeting but did not talk. He knew Jenny already and expressed pleasure on seeing her with me. Mrs. Jory (Gwen) said I was welcome to read any of their books. The first I chose was Plato. Gwen wasn't away long enough for me to read it all so she loaned me the book to read at home.

Tom smirked when I showed the book to him. Plato was old hat to him. He became convulsed with mirth when I exhibited surprise at finding that Asclepius was a Greek god. From my elementary school days I had held the belief that Asclepius was just a kind neighbour of Socrates. Hell, I could not see the sense of sacrificing cocks to gods. It always seemed to me that a god can take any cock or tree or man any old time he wants to. I can't understand why people think gods demand sacrifices of humans other than their own obedience or love.

I had received the impression from my schoolteachers that Socrates was a truly great philosopher and nobody disagreed with him. I was not very impressed; his attitude toward the state was silly.

The state, or society, is dependent upon its creator, man, for its maintenance, not man upon it. And as a dependent it should serve equally all those upon whom it depends equally for existence.

We are not responsible for the society we are born to and its laws. For our first few years we are in a dependent, subordinate state and have to take whatever society dishes out. Should we be grateful for that? No. Society seeks its own good just as individual people do.

Of course we owe support to the state if we expect support from it, and vice versa. But the state belongs to us, not we to it. We belong to nature.

To my great anger I see that Canada does not even try to serve all of us equally. Fortunately it has given us the legal right to fight parliamentarily for better and better service. To me that is a good thing.

Reading Plato did not change my views but it helped me understand why they had killed Socrates; he drove them to it, deliberately. He did not try to defend himself seriously; instead he laughed at his judges and made them appear fools in their own eyes. Their egos could not survive the blow he dealt them through their own mental processes. While they could not destroy the truth of his arguments they could get rid of the one who would always be a reminder of their folly. He must have known what he was doing and all that talk about his debt to his state had to be the product of a lesser mind or a ploy to keep lesser men out of trouble.

I tried to discuss the book with Tom but he was not interested.

"They're doing the same today," he said. "Man doesn't want to hear the truth."

I became concerned about Billy. His part-time job entailed

work after school from four to ten most week nights and from four to twelve or one a.m. on Friday and Saturday nights. Sometimes, but not always, he got a short break.

One evening he failed to return from school. That didn't worry me. He was fifteen years old, had a little money in the bank, and usually carried a few dollars on him.

At four p.m. his boss began calling to see if he was home and asking me to tell Billy when he did arrive to please go right in to work. Billy's boss called periodically all evening. Tom was home and took half the calls. He began to rage and rant about Billy's irresponsibility, etc., etc.

Johnny leaped to his brother's defense. Billy had a lousy job and he, Johnny, wouldn't work at it. It was the kind where a boy or a man was expected to drop everything and come running whenever the restaurant got busy, and for a dollar an hour that was too much.

"Well why doesn't he quit?" Tom roared.

"Maybe he has," I said. "Or why doesn't Joe fire him?"

"Billy won't quit because the job is close, and Joe won't fire him because he can't get anyone to take that shitty shift for long and he won't pay a man a decent wage," Johnny said.

"Well Bill'll have to quit or do better," Tom swore. "I'm not putting up with this. Calls every half hour—and he should come right home from school anyway."

Billy arrived home about nine. Tom was out by then.

"Did my boss call?" he asked.

"That's all he's been doing all evening," I said. "Where were you?"

"Out. Playing pool with the guys. Listen, if he calls again tell him I'm not here. Tell him I'm at Uncle George's in Port Credit and won't be back until tomorrow. I'm going to bed."

I did as Billy asked. Joe wasn't satisfied. He wanted me to ask Billy to try to catch a streetcar home. I said I would. I reported to Billy. He swore. "If he calls again," he said, "tell him I'm out with my cousins or something. I don't want to work tonight. He's gonna give me hell because I'm late."

"Well Billy, why don't you quit?" I asked.

"I've tried to quit. He keeps asking me to go back. This time he can fire me."

Next call I told Joe I couldn't contact Billy. I said he had left his uncle's and might be on his way home.

"All right," Joe said. "If he arrives soon will you please send him to work? I really need him."

I had heard Jenny leave the house while I was on the phone and I thought she was going out to watch the night lights from the verandah. She came in a few minutes after I hung up.

"Mamma," she called.

I went to her.

"I've got something to tell you," she said. "Promise you won't be mad."

"Oh, I won't promise," I said, "but let's hear it."

"You'll be mad, I know. I did something bad."

"It can't be so bad," I assured her.

"Well–uh–well–Mamma I went over and told Joe on Billy." Jenny was abject.

"What?" I roared. "What did you tell Joe?"

Jenny was on the brink of tears.

"I told him Billy was in his room and didn't want to go to work. That's all. I know it's bad and I'm sorry now. But he teases me all the time."

My mind had somersaulted.

"Get to your room!" I roared. Now what would I tell Joe if he called again? Oh well, better notify Billy of his predicament.

Billy was a bit displeased when I told him of Jenny's interference. He threatened to kill her. Tom came in and found out everything. He didn't start roaring but he was more than a little angry at all the fuss.

Joe called again. I told him that Billy was home now, that he was tired and did not feel up to facing an angry boss. I suggested that Joe fire him and get a more reliable worker. Joe said he'd not berate Billy and asked me to ask Billy to please go to work.

After a little discussion Billy went off to work. It was nearly ten p.m. Johnny saw humour in the whole thing.

I apologized to Jenny for my anger. She admitted she had been afraid to tell what she'd done at first but had made up her mind to be brave. I praised her for that and suggested that in similar future situations she try to be brave again and do what she could to soften the consequences.

The following morning Tom went after Billy about squandering his money on pool and neglecting his job.

"It's no good!" Tom bellowed. "You're just like the rest. You don't want to work."

"Look Dad!" Billy yelled. "It's my job. And my business. If Joe doesn't like what I do he can fire me."

"That's right, Billy," I said. "Tom you're screaming and howling isn't doing any good. What in hell is it—are you on Joe's side or what? If Joe was a decent employer he'd have given Billy a raise by now."

"He can't be worth a raise," Tom said.

"Oh no?" Billy cried. "Well Joe gave me a raise already— "

"He did?" Tom asked, pleased. "How much?"

"Let me finish, eh?" said Billy. "Or I won't tell you at all. He raised me a quarter an hour. Then he took it back because he said it caused inflation."

"What?!" from Tom. It sounded like a strangled howl. "The cocksucking son of a bitch! Quit him, Billy. Quit him flat! The dirty mangy dog! To do that to a kid. The rotten bastard!"

"Oh I'm going to quit," Billy said. "After a while. I've got a good job lined up already. Only I might have to quit school."

"Oh Billy, don't quit school yet," I said. "Finish this year anyway. You're doing all right."

"Well I wasn't going to quit yet. But if Dad doesn't get off my back I'll quit and move out. I don't have to take shit all around."

"Move to hell out if you want," Tom roared. "I can't stop you. But I don't give a damn about Joe's job now. To hell with that bastard. He's worse than a thief. Exploitin' a kid."

"Will you shut up, Dad?" Billy demanded. "It's my job. Not yours. What's exploitin' huh? Maybe I'm exploitin' Joe. Maybe you're the one being exploited. Not me!"

"Well maybe you're right," Tom said solemnly. "But I've got to take it. I've got dependents. But Joe! I never thought he was like that."

"You can think it now," I said. "And while you're doing that perhaps you'll stop that ear-breaking yelling. You'll have just the four walls to yell at soon enough."

"I've got plenty to yell about," Tom growled. "He has no business playing pool. Those guys'll gang up on him and take his money. I know them. They're coloured and they work in gangs."

"Oh Dad. They're not all like that. Besides the guys I play with aren't all coloured," Billy objected. "You don't know them."

"Tom, it's all right to warn the kids and give them advice but you can't put your head on their shoulders. Screaming and howling doesn't make them wiser any faster. You can't stop them from having some trouble. So just leave him alone. He doesn't smoke or drink yet."

"All right. Let him go. Let him do what he wants. He'll learn." Tom closed the subject. "Do you want anything from Martha's?" he asked putting on his heavy coat.

"Yuh. Some earplugs," I said.

"Ah to hell with the whole pack," Tom muttered and walked out. After that I enjoyed a lull between storms.

At last to the relief of all Johnny had his trial—such as it was.

Tom went with him and both came home bitterly angry—Tom because Johnny wouldn't let him talk, and Johnny because the judge wouldn't let the police witnesses answer his questions about hypoglycaemia.

After all that time Johnny was convicted and given a suspended sentence.

I returned from the doctor's to find Tom and Johnny in a row. Tom was berating Johnny over his squandering of money. I arrived in time to hear Tom bring up the subject of the weight lifts and last year's old car. Johnny had had enough. He hunted up a cheque book, wrote his father a cheque for fifty dollars and threw it on the table.

"There!" he said. "I'm paying you in advance for five weeks board. By then I'll be done school and I'm getting out. This crazy life's not for me." Johnny stamped away upstairs.

I sat down and glared at my husband.

"What was that over?" I asked coldly.

"Oh never mind. What did the doctor say?"

"You never mind. I asked first."

"All right. He's talking about getting a motorcycle, another waste of money. I was just trying to talk him out of it."

"I bet. You never learned how to talk. You sure must have been screaming. Oh well, I'm better but I'm going to have an operation, after school's out. He'll phone me in a few days."

"Well I hope it's before I'm laid off so the insurance'll cover it."

"Oh you'll not be laid off. Who says you're gonna be laid off?"

"I know. We all know. The company's closing the other plant and a guy there has more seniority. He'll be moved over to take my place. Of course they might find me another job or give a couple hundred dollars severance pay—but we'll have no medical insurance."

"Oh well. There's no need to fret yet. By the time you're laid off we might have medicare. There's OMSIP anyway. So don't make a big mountain out of nothing."

"Well maybe so. Are you going to get supper? I'm hungry."

"Yes, I'm going to get supper. Just as soon as I can get out of this dress and into my old work skirt. If you're so hungry why didn't you get supper instead of wasting energy fighting with Johnny?"

"Get supper. I'm going out for a paper."

Tom got up from his chair, tore up Johnny's cheque and dropped it in the garbage. He put on his cap and went out.

I prepared a meal of beans and wieners. We ate in peace and pretty good humour.

When Tom had gone Johnny and I talked. Johnny had made up his mind to quit school right away and get a good job. He just wanted enough money to go to Alberta. He seemed to have thought long and hard about it.

My heart sank. I figured there was nothing I could say to change his mind.

Sadly I told him, "It's your life Johnny. You shouldn't need much more money. Dad tore up the cheque, did I tell you?"

Johnny gave a look of surprise. "Did he? Well, goddamn. He didn't have to. I gave it to him."

"I know, but I find Tom acting kind of different lately. There's something happening to him. But anyway about you. Johnny are you sure you can't stand it for another few weeks? Remember Harold and that harridan of a teacher who caused him to quit halfway through his last year? But he said he knew he was going to fail. He hasn't studied a book since."

"Oh Harold and me are different. I'm not in danger of failing. It's the continual fighting and rowing here. And Dad tries to blame it all on everyone but himself. He makes me so mad sometimes I could hit him. I don't want to but I'm scared I will. And I might hurt him bad. That's why I've got to get out."

"All right. I understand. I won't talk about it anymore."

I left Johnny's room almost in tears.

Johnny didn't quit school exactly. He stayed out a day-and-a-half and looked for a better job.

The school called. I told them Johnny wasn't home. The second afternoon Johnny went back to school for his books.

He stayed for classes and next day resumed regular attendance. Don finally got to court. The case was dismissed.

By July there was no longer a good reason for putting off my operation. I went to my gynecologist and he arranged for my admittance to a hospital. Luckily Don was going on vacation the day before I was to be admitted. He planned to drive with his girlfriend and Jenny to New Brunswick. It was expected that by the time they returned I would be over the operation and ready to come home. I thought Tom and my other three could run the house and look after themselves for that two weeks.

With an easy mind I entered the hospital. The operation went smoothly and I gained strength rapidly. Every day I would have one or two visitors. On the fourth day my sister and Don called from New Brunswick. I was greatly pleased.

For the first two days at home I did not work at all. I lay or sat around much of the day out in the front yard. The weather was very good. Tom was managing fine. He hadn't a great deal of work as the house was pretty clean and each person had the responsibility of his own room and laundry.

Tom began looking about for more time-filling projects. He started fashioning a laundry cart. I lazed around, putting in many quiet hours watching Jenny and her friends play in the yards and lane where traffic was rare and slow.

One nice evening as Tom worked on his cart in the back yard and I watched the kids from the front yard, a young woman holding a little girl by the hand came down the street and stopped by our fence where I was sitting.

"Are you Mrs. Firth?" she asked.

"Yes," I answered. "What can– ?"

She interrupted me, speaking quickly. "Mrs. Firth, excuse me—I'm in a hurry. I have to be at work in a few minutes. The woman at the store said you might be able to mind Joanie for a couple of hours. This is Joanie; she's six. I'm Mrs. Pine. Call me Angie. I know Martha and I thought she could mind her but she can't right now. Joanie won't be much trouble. Martha said you have a little girl. But maybe you aren't feeling strong yet. I work just over there, at the Victory."

"I think I can mind her. Would you like to stay here Joanie? Will you be good?"

The little girl had been talking to Jenny while her mother explained.

"Yes," she answered me happily. "I'd like to stay."

Tom came down the verandah steps.

"What's this?" he asked.

"Martha sent her here to see if I could mind her little girl a couple of hours. I guess it'll be okay. The lady's in a hurry."

"Oh. Where do you work?" said Tom.

"At the Victory," Angie told him.

"Oh," said Tom with a knowing smirk. "What's your job?"

Angie put one hand to the side of her mouth to indicate secrecy. She glanced at Jenny and Joanie, then leaned close to Tom and whispered, "I strip and do a little dance."

Tom chuckled. Angie relaxed and whispered again. "Joanie doesn't know what I do. I'm not ashamed but—well, you understand."

"Yes," I said. "There would be problems—neighbours' attitudes. Well the girls seem to be getting along. Maybe we'll have time to talk later."

"Oh yes. I have a break about ten. You can tell me then how much you charge, okay? Thanks. Good-bye, Joanie. Be a good girl," Angie said, waved, turned and crossed the street.

Joanie was quite different from Jenny. She was tall for her age, Jenny short. Joanie was predominately extroverted, Jenny less so. Joanie preferred active games; Jenny also liked games requiring mental ability. Joanie was obviously eager for approval and was quick to accept blame and to make up. Jenny appeared more concerned with whether or not other people merited her approval. Joanie was far more polite to adults, and showed less respect for others' possessions and expected less for hers.

When darkness fell the two girls went to Jenny's room to play quiet games. Within a few minutes there came an angry howl from Jenny.

"See what's the matter," Tom yelled from our bedroom as I hurried upstairs.

I found Jenny huddled in a big chair with a book and Joanie standing near. They were looking unhappily at each other.

It seemed Joanie had been playing with Jenny's bride doll after being asked not to. Jenny wanted to read.

"We'll just have to try to find something you both like to do. How about lunch? A glass of milk? Then we can sit outdoors again if it isn't too cold," I suggested.

Joanie and I trooped down to the kitchen. Tom talked with Joanie while I prepared lunch. As we began eating Jenny came down.

"Nah," she said, "I'm not hungry. Oh well, make me a peanut butter sandwich and give me a glass of milk."

I passed Jenny the peanut butter and a knife.

"Make your own," I said. "You make your own at Gloria's so make it here. I'll get you the milk."

When we were finished eating the two girls accompanied me outside. I sat on the verandah awhile smoking a cigarette and drinking my tea while they played tag in the yard. There was plenty of light from the street lamps and our own front windows.

After a while, tiring of tag and seeing that I had finished my tea the girls came up to me and asked me to suggest a new game.

I said, "Both you girls have travelled to different places and done different things so why don't you sit down here and we can all tell interesting stories."

That idea had little appeal. The girls shrugged it off.

"Well then," I said, "how about teaching one another songs, but not too loud. Jenny, remember the one your cousins taught you this summer– ?"

"Oh yes," Jenny laughed. "Joanie, do you want to hear a song? I'll sing it."

Joanie laughed at the song and when Jenny repeated it she

joined in. After a few repeats Joanie had memorized the song. Then she taught Jenny one.

When they grew tired of singing they sat on the steps with me and we drifted into a conversation about holidays and schools and things they liked to do. A bit before ten Angie returned. Joanie rushed to her mother gushing delight at having found new friends.

Angie could stay a bare ten minutes. She told Tom and me that her husband was a sailor in the United States Navy and she expected him to be in Toronto the next week on a ten-day leave. She and Joanie had just arrived in town. They had an apartment but it was only partly furnished. She hadn't had time to unpack. Angie said she greatly appreciated my help. It was very kind of me, she a stranger and all. She thought seventy-five cents an hour was a reasonable babysitting fee.

Angie returned at 11:30 to take her tired young daughter home. Tom was impatient to learn more about our new acquaintance. I was not so curious. Over tea Tom plied her with questions about her life and her family.

Angie had been born in Ontario, had dropped out of school at an early age and gone to work to support herself. As she developed in her teens she discovered she had an attractive body and a bit of acting talent. Young, naive and ambitious, she had tried with similarly-endowed girlfriends to get into show business but had failed auditions regularly. Discouraged but still seeking a way to make a good living by some means other than manual labour at low wages she had seized a chance to do burlesque in a small tavern.

"If people want to pay to look at me I see no harm in it," Angie said. "But I'm going to quit soon. Joanie is of school age. She started last year. Roger is quitting the boats too, so we're goin' to settle down here. I'm tired of that job anyway. There's a lot of travelling."

"You play all the big cities?" asked Tom.

"Some. Montreal, Chicago, New York, and some smaller places too."

"How long have you been in that profession?"

"About nine years. I was nineteen when I started. I didn't expect to stay so long. I guess we all say that."

Tom's prying in the presence of the two little girls seemed to upset Angie. Tom didn't notice or didn't care. I sent both kids up to Jenny's room for a few minutes.

When they'd gone I said, "I suppose your relatives disapprove of your profession. Does Joanie understand what your work is?"

"Joanie doesn't know yet. I told her I take tickets. Some of my relatives don't mind. They even come to see me when I'm playing their city. I don't think my mother knows. But you can't please everyone."

"You must be exhausted. Don't let us keep you. Tom, there, could talk all night. History was his favourite subject, I think," I said.

"Oh I don't mind talking. Joanie must be pretty tired, though. Could you mind her tomorrow night again? After that I'll have a few days free."

I agreed and suggested she bring some of Joanie's toys next time in case Jenny, who was older, didn't want to play. Angie said she'd dig out some things from their still-unpacked boxes.

They didn't return the next evening but two days later they paid a visit in the afternoon. Joanie had been ill, Angie said, and she hadn't known our number to call and let us know. The doctor had explained that the change of water or food had upset Joanie's system. She was fine again but the landlady had been minding her.

"I thought you might be wondering what had happened to us," Angie said, "and Joanie wanted to see Jennie again."

I sent the two girls out to play in the front yard so Angie and I could talk without watching our topics.

"And don't keep running in to hear what we're talking about," I told Jenny as she left the room.

"Oh we won't," Jenny called back to me. "Who wants to listen to your old gossip?"

"You allow her to talk like that to you?" Angie asked, shocked.

"That's mild. You should hear her when she's really put out. She calls me an old bully and not long ago she called Johnny a fuckin' bitch."

"Did you raise all your children like that?"

"Pretty much. Certain words are taboo when they're little, mainly because their habitual use will cause trouble with adults and lose them friends. I explain that to the children and they watch their language away from home."

"I'm very strict with Joanie but I wonder if it's good. I want to raise her well but there's so many problems. I don't know how to answer all her questions. Now she's old enough to understand certain things. I worry how she'll take it when she finds out what I do. I'm not ashamed. I don't want her to feel ashamed. But—some people can be pretty dirty. They like to say things to hurt a kid."

"Yes, I've had that experience often enough. All I could do was try to help my children be strong enough to disregard other people's prejudiced opinions. Lots of kids have criminals and alcoholics and worse for parents. If there is love in the family the kids can even take their parents' side. Your own attitude may count more than the gossips', Angie."

Tom joined us.

"I think I haven't given Joanie enough attention," Angie continued. "It's hard when you've got a job. My husband will be home next week. We're going to take her to the CNE. We always take her lots of places. There's no neglect there, but in other ways, maybe. I wish I could get some professional advice. Do you know any counsellors, psychologists, or somebody who helps parents with questions?"

"No. But there are some around I guess. You might get some help by reading books on the subject. We have some good books written by doctors. At least that's the claim. These books have questions and answers. They explain why people act like they do and hold certain beliefs and attitudes. Oh, they don't explain everything but they help. I'll go get a book and you can look it over."

Tom began to discuss his books: luridly sexy novels.

When Angie examined the book I brought her she was pleased.

"Can I borrow this one? It may help me," she exclaimed.

"It's really Tom's," I told her. "Once in awhile he looks up an answer. You should be able to buy it."

"Oh let her have it," Tom said. "But I want it back. I'll get some more you can borrow." He went to our bedroom.

Angie gave her attention to the book and I went to check on the children. The kids were playing hop-scotch happily. Joyce came into the yard as I watched.

"Who's the little girl with Jenny?" she asked, climbing the steps.

"Joanie Pine," I said, speaking low. "Her mother does a strip at the Victory. She doesn't want her little girl to know yet. Her mother's in the house."

Joyce hurried in.

"Hi," she greeted Angie. "I'm Joyce. Do you really work at the Victory Theatre?"

"Yes," Angie said, looking curiously at Joyce. "It's just a little dance. Do you still go to school?"

"Well last year I did. I'm twenty and still only in grade eleven." Joyce sounded a little ashamed.

"That's because you've been dropping out and working and running off to Edmonton and places," I reminded Joyce.

"I never finished grade eight," Angie said. "Maybe I was stupid. I never seemed able to study hard."

"I don't like to study," Joyce told her. "Would you tell me about your job? I've never been in one of those theatres. What's it like? Stripping, I mean? Aren't you shy? Do the men bother you?"

Angie seemed slightly nonplussed at Joyce's attitude and eager questions.

"The job isn't hard," she said. "I'm not shy now of course. I'm used to it. Some men are a bother–they call out things but that's part of the game. A few have tried to climb right on the stage but we're pretty well protected. I've never had much trouble."

"Does your husband know you work there? Does he mind?"

"He knows. He knew it before we married. He doesn't say much, but he wants me to quit because Joanie is getting older. I am quitting soon."

"Do you think I could do your job? Is my figure good enough?"

"Your figure's good enough," Angie told Joyce. "It's not hard to get that kind of a job when you're young. But there's a lot of work to it–not difficult but exhausting."

"You're not cut out for that work, Joyce," I said. "There'd be a lot of talk you wouldn't like. I don't think you have the right attitude to succeed anyway."

Tom entered the room with an armload of books. It had taken him awhile to pick out the ones he did not mind losing in case they were never returned.

"Here's some good books." Tom placed his load on the table near Angie.

"Oh I'd never read all of those," Angie protested. "I'll take the top one. That and this one," she said, holding up the book I had brought her, "will be enough." As Tom tried to force them on her, "No, no. Really, I'll never read them."

"Put them away, Tom," I ordered. "Everybody isn't a reader like you. She has a young child to look after. She can't lay around much reading. She's probably heard better in real life anyway."

Angie gave me a wary look. Reluctantly Tom carried his precious books back to the room.

The sound of voices at the front door drew our attention. It was Gloria and Bob. I felt sudden mirth. Bob was always suggesting a group of us go to watch the go-go girls downtown.

"Come right on in Gloria, Bob," I called.

"I thought I'd catch you in bed," Gloria joked at me. "Every time I phone here you're in bed."

"Try phoning at night," I said. "In twenty-four hours I stay up the same amount of time as you and get as much done." I made the introductions.

"Is that your little girl playing with Jenny? Nancy, that's my baby, stayed out with them."

"Well Joanie was out there. How old is your baby?"

"Ten. I just call her my baby. Do you work, Angie?"

"Yes. I have a job. A part-time job."

"Where do you work? Is it an office or plain labour like the rest of us?"

"It's not an office." Angie told her. "I'm a dancer."

"A dancer? You mean like in shows?" It was easy to see Gloria was puzzled. I hadn't mentioned knowing any dancers or actors. I thought it would ease everybody if I told it plain and quick.

"A special kind of show," I said. "Like at the Victory."

For a second my two old friends were silent. Then in disbelief

Gloria exploded. "The Victory?! You mean you strip?" Bob was glancing from Gloria to Angie and back again. I wondered if he were comparing the two women. He was grinning.

"What else do they do at the Victory?" I asked. "Angie, don't mind them. Gloria and I have joked about stripping but we're too old and haven't the figure."

"Oh *I* have the figure," Gloria exclaimed.

"Who'd pay to look at you?" Bob asked sarcastically.

"You'd be surprised," Gloria retorted. "My stomach sticks out a little but I'm not fat. My legs are good. Anyway the men might like a change."

"You're right, Gloria," I said. "You see the manager and test him out. If you get a job I might audition," I laughed.

"There's amateur night," Angie said smiling.

"Amateur night? Maybe I should go," Joyce cried excitedly. "When is it?"

"It's advertised," I said. "If you sincerely want to go you should ask the manager quite a bit ahead of time. But Joyce, you're too impulsive. If you get in that profession you might regret it. Some people look down on burlesque and you know how they treat strippers."

"Yes, Joyce," Angie said soberly. "Don't rush into things. I could take you over some night to let you watch. I can get passes. I'll come and get you if you really want to come."

"Get us all passes," Gloria cried. "I've never seen burlesque. We can all go."

"Gloria, do you want to break the theatre?" Tom cried. "It only costs a dollar-fifty."

"You pay your way then," Gloria cried, turning to Tom. "Or give me and Sophia the money. We'll go ourselves."

"Don't make plans for me," I interjected. "I think I'd rather read a book. I'm not really interested in that kind of entertainment. I'm not against it but it seems pretty dull to me."

"Oh you're not interested in anything. You don't want to see go-go girls. You don't like bingo. To hell with you all then. I'll go by myself some night," Gloria said petulantly.

Later Gloria offered Angie a ride home. "Joyce, are you coming up with us? I don't want you to help with the housework. I have a couple of dresses that might fit you. They're nice and almost new."

"Yeah, I'm going. Wait a second." Joyce ran for her purse as the others rose to leave. Angie took along the books.

For over a year we had been aware of racial storms brewing at the centre where Joyce worked as a youth counsellor. Joyce had spoken a few words off and on about it; I had heard her on the telephone with other workers discussing fights and deliberate acts of destruction, and she had sought my advice on dealing with troubled and troublesome teenagers.

I was proud of her but feared for her safety. She was barely out of her teens herself and not a large or "tough" girl. Violence, while not the most common method used by the youngsters to settle their disputes, was resorted to at times and it was Joyce's job to try to keep such indulgences down and encourage quieter, more constructive means of solving problems and disagreements.

For some time the occasions of violence and assault had been increasing in number and intensity. The supervising adults had taken a hands-off policy and were leaving the settlement of issues to the young people.

Time and again one or another of us had predicted disaster for Joyce and asked her to quit that job. She refused.

"I'm not a quitter!" she said. "These are basically good kids and they're no worse than the establishment. Look at the wars of this century. Look at Vietnam, Biafra, and America. How can you expect us to be better than the adults?"

Actually I thought Joyce deserved praise, not censure, for what she was trying to do. But I feared.

My fears were realized one night in mid-August. It was about 11:30 p.m. It was Tom's night off. He was in bed. Billy and Jenny were in bed too. Don and Johnny were out, as was Joyce. I was almost ready for bed myself but it was a warm night and I went out to the yard for a last cigarette.

We had an old cushionless armchair on the verandah where one could sit, enjoy coffee and cigarettes, or whatever, and view a busy part of two streets, the lane and a bit of sky. As I sat there relaxing with the stars twinkling down on the city a car pulled up to our yard, stopped, and Joyce got out. The car drove on and Joyce entered the yard.

Catching sight of me she came slowly forward. When I saw her face in the light from our window I felt shock and sorrow.

Both of her eyes were swollen and discoloured, her face was bruised and lacerated, her lips were cut, and her clothes were dirty and dishevelled. I made motions to go to her but she called, calmly enough, "It's O.K.," and gave me a painful little grin that told me she did not feel too badly and expected some I-told-you-so's.

When she came close I whispered, "Don't talk loud because I don't want your father rampaging tonight. Is it very painful? Do you want to tell me or not?"

"Oh, I don't mind telling." Joyce spoke in a low voice. "Give me a cigarette. I just got beat up but it's partly my own fault. I wouldn't run, I wouldn't cry and I wouldn't hit back." She lit her cigarette.

"Tell the story as it happened. What started the trouble?" I said.

"Well! You see we have a TV room at the youth centre. It's supposed to be for everyone. We all have a right to use it. Some kids were using it. They're younger'n me. It's my job to supervise them. I went in and talked to them awhile about the show. Then I went to another room. They stayed and later I came back. They were still watching so I asked them about the show and they told me about it so I knew they were really paying attention. Then George came in, and Harry, and Kathy. They wanted to use the TV room so George ordered the kids out. That isn't right. I told George it wasn't and asked him why he wanted the kids out. He said he had business. Well for private talks there is another room and I didn't think he should be allowed to take over the TV room like that. George is a counsellor too, he gets paid, and is supposed to teach other kids respect for people's rights. So I told the kids they didn't have to go, that I was staying and they could too.

"Well then George turned on me and ordered me out too. I wouldn't go and we argued, then he spit at me. I said, 'That makes you a big man, doesn't it George?' Some of the kids had stayed and they giggled a bit. Then George slapped my face and I said, 'They slapped Jesus too and spit at him, and they shot Martin Luther King.' Then Harry started pushing and slapping me around and saying, 'You're pretty stubborn, little white girl. You think you're smart.' Harry and George used dirty words too.

Then Kathy tried to pick a fight. She kept hitting and pushing and someone turned out the lights. I didn't want to hit them back because it would have been worse. I couldn't beat all of them but I'm supposed to set an example. So is George. It's his job to stop such things. So when the lights were out I began to pray; that was so I wouldn't cry because that's what they wanted and I wanted to show the younger kids they don't always have to hit back if they're pushed around. I guess George heard me saying the Lord's Prayer and he got scared and made them turn on the lights. Then he stopped hitting me but he didn't try to stop the other kids. Harry stopped too but Kathy kept on.

"Then Ivan Mallon came. He's over us all. Some kids must have called him. Ivan made them all stop. Then I got ready to come home; it was time anyway. I had done my stint for the period. Outside Kathy kept daring me to fight her and I wouldn't. Ivan told her to leave me alone, then he offered me a lift home. I know I must look bad but I don't really feel so bad. Maybe tomorrow it'll be worse. Both eyes are black aren't they?"

"Well they're swollen and discoloured but I don't think they're black yet. I can't tell in this light. Now, are you going to the police or not?"

"I don't know. I think I should go to the police but I don't want to get back at them. I'm not even really mad at them, but they aren't doing right. Especially George. He's beat up other girls. So have Harry and Kathy. And George has even beat up Harry so Harry's afraid of him. I've been telling the other girls they shouldn't take beatings from the boys–they should lay charges. But they're afraid to do that. They think the boys'll get them later–and they might too. Some of them are pretty dirty. Do you think I should lay charges?"

"Well, Joyce, it's hard to know what to do." I paused to light a cigarette and think. "Actually I'd like to be able to give all three bullies a good licking myself but that would only give me a small measure of satisfaction. It probably wouldn't achieve much. Now before you decide what to do can you explain what you really want to accomplish, well, like why would you lay charges?"

"Oh I know what I want. I just want to do whatever I can to make it better for all the kids. I want to get George and Harry and Kathy and some other kids to stop beating and bossing smaller kids. They are making it bad for all the kids because some of the younger kids admire George and they copy him."

"Well, then you may have to lay charges. Not to get revenge but to make these bullies realize how they're hurting themselves. These kids may have to be made to suffer the unpleasant consequences of their deeds before they'll change their tactics. They may think they know all about the law and courts but they can't know how it feels to be up before a judge, or stuck in jail, or having a suspended sentence hanging over their heads. They might think they can imagine it but they just might not have a good enough imagination." I wondered just how able Joyce was to handle the problem herself and how far I should go in trying to influence her decision. I was very proud of the way she had handled it so far.

Joyce said, very thoughtfully, "Uh-huh. I have a pretty good imagination but I know other people haven't. It's true that some people can't realize what a thing is like until they actually go through it. I think I'll have to take the kids to court."

"Right now they may be feeling very remorseful and scared. They might actually be feeling sick with shame and worry," I reasoned.

"I don't think they're that kind. They try to talk tough. Hit first and fast and hard. That's their idea. Kathy's anyway. She says Whitey does. I'll just bet Kathy is bragging away to her friends how she gave one white girl a good going over. I think court's the only thing that might change her but it might just make her attitude worse. She won't admit she's to blame, I know. If I go up to the police station will you come with me, Mum?"

I felt a twinge of anxiety and frustration.

"Oh, Joyce, dear," I said unhappily, "let me think. I'd like to go. You had better report it tonight but I don't know if I can leave. I can't wake Dad because he'll have a screaming fit over this and if he wakes and finds me gone he'll have a screaming fit too. The station is just up on College. That street's well lighted. How about if I go halfway with you? Or maybe you could go by bus."

"No. I don't want to wait on buses. Besides—well—I must

look awful. I'd be embarrassed with people all staring at me. I'm not very scared. I just imagine drunks or maniacs are going to jump out of the dark lanes and grab me. If I had someone with me I wouldn't imagine. Beverley is well lighted too. I could go to the next street, then down to Beverley and up. Would you watch until I reach Beverley?"

"Okay. Take these tickets. Now don't walk home."

Joyce put the streetcar tickets into her jeans pocket.

A handsome young policeman drove Joyce home. I was still sitting outside. I spoke with him a few minutes.

"Your daughter should lay charges," he told me. "It's a bad crime. They might get off, anyway. Our courts today!" The man shook his head as he continued. "Cases of this kind are increasing and this is the worst area now."

"I know. And the trouble is we can't be sure what course of action will help these kids, and our whole miserable society."

"That's true. We do our best, picking them up, laying charges. They get suspended sentences and we have to do it all over again. Joyce should see a doctor."

"Oh, she will. Goodnight and thanks very much."

The next morning Tom learned of Joyce's beating. His outburst was milder than I expected probably because his mind was preoccupied with pleasanter matters–a trip to the races soon.

Gloria and her husband called to see us in the morning.

"My God!" Gloria exclaimed at the sight of Joyce. "Were you hit by a truck?"

"No. I just got beat up, that's all," Joyce replied, trying to smile.

"Yes. By them goddam niggers she hangs around with. It's her own fault. I warned her," Tom growled.

"Coloured people? How many?" Gloria asked.

"Three," Joyce said.

"Three. It surely didn't take three to beat you, unless they were kids."

I spoke up. "They weren't kids. But you see they were only trying to boss her around, to break her will–not hurt her seriously. It happened over at that Hi-C place where she is a counsellor. Some dictators have been trying to run it and walk all over the smaller kids. Last night Joyce stood up for her rights and theirs too."

"You're gonna lay charges aren't you? Did you report it? Did you go to a doctor?"

"Yes I reported it. I'm gonna see a doctor today. I think I'll lay charges."

"Think. What's there to think about? You can't let them get away with that."

"Why not? Older people have been let get away with lots more. What about Trudeau? What about the guys in that Atlantic thing – that lost poor people's money? Sure it's wrong to beat people up but it's just as wrong to put them in jail and make them worse. I want to help those kids."

"Well do you think letting them beat you up is gonna help them? Sure it may give them satisfaction, make them feel big, but some day they'll pick on the wrong one. And what if your eyes are damaged? Or if they get away with beating you they go out and beat up some other kid?"

"Oh shut up, Gloria. It's her business," Bob said. "She don't have to lay charges if she don't want."

Gloria subsided.

Tom sneered. "She won't lay charges. She's too stupid."

"I'm not stupid," Joyce screamed. "What's laying charges gonna do? Tell me that, huh? What if I can't even prove they did it?"

"Well," Tom said and faltered. He hadn't much faith in our judicial system. "Well stay clear of them then. Some day you'll be found with your throat cut. That's what'll happen."

"Oh, shut up, Tom. You're out of your element. It's always been your way–run or ignore problems you can't solve. At least Joyce has the grit to get right in the dirt and try to make changes," I said.

"Yuh. You know it all. You run it then. A fine pack you raised," said Tom.

"No. I don't know it all," I roared. "But I'm not narrow-minded like you. I can see more sides to a problem than you. That's the difference. You're a good mathematician but when it comes to people you're lost. All you know is what you were taught and some of that doesn't work any more."

"You ready Gloria? I gotta go," Bob said.

"Yes. I'm ready. Joyce, why don't you go to emergency at

Western? We can give you a ride there," Gloria said.

"Yes, Joyce. That's it. Go to Western. Go now and have it done. Have you still got tickets? Here, I'll give you the insurance and hospital cards. They cover you." As I went for the papers I heard Gloria say:

"C'mon, Joyce. Oh you don't need to change clothes. They go into emergency every old how. Just grab a jacket and c'mon."

I returned to the kitchen and gave Joyce the insurance papers. She left with Gloria and Bob.

She returned in better spirits. The doctor assured her she'd suffer no permanent damage to her eyes or face. He had advised her to lay charges but Joyce was still hesitant.

She sought the opinions of older workers in the organization, her friends and a few of our more intimate neighbours. Most seemed as baffled as we about the best thing to do but all agreed that something had to be done.

"I wish there was an easy way to handle this," said Joyce. "Anyway, I'll soon see what their attitude is. All the kids know about the trouble. They'll be talking and they'll tell me what George and Harry and Kathy are saying. I'm on duty tonight so I'm bound to find out, and if they're braggin'—well! we'll see."

That night Tom went to work. Joyce returned from Hi-C and we discussed the situation again.

Joyce hadn't liked what she'd heard. The boys weren't talking much, but they hadn't showed any sign of regret or offered an apology. They hadn't even enquired about Joyce's health. Kathy was threatening to beat her up again and anyone else who crossed her; also Kathy vowed she wouldn't go to court for any white person.

I gathered that the atmosphere among the young people was very tense. Some of them identified with George and his cohorts—some with Joyce. The latter were worried—and hopeful. Some of the most outspoken had bitterly thrown her own words back at her.

One fifteen year old coloured lass, a sometimes victim of beatings, challenged: "You tell us we don't have to stand for pushing around. We should lay charges! Hah. Now it's your turn. Let's see you lay charges, or are you scared too?"

Joyce's tone told me she was favouring court action more. I added another persuasion.

"Joyce," I said, "why don't you simply stop hemming and hawing? Lay the charges, then put the whole thing out of your mind until court day. Laying the charges won't give the kids a record. And if something happens to make you change your mind, you can drop the charges."

"Oh, I never thought about that. But if I lay charges and drop them won't that get me in trouble? Will the judge be mad?"

"Probably. I've read in the papers complaints of judges or police about women who lay charges against their husbands then suddenly drop them, then when the husband goes on another rampage they go through the process again, complain, charge and forgive. But legally we are within our rights to withdraw charges. So all the old judge can do is hand you a lecture. These judges don't make the laws, they just uphold them—or are supposed to. Judges are subject to laws too."

"Oh well, I can take a lecture. I'm used to them." Joyce laughed, a happier laugh than she'd enjoyed for days. I took it as a sign that her mind had been freed of a great load.

Joyce found it not as easy to lay charges as I had believed. She returned from a trip to court to report that an officer of the law had informed her that she had to get the names and addresses of those she was laying charges against. I was aghast.

"Joyce are you sure you understood him? I thought it was the duty of the police to help get the addresses. Good heavens, sometimes victims don't even know the names of their assailants let alone the addresses."

"Well that's what I was told. I'm not lying. I have to get the addresses before I can lay charges," Joyce insisted.

"Didn't he offer any assistance? Maybe you should go back to the police station. It must be their duty to help you find out where these kids live."

"Oh I can find out myself. Their names and addresses are on record at St. Chris' House. I'll phone Miss Henderson. She can look them up and tell me."

Finally the charge of assault was laid against George, Harry and Kathy. The trial date was for early in September a few days after school was to open.

"Now, Joyce, relax and let them worry. And if the kids don't, some of their relatives will," I told her.

"Will they really? How can you be sure?" she asked.

"Joyce, dear, I haven't lived all these years without learning a little about people. We all have many things in common. The big difference between people is not in our kinds of inherited properties but in the quantity of those properties, or characteristics if you wish. Parents and anyone who cares will be grieved to hear that their relatives are in trouble. They'll rally to their defense—you'll see. So for now you should try to put the whole thing aside, force yourself to think of other things and just wait."

"I will. Mamma I've heard that the welfare helps poor kids to continue school. One of my friends is going to try it. A girl she knows got help last year. I think I'll see if they'll help me. But I guess I'll have to move out and get a room."

"Well, why not? Yes that sounds like a darn good idea. It'll be good for you and for me too. You and Dad get into some awful arguments and I'm tired of them."

"The boys have as many arguments with him as me. Aren't you tired of them too?"

"Yes, but when it comes to you I'm afraid Dad will hurt you sometime in a blind rage. Don and Johnny can defend themselves. Maybe not Billy yet—but even he is stronger than you."

"I know. But I'm not scared of him. Anyway I'm sick of this damned, falling-down shack. I want to get out. So I'm going to look for a room and then see about welfare."

"Try Gloria. I'm sure she wouldn't want the rent in advance."

"That's right. If I don't get welfare I can do work for her until she's paid. If I can't go to school I'll have to get a job. And I'm moving out for sure. I'm ashamed to bring my friends here."

I said no more. Joyce saw I wasn't interested in listening to a tirade of complaints. She left the kitchen and went to her room.

The end of August neared. School again became a common topic of conversation. Jenny told us that she hated school, especially Olde Orde. She began to plead with me to move to a new district so she could go to a new school. We hadn't saved enough money for a security deposit and a month's rent in advance which most landlords asked and we didn't care to borrow it.

Then Schmidt offered us another of his houses on Huron Street, No. 75. He said he'd repair it well before we moved in, then he'd repair 79 and when it was ready we could move back to it. The family decided collectively to give Schmidt's offer a trial.

Four days before the end of August Joyce received a phone call from the brother of one of the boys, George, she had charged with assault. The brother was a policeman. He was shocked and worried not only for George but his own image. George hadn't received a summons yet but a friend in the police department had seen his name in the book.

He called, he said, because he wanted to talk to Joyce. Joyce invited him to the house.

"I bet he wants me to drop the charges," Joyce commented after she hung up the phone. "I won't unless George improves. He can't be allowed to go on like he has been. His brother's name is Jerry."

The man was not in uniform when he came. Joyce was not at home but was expected soon. I invited him into the kitchen. Tom was home. He declined to join the discussion. Jerry was polite until we got to the reason for his visit.

"That's a very serious charge," he said. "Do you understand how a conviction could hurt my brother? It might ruin his life."

"Oh, I don't think the conviction itself can ruin his life. That is only a consequence. What part does the man's own action play?"

"Well I'm not saying he isn't to blame. He is, but do you really think it's necessary to take him to court? That could hurt his career very much."

"That's true," I said, "but Joyce could have been injured permanently. Does he realize that?"

"I think he does. I haven't discussed this deeply with him yet but I intend to. I wanted to hear Joyce's version of the incident first. When I was told George was up for assault, I couldn't believe it. I just couldn't."

"But as a policeman you must have known there's a bad situation there at Hi-C. This is not the first bit of trouble among those young people. This just brings it home to us how bad the trouble is."

"I guess that's right. The fact is I've gotten involved with some of those kids before. They've been warned. George too. He must have been out of his mind to do that."

"Well, rage and frustration can do that. I am afraid sometimes my own boys will get in a similar scrape. Even Joyce could. She has a terrible temper too and is very stubborn. She won't take pushing around. But how can we give our children self-control?"

"It's a hard problem. Do you expect Joyce soon?"

"Yes. But don't expect her to decide right away. She has us to consider too. There's her little sister Jenny growing up who might meet the same trouble in the same place. And there's Billy who is fifteen. If he should want to visit that drop-in centre what kind of treatment do you think he'd receive? What of the younger people dropping in there now? Some of them are looking to Joyce to set an example of how to deal with the bullies and dictators."

"I never thought George was a bully and dictator. We used to be close but I've been neglecting him the last couple of years. I guess I shouldn't have. I'll have to pay more attention to him."

"That may help but George and the others are not little kids anymore. I think it's time someone made them face up to their own faults and their responsibilities to others."

Joyce arrived then. I let Jerry and her talk but I listened awhile to see what attitude she'd take. It was soon apparent she'd been thinking deeply and wasn't going to be swayed easily. She asked Jerry why George couldn't plead his own case. I gave her a silent cheer.

Jerry suggested they both go to see George. Joyce thought it was a good idea but she insisted they also visit Kathy if possible. Jerry agreed to that as a matter of course. The trip was almost fruitless. They had been able to see only one of the assailants, George. Joyce hadn't been favourably impressed by his show of repentance. She thought he was shamming.

Tom was angry. "Calls himself a policeman, an upholder of the law, and he's trying to get you to let them outlaws off the hook? Don't listen to him."

"He's human too," Joyce flared. "Policemen have feelings too. You're not so good yourself."

"Joyce," I said, "Dad is not in the same position. Jerry volunteered to enforce our laws. What kind of a policeman sets his relatives above the law, or shields one lawbreaker and not another?" As Tom made to speak I interrupted him, "Tom shut up. You argue with the boys, I'll argue with Joyce."

"Perhaps Jerry is doing wrong," Joyce said slowly, "but there's George's mother. She was talking to me. She feels pretty bad. She said George had a chance for a scholarship. A record will ruin his chances.'

"Where is his father? What did he say?" I asked.

"Oh his parents are separated now. His father moved out."

"But that doesn't mean he doesn't care about his children. Did anyone bother to let him know his son is in trouble?"

"I don't know but I don't think so."

"Well they should. It's his business. If he doesn't care they can't make him care but the boy is only twenty. The father might care more than they know. And he just might have more influence on George in this instance than anyone else. Do you suppose George is subconsciously trying to hurt his father and family?"

Joyce was silent, apparently busy pondering this question. I wanted to end the conversation. I said, "It's something to think about. The poor kid. Well if it's attention he wanted he'll get it now though he mightn't like it all. Well anyway the right course to take is beyond me, and I don't want to hear anymore about it for a while."

I pushed Joyce's problems to the back of my mind during the next few days.

Then it was back to school. Jenny and Billy went, reluctantly. Joyce moved to Gloria's, registered for classes at her former school and applied for welfare. Johnny refused to return. He'd continue working he said and get his grade thirteen credits through night school. Don finally started to attempt a repair on the TV.

The date of trial for Joyce's assailants arrived bright and warm. She went down to withdraw the charges. She found the summonses hadn't been served. Couldn't she withdraw the charges she asked. No, she was told. A trial date was set for October.

"Why don't you let it go through?" I asked. "You're doing all the running around and they're probably at home smirking."

During the same week, Don, Tom and I received in hand an envelope containing a copy of a city housing bylaw and a list of the required repairs to be done to 79. The papers noted that copies had been delivered to certain other parties too; Schmidt was one of them. We looked over the list of repairs, and laughed. There were nearly forty small repairs: missing tile in kitchen floor, broken tiles in bathroom floor, broken tile in room upstairs, cracks in wall, deteriorated woodwork on windows, missing hardware on windows, and such like annoyances. We considered the house to be in a crummy but not condemnable state. We all ignored the notices. Schmidt had hired a helper and was repairing 75. We were ready to move in.

It turned out I was wrong about Joyce doing all the running around. Jerry was doing some and his sister. When she'd heard of George's trouble she had come up from the U.S. to see what was happening to the brother she had, like Jerry and Mrs. Peterson, had such high ambitions for. The sister couldn't remain in town long but she did attend a family conference to which Joyce was invited. Joyce explained why the charges hadn't been dropped but assured the concerned relatives they would be. A day later Joyce changed her mind. She had both heard and observed things that caused her to believe George, Harry and Kathy should not be let off. She informed Jerry and his mother of her change in plans. Another conference was called at a drop-in centre. Joyce asked me to attend. I went but I was late. It was nearly over. Joyce had promised again to drop the charges. I met Mrs. Peterson and George for the first time. I spoke with them a little while. Take away their colour and they were just like us. Mrs. Peterson struck me as a proud, unhappy, worried mother. She was intelligent, well-groomed, well-mannered and self-assured. I wished I could say the same for George. I got the impression he regarded his crime as no worse than swiping cookies from his mother's pantry.

He seemed childishly amused at the great concern over the assault on Joyce. I felt pity for him and sympathy for his mother. I told Joyce that I felt George's mother was suffering the most. Joyce agreed. "It's to save her I'm dropping the charges."

Mrs. Peterson and I left the building at the same time. We stood in the yard together waiting for our children. We talked quietly of the weather, and the monetary troubles with which we were beset.

As we were engaged thus a car drew up near us, a woman got out and went into the building.

"That's Mrs. Campbell," said Mrs. Peterson. "There's some kind of a business meeting here tonight. I heard she was invited."

"The Mrs. Campbell who's running for mayor?" I asked. "Was that her?"

"Yes. That's the one. Didn't you recognize her?"

"No. Well I've never met her and I don't remember seeing her picture. Have you met her?"

"No."

"Well let's go meet her. I want to wish her luck and thank her for running. An intelligent woman in the race ought to make a nice change from the last election."

"Oh, no. I couldn't."

"Well I can. So long then."

On re-entering the building I saw Joyce in the hall. She was talking to a tall, young, black man. She called me to her side.

"Mum. This is Boyd. He works here. That is he did until today. He's been fired but he doesn't know why."

The young man fidgeted.

"Oh, Joyce. It's all right. Just one of those things," he said.

"Well it shouldn't be," I exclaimed. "A man has a right to know why he's fired or laid off. Do you mind telling me if you've had trouble with other workers?"

"I've had disagreements on methods and policies but nothing I expected to be fired for. I'm going to ask them for a reason."

"You should. I don't like that method of firing a man without giving the reason. Our taxes help to support this organization so I think I have a right to know the reason too. I'll try to find it out."

"Well thanks for your support, Mrs. Firth. I was thinking of looking for another job anyway."

"This could hurt your career though. You better make a fight. Well I want to see Mrs. Campbell, so—goodbye then and good luck."

Seats had been arranged in a big room off the hall to the left of us. Mrs. Campbell was sitting near the back conversing with another lady.

I walked over to them and when there came a pause in their conversation I introduced myself.

"How do you do," said the lady. "Would you care to work with us?"

"I don't know if I'd be able to. I have a ten-year-old girl and I had an operation two months ago but I'm certainly glad we have a woman in the race. Thank you very much."

"Thank you, Mrs. Firth." The lady smiled, then turning slightly aside, "Oh, hello Boyd. How are you?"

I turned around. Boyd had come up behind me. He and Mrs. Campbell were shaking hands.

"I'm fine thank you, Mrs. Campbell. How is your campaign going?"

"Well we have not started seriously yet. I've been busy with meetings like this one. Meeting people consumes an enormous amount of my time."

When she paused I broke in. "Mrs. Campbell, Boyd says he's fine, but I just found out he lost his job today. He was fired without a reason. I think that's lousy treatment. Don't we all support this place?"

"We certainly do!" cried Mrs. Campbell. "I want to hear more about this. I'll look into it right now."

She rose determinedly to her feet and started away.

Boyd looked uncertainly about for a moment. I felt he was embarrassed.

"Go on Boyd. Now's your chance to find out who wants you out of here. Perhaps I'll go with Mrs. Campbell myself."

Boyd started. "Perhaps I should go along. It's my problem. Well good-bye, Mrs. Firth. It was nice meeting you." He hurried to catch Mrs. Campbell.

I turned to the other lady who had remained silent after I caught Mrs. Campbell's attention.

"Did you hear what that was all about?"

"Some. Did those bureaucrats have the nerve to fire that young man for nothing?"

"Well it looks like someone around here doesn't like him. But we'll see, rather our friend Mrs. Campbell will see. Now I have to be going. I told my little girl I wouldn't be long. I'm glad to have met you. Good-bye."

I left, satisfied I had acted properly in bringing Boyd's problem to our alderman's notice while it was a fresh issue.

Near the middle of September, officials from City Hall came and nailed in the center of our front door a list of the repairs to be done to the house. The papers could be seen from the street though the printing was illegible from that distance. People began asking me if there was an election coming up; a few bold ones came onto the verandah to read for themselves, and went away muttering and shaking their heads. Neighbours began to check their homes for faults; some observed aloud that the City would be wiser to repair its own buildings. The neighbours seemed more angry than we.

At last it occurred to me that the repairs on 75 were progressing too slowly. I decided to help. The cupboards and clothes closets needed painting. I told Schmidt I would do them. He was dubious about my ability but he supplied the paint and I did them. Schmidt showed me greater respect.

Two evenings later the boys helped me move some items to the other house. It took two days of walking back and forth from house to house before we had everything moved and Schmidt had finished the inside repairs. And I lost my teakettle in the process. The last night as I took down the curtains from 79 somebody set the teakettle to boil and forgot about it. I returned from 75 to find an unfamiliar smell pervading 79. The bottom had melted out of my kettle on the electric stove. Oddly, Tom showed little anger.

The next day, though, when he had to heat water in a pot he began to rail at me for my carelessness. He was suddenly disconcerted when Johnny took the blame for the loss. I was not sure that was the way of it but the comical expression on Tom's face kept me silent.

Two days after we were into our new house a real estate agent planted a sign in the front yard advertising the house for sale. We were nonplussed. We said nothing to Schmidt but resolved to do without and save money to lease another place.

Schmidt must have been satisfied with our tenancy. He told us he would try to see that 79 was repaired before 75 would be sold. He had to sell one house, he explained, to get money to repair the other.

"I won't go back to 79 until I have a good stove," I warned. "I'll go back to New Brunswick and a wood-burner." The stove at 75 was very good. It used gas.

For the next two weeks prospective buyers marched daily through our house. Then the "for sale" signs were replaced by "sold" signs.

"The deal isn't final," Schmidt told us. The parade of City Hall inspectors and house-buyers stopped, to our relief.

13

A group of us sat around Gloria's living room jabbering and half-heartedly watching a TV program that none of us liked.

"Why you watch TV so much?" asked Bob Dubé. "It's crazy. Every night you gotta watch TV. You have it on all the time. It makes me sick."

"Oh, Bob," cried Gloria. "We gotta have something to do. Sometimes there are really good shows and funny ones."

"We should write to the Government and the CBC," I said. "I think the trouble is too many people put up with the damn garbage. We haven't even bothered to buy a TV."

"Oh yes, you read," said Gloria. "You can't tell me you don't read some lousy books. I know Tom does. I've seen them."

"Don't judge me by Tom," I cried. "I've never read a lousy book in my life. Oh I've studied a few, looked over a few, but never have I read one for pleasure. That's one good thing about reading. Everyone has their choice and there are no commercials. Besides we can skip parts if it suits us."

"Sometimes the commercials are the funniest part," said Howie. "But they get boring after you've seen them a coupla times."

"You are all willing to criticize TV," said Johnny, "but have you considered the work it takes to put on a TV show? What kind of a show would any one of you put on? Do you think you could do any better?"

"Someone could," cried Gloria. "There must be someone who could put on better shows."

"Someone is not you, Gloria," said Johnny. "Come on, tell us what you'd show."

"Well, that party we had tonight would make a better show than that thing they've got on," laughed Gloria.

Remembering, we all laughed with her.

"Why don't you write it out and send it to the CBC, Mamma?" joked Brucie.

"What? How could I write it? Perhaps Alice or Johnny. They're getting education," Gloria said.

"I could," said Alice. "I might need a little help. But I could do it."

"Then do it!" said Johnny.

"What good is it to write about one party?" asked Gloria. "We've had better. Someone should write a book about us. All about the fights and drunks and foolish things."

"You mean all of us and all the people we know? What a helluva book," laughed Alice. "But we should do it."

"But who'd do the writing?" asked Howie. "It's all right to talk but it takes brains to write a book."

"Oh, not so much brains, Howie," I said, "as persistence. You couldn't write a book about us in a day. There's too much to tell."

"I suppose you could write a book," Gloria spoke directly to me, sarcastically, I thought.

Piqued, I said, "Yes, I suppose I could. I've had a little education too, you know."

"Oh I've had enough education, too, to write the kind of book you're talking about. But what kind would that be? Some book!" retorted Gloria.

"Well it would be good enough for our relatives and friends. I could sell enough to them to pay the costs," I said seriously.

"Humph. But you wouldn't make any money," Gloria laughed.

"Who'd write to make money? Not me. I'd write for my own pleasure and to give pleasure," I said.

"Well then," said Gloria in a bored tone, "why don't you do it?"

"Well actually I have been doing it—though not as a book. Just a chapter now and then and sending them out as letters to people back home. But now I think I'll do the story properly and have my letters bound in a book."

"Do it, Mother!" cried Johnny enthusiastically. "I'll help you get it typed."

"Yes, do it, Mrs. Firth!" cried Alice as enthusiastically as Johnny. "I'll type it. Dad got me a new typewriter."

"And I'll tell you interesting stories you don't know; about us and Norman, and working at Joey's before you came up," cried Gloria catching the kids' excitement. "I can't write much but I'll tell you and you write. We'll sell it and get rich."

"No we won't," I said. "If you want to get rich—write your own book."

"Where'd I get time?" asked Gloria.

"Take time. Forget everything and just write," I said. "You just might produce a masterpiece."

Johnny, Howie, and Alice went into paroxysms of laughter. Bob and Brucie appeared quite amused. Gloria and I smiled benignly at them and began talking about the Tupperware party to be held at my house.

The next day I began to write with a pencil and a ten-cent writing pad from Martha's.

I wrote in bits and pieces, a few minutes at a time. I would have loved to sit down and work for hours but that would have upset our family life too much.

The Tupperware party with me as hostess went off well.

The next day Billy got himself kicked out of school for a few days.

"They won't let me back in until you or Dad go to see them," Billy told me.

"Okay," I said. "Do you really want to go back?"

"Yes," he said.

I called the school to make an appointment to discuss Billy's behaviour.

"You'll receive a notice," I was told.

"I want to make the appointment now. Do I have to wait for a letter? Billy told me a story," I said.

"Oh all right. Yes. We can make an appointment now," the telephone voice said.

So it was arranged.

I spoke first with the vice-principal.

"Have you the confidential reports on my son?" I asked, politely, I thought.

"Yes I have them," the vice-principal said and proceeded to read them to me. That little trick annoyed me no end. I had asked for those reports for myself—the previous term another set had been sent through the mails to me—now here was this young man reading aloud to me.

"I see," I said. "I understand that when students get used to respect from adults at home and on jobs and are earning enough money to help support themselves and enjoy a measure of independence they don't like to come to school and be subjected to less respect from teachers and secretaries."

"Then you think the teachers and secretaries must put up with rudeness and disobedience?" asked the VP.

"To some extent, yes," I said. "Even though these students have some adult responsibilities and privileges they are not adult. You are supposed to set an example. Here—I have something I copied from a book at the library."

From my purse I pulled a paper on which I had copied some laws and rules regarding the conduct of teachers in school. I read my notes aloud to Mr. VP.

"Now it seems to me," I elaborated, "that you lost your temper and perhaps for a moment, we could say, you were not sober. I've checked that word too."

"Well," he excused himself lamely, "we are only human. We do lose our tempers."

"Well why don't you allow for that? And if adults can lose their tempers why not children, and children more often because they haven't had as much time to develop better self-control?" I asked, watching him closely.

"I agree there, and I admit I lost my temper but Miss Jones was very upset. Would you like to talk to the principal?"

"Yes, I would."

To brighten the school picture Johnny received word that he had received the highest prize for chemistry in grade twelve. We were all delighted. Johnny ordered a made-to-measure suit for the graduation exercises.

And then one day as I basked in the pride of Johnny's achievement a man from the Hydro came to my door and informed me that our electric power was soon to be cut off until a new service was installed. We had one week to scrounge up some extra money and move out.

I told the family. Everyone was angry. But unhappier events captured our attention.

Gloria called me up one morning to ask me to please go up and mind her house until her husband could get home from work. She had to go to the mental health centre; she couldn't take any more, she couldn't do her work, couldn't mind her kids, couldn't stand to be in the house. She was crying as she explained over the telephone.

I hurried to her side. She was very depressed. I went with her to the hospital and after she was admitted I returned to her house to wait for Bob. He was pretty upset.

For the next few days all of us were more concerned with Gloria and her problems than with the Hydro.

Then Billy got a job, hopper on a newspaper delivery truck. He was finished with school. That very day they came and cut off our power.

Martha carried candles in her store. We started buying. When the boys came home we ate supper by candlelight.

"What in hell is going on anyway?" Don asked.

"The Hydro told me they had ordered Schmidt to repair the wires and outlets," I said.

"He did that," Tom said. "Now they want a new service put in. This old one is too small. It can't take a big enough load."

"But can they make Schmidt change the service?" I asked in surprise.

"They can do anything at all," Tom answered. "We'll have to move out I guess."

Schmidt was angry at finding the power cut off. At my insistence he paid for our candles. But he did not want to pay for a new service. He argued with Hydro that the old one was good enough. Hydro insisted it had to be replaced. There was trouble.

I did not like being the victim of a war between our landlord and Hydro. I had the idea that Hydro should have given us more time to move.

I went to our public library and looked up the laws concerning Hydro's authority. To my amazement it was written as Tom had told me: the Ontario Hydro Commission had the power to cut off a consumer's electric power at any time for many reasons, and they could make repairs and installations themselves and charge the cost to the consumer. That commission, it seemed to me, had more power than its creator, the Government.

I no longer wondered why the aldermen and controllers I had been complaining to weren't helping us. They could not. I was appalled.

With the hydro off our gas furnace did not work very well. Jenny caught pneumonia. Hydro gave us emergency lighting for the week-end.

That night I attended the commencement exercises at Johnny's school. I felt great watching him walk across the stage and receive his prize and diploma. Speaking with his teachers after the ceremonies I discovered most of them were very proud of him. I thanked them for their care and efforts with Johnny.

"We had good material to work with," I was told with a smile.

"And so was Billy, only different," I said. But those teachers had not got Billy.

Johnny's prize was 200 dollars' worth of chemistry books. Johnny hired a cab for me and I took the books home. He stayed for the dance.

At home I found Tom at the end of the table, flopped on a chair, drunk.

"What'd Johnny get?" he asked. "Not just books? The bastards. They should have given him money. He could pick out his own books. Oh well, he earned them."

Tom put his head on his arms on the table and began to cry.

"I couldn't go to see Johnny get his prize," he sobbed. "Like a pig I had to get drunk."

I felt sudden grief for Tom and the things he had missed. I said, "It's all right. You helped him. Remember the time you took him all over the boat in Campbellton when he was little?"

"Yeah. He wanted to see everything. He's a smart boy. I wish he wasn't sick." Tom broke into deep sobs.

"Oh well," I said. "I'm hungry. Want a lunch?"

"Yes," Tom said, the crying stopped. He got up from the chair and began to examine the prize books.

"Don't dirty his prize," I laughed.

"What do you think I am?" Tom asked gruffly. "Here. Put them away, and get me a lunch."

Joyce found herself a rooming house– "where it was peaceful and quiet."

Don changed jobs and bought a beautiful big car.

Schmidt hired an electrician to change the service.

Tom got laid off. It was a relief to have the uncertainty ended. He applied for UIC benefits and got right down to the business of finding another job.

In December Don's new company transferred him to Windsor for a few weeks. While he was away Tom got a job with the City in its Property Department. Tom was assured that he could expect the job to last until spring. That took a great load off our minds.

Tom's job did not last long. He had merely been replacing a man who had fallen sick. The man recovered within a few weeks and returned to work.

Tom had to wait a week for his pay. Most of that time he spent grumbling around the house. When finally his paycheque came, a mistake had been made in it. Tom was short the money he was counting on for Christmas gifts. He was very angry.

December 19 we had a little ruckus at our house. The day before I had made arrangements to have Uncle Arthur Ross, my father's only living brother, in for a visit. Tom had gone out and got a twenty-six ounce bottle of rum to treat the old man. It was in the refrigerator, along with a mixer.

In the morning Tom went out to make an attempt to get his money from City Hall or the Welfare Department. While he was away on that business Don and I waited for a call from Uncle Arthur to tell us when he'd be ready for Don to pick him up. When he called it was to let us know he couldn't come after all.

Tom arrived back about noon. He opened Uncle Arthur's

bottle and began to drink.

Norman came in and asked if he could come back and board with us again for a while. Tom said he could on condition he was not to get drunk or keep late hours at night. Norman agreed to that. He said he knew he hadn't been doing himself any good by drinking and going to bed at one or two a.m. Tom said he could move back in that very evening after work.

After lunch Tom was supposed to go with Don to mail a couple of parcels to my parents. Instead, Tom over-drank. He progressed from a mood of jollity to one of vulgarity. I told him the only place he was fit for was bed. He refused to go but after a while, still dressed for the outdoors, he fell asleep at the end of the table. Don and I left him there like that, alone in the house, and went out to get the parcels away.

When I returned home Tom had taken off his outdoor clothes and gone to bed.

Later that evening Schmidt came in for the rent. Tom explained to him about the mistake in his pay. Schmidt said he needed his money. I asked him if he had received the tax rebate for his houses yet for 1969.

Schmidt pretended ignorance of the meaning of a tax rebate. Tom's back wages and the tax rebate that was due us would easily take care of our rent to the end of the year. I tried to explain that to Schmidt. He said he hadn't received a rebate. I asked him if he had let it be deducted from his property taxes.

He evaded my question but asked where one would go to enquire about the rebate. I told him and offered to accompany him. He said that would be good and we set the date for the coming Monday.

Billy arrived home from his job. He loaned me twenty-five dollars which I gave Schmidt for partial rent.

Tom began teasing. I was in no mood for playing around. I told Tom to go to bed and let me get my work done. He refused and continued yakking in an obvious attempt to get me angry.

I tried to work quietly. Tom continued to drink and make cutting remarks about me and my relatives. I replied in kind.

Tom became really abusive. He accused all of us of being against him, of trying to ruin his life, and of wanting to be rid of him. He ordered all of us to leave.

Johnny decided to go. He feared his own temper might rise and he'd injure his father if Tom attempted to act out his threats. I asked Johnny to take Jenny to Gloria's until Tom could sober up. I suggested to Billy that he and I leave also. Billy elected to stay. Johnny gave me some money in case I might need it. Then he and Jenny went out.

Billy went off to his room. I felt like going to Gloria's but I feared Tom's mood would become uglier and he might hurt Billy with some kind of weapon. He has a penchant for throwing things when he gets in a blind rage.

I sat in the kitchen and Tom continued his verbal attack. I developed an urge to laugh.

"I should kill you, you bitch," he slurred, "but you aren't worth it."

I burst into laughter. "Well instead why don't you do like Doug, your friend in Campbellton, and break up the furniture? That'd be brilliant. There, start with the stove."

Tom screamed an invective and lunged at me. He reached for my throat. I threw up my arms in defense. He grabbed me by the hair but didn't get a good grip because it was short. He knocked my head against the wall and I became very angry. I kicked out at him and pushed hard at his chest. He reeled back and I got to my feet. He made another lunge. I stood still and tried to kick him. I succeeded but he managed to grab me and attempt a good shaking.

Then Billy was there, grabbing Tom and wrenching him away. I felt myself free, and not about to miss the chance, I aimed a good blow at Tom's last remaining tooth. It was loose I knew, and about ready to fall out by itself. The tooth fell to the floor, to my glee.

Holding his father almost helpless Billy turned angrily to me. "Why'd you hit him again? You could see I had him!"

"I wanted to help him get rid of that damn tooth," I said. "He wanted Don to pull it with the pliers a few days ago. He won't go to a dentist. Anyway he deserved it for hurting my head."

"Let me go!" Tom howled furiously. "Let me. Get out. Go on. Get out! Both of you."

Billy released his father, but stood in front of me.

"Wipe your mouth, Dad," Billy said. "It's bleeding."

Tom wiped at his face. He muttered a few words that I did not hear clearly. He leaned over the sink and spat.

"Now why don't you go up to Gloria's?" Billy said. "I can handle Dad."

"I was thinking of going. I guess I will."

Tom swung around from the sink and tried to swing a heavy metal chair at Billy.

I spoke a warning but Billy was alert. He leaped swiftly behind his father, caught Tom's two arms and pinned them to his sides. Tom fumed, and wriggled about, impotent to strike at anything.

"Are you going to be quiet?" Billy demanded. "If you'll be quiet I'll let you go. You can see you can't do anything."

Tom made no promises but he stopped name-calling and swearing. Billy released him. Tom hunted up his cap and staggered out of the house.

"Where's he going?" Billy asked me.

"Probably to Martha's to cut off my credit," I said. "Let him go. The cold air might help to sober him. This mood'll soon wear off. Just don't let him do too much damage and it'll be okay."

"Well if you wouldn't say anything to get him mad perhaps he wouldn't try to fight," Billy said.

"No Billy, that isn't right. He works himself into a crazy rage. He isn't really mad at any of us. It's City Hall or whoever made the mistake in his pay. He was counting on that money and he's disappointed. He can't take these things so easy now. He was mad when he started drinking but not at his family. And he can't take liquor too well either. But you're handling him fine."

"Well why don't you go out then? Up to Gloria's."

"No, I'll go later. I want to wait and see if he gets worse or better."

Billy picked up a book and began to read.

I sat down and lit a cigarette.

The telephone rang. Billy answered.

"Hello," he said, "who's this?" Pause. "Where's my father? Where'd he go?"

Billy passed me the phone, pulled on his jacket and started out.

I spoke into the phone. It was Martha.

"What's wrong with Tom?" she asked.

"He's just drunk and fighting," I said.

"What happened? Why is he bleeding?" she asked.

"Oh he tried to wring my neck and I knocked out his tooth."

"He said it was Billy."

"Ah, he's ashamed to tell the truth. Billy never hit him. He's just trying to prevent big trouble. Anyway I can't talk now."

"Okay, okay. I just thought you might not know what he's doing. He shouldn't be staggering around the streets. He'll get picked up."

"Well let him. It might save a lot of trouble. Good-bye now." I hung up.

I put on my coat and went outside. The lady next door was peeking out the glass window in her front door. I waved at her. She dropped the curtain fast.

I expected to see Billy come wrestling Tom along the street. But no. Tom came lurching around the corner alone. I moved out of his reach as he neared the house.

"Go on, bitch," he shouted. "You'll not get back in this house. No one gets in here tonight."

I did not reply. Tom went into the house and slammed the door. The catch was functioning poorly. He slammed it twice before it held.

Billy came around the other corner. When he drew near he asked, "Have you seen Dad?"

"Sure. He's back in the house. He doesn't want us in."

"Well I'm going in," Billy vowed.

"Okay. But I'll wait awhile," I said. I was beginning to feel cold, though.

After a few minutes I peeked in. Between the curtains I could see a little. Tom was leaning, half asleep, over the railing at the side of the stairs. He looked sick. I went in and walked past him up the stairs. Tom neither moved nor spoke.

I went into Billy's room.

"Billy," I said. "Dad might need a doctor. Or maybe you can get him to lie down. He's not so drunk. Perhaps we'd better call Johnny to come home."

"What about Don? You call someone."

"No. He might try to fight me yet. Leave Don. He's a long

way out. Johnny can be here in a few minutes. He'll help me put Dad to bed."

Billy made the call. It was very short. Tom stubbornly resisted efforts to help him at first but Billy got a damp cloth and began to clean his father's face. Then Tom let Billy help him to bed. When Johnny arrived the house was quiet.

"What happened? Where's Dad?" he asked.

"He's in bed now," I told him. "But he started fighting."

"Did he hit you?"

"Yes, but not much. Billy was able to handle him. I managed to knock out his tooth so he'll not be bothered with that anymore. Now he might sleep it off."

"Well goddamn. He'll never learn."

"There'll be plenty scenes like this around town for the next two weeks. The main thing is try to keep calm and see they don't do much damage until they sober up. Billy was really manly. I was surprised."

"Good. Then I guess I'll read awhile. Are you going up to Gloria's for Jenny?"

"Yes, I can go now. You'll stay with Billy won't you?"

"Yes, I'll stay."

"Okay. Dad won't try much with both of you here. Not now anyway. The worst is over."

The pair of shoes I wanted were not where I had left them. Sometimes Jenny would use my shoes and dresses to play grown-up. I went upstairs to look in her room.

At the top of the stairs I was arrested by the sounds of low sobbing. Quietly I checked the boys' rooms. Johnny and Billy were both crying, each in his bed, face down, with his head cradled in his arms.

Instantly I felt a desire to comfort them but I hesitated for fear I would say the wrong thing.

Finally I approached Billy.

"It's not so bad, Billy," I said. "You were really great. These things are common. We have to learn to deal with them. His drunk will wear off. The main thing is to keep him from doing damage if we can. Dad will be all right soon. I'm going up to Gloria's now that Johnny's here with you."

Billy continued to cry quietly to himself.

I went to Johnny's room and spoke to him as I had to Billy. He said nothing, either.

Downstairs I found Tom trying to explain to Lee on the phone. He was calmer and full of self-pity. I heard him ask her if she and George would give him a room. He began a jeremiad of his family troubles; how the boys were punching him around; how I'd threatened to kill him; how he had to put up with lousy house-keeping, etc.

Lee insisted on speaking to me. I told her a bit of the trouble, playing it down as much as the facts would allow.

"By Gawd," she said, "if he had tried to put my head through the wall I'd have killed him."

"Oh," I said, "I couldn't get really mad at the poor drunken slob. Tomorrow he'll be all shamefaced. He didn't do much damage. He got the worst actually. However I'm not putting up with such ridiculous goings-on. I've got to go now to get Jenny at Gloria's. He'll be good and sober before I come home again. Lee, he wants to talk to you again."

Tom took the phone quietly from me.

"Hell," he said. "You know it's not all my fault. She's spoiled those kids– "

I walked out.

At Gloria's I had to tell all about it.

Next day Tom was quite averse to talking about his drunken spree. I alluded to the subject often. Lee called. I described the epic as well as I could and loud enough for Tom to hear. Tom was grimacing as he moved about the kitchen. I could hear Lee laughing at the other end of the phone.

"Ask Tom does he still want a room," she said.

I asked him. "Piss on Lee," he answered.

"No, he doesn't want a room," I told her.

"Then does he want to cry on my shoulder today? Tell him I can listen better this morning," she laughed.

"Here Tom," I called, laughing, "Lee wants to talk to you."

"Well I don't want to talk to her," Tom growled. "I don't want to rehash that shit."

"He doesn't want to rehash his Waterloo," I told Lee. "But he'll rehash it to the counsellor."

"Counsellor? You mean a marriage counsellor?" Lee said. "Is

that what you're gonna do? Take your troubles to one of them?"

"Well, that's what they're for. Your money and mine go to pay them whether they help or not."

"Tell old Tom he's lucky I wouldn't wake George last night. He'd have been right down there to clobber him for trying to get me mixed up in a family quarrel."

"Oh Lee, that's what families are for. It's certainly your right to butt in and prevent bad trouble or murder. You can be proud that Tom called you instead of his own relatives."

"Yes, well tell Tom next time my kids get arguing or fighting I'll call him to come be the referee, even if it's two a.m. I better let you go now. I just wondered how it all ended and whether everybody had left the house to Tom or what. Have a Merry Christmas, and a quiet one I hope."

Shortly Tom went out and put my credit back on at Martha's and the drugstore. Furthermore he bought two pairs of light but warm blankets, and a cookie sheet I had been asking for since the move.

As Gloria said, he was making peace offerings, or in Johnny's opinion, salving his conscience. On top of purchasing the new things Tom cooked a very good supper for the family.

We recovered rapidly from our shake-up. On the second day Tom sat down with Don and Billy for a few hands of poker. He won ten dollars off them. That lifted his spirits.

Christmas Eve Tom got a job at a dairy. He was to begin work in January.

The new year began quietly and well. I received letters from New Brunswick assuring me all of my relatives there were well and cheerful.

At the end of January my mother phoned and told me my father was in the hospital and would probably lose his leg.

"Your father's eighty-five," Tom said. "If they amputate his other leg he won't live long. Are you going down?"

"Not yet," I said. "If I go now he might be fine while I'm there, then after I got back I might get word he's died and I'd have to go right back. I can't afford two trips and when I go I'd like to be able to stay a month or two."

Tom was called back to work by his old company. Next day,

to my relief, Norman moved out.

I received a letter from Mother. Father's leg had been amputated; he was doing well.

Don and Johnny said they would pay my return fare. I was not eager to go because of the season but I began to prepare for a trip east. I did a bit of housecleaning and clothes-repairing so that the house would be in good order when I left.

A spell of warm weather delighted me. I began to look forward to spring and a trip east.

Then late one night the telephone rang. It was Nell. Dad, she told me, had become very ill suddenly. Mother had been with him all day. He was very low.

"I'll come down," I told my sister. "I'll leave tomorrow. Tell Mother."

Fifteen minutes later Nell called again. My father had just died. Nell was crying.

Tom was at work and I could not reach him by phone. Don drove up to the plant to tell him. A few minutes later George phoned and asked if I could be ready in an hour to leave for New Brunswick. He was driving down.

Tom phoned. I told him that George and I would be leaving in the car shortly and I would be taking Jenny. He said he would finish his shift rather than bother getting a man to replace him.

"Take some money," he said. "I'll send you some more in a couple of days."

I woke Jenny and began hurriedly packing suitcases. At 3:15 George arrived and we left.

In Campbellton the weather was bitterly cold but not stormy.

It was a military funeral with a small group of mourners. When "The Last Post" was played I started to cry. Mamma was crying quietly too. I left the vault and went out to the car. The next day George drove back to Toronto.

That night a few people gathered at Mother's house. We held a séance. Lois was the instigator; she had participated in some and knew the procedure.

I was nervous at first and refused to join Lois, Mother, Nell, Jenny, and three others who sat around a wooden table and tried to move it with just their fingers resting lightly on the top.

As I watched with curiosity as nothing happened, my fear left me. I walked over and sat down beside Mother, opposite Lois and Nell, and put my hands on the table.

"We may have to wait quite awhile before anything happens," Lois said. "Maybe there are no spirits here tonight. If there are they might not want to talk to us."

"Maybe we should put the lights off," said Harry Doucet, age fifteen. "And the TV."

"No!" I said firmly, unnecessarily loud. "The spirits can visit us in the light, and let them see what we get on TV."

"Let's be quieter then. Make the kids sit down," said Jenny. The kids were Nell's three youngest.

"No, let's be natural," I said. "I'm nervous enough as it is. I bet if we had some Demerara rum there'd be at least one spirit here."

"Yes," said Lois, laughing lightly.

The table moved.

"They are here!" exclaimed Lois. Everyone became very quiet. "Now I'll ask questions."

She began to explain a plan to us and the invisible force. "When I ask a question and the answer is no, tip the table toward me. If the answer is yes, tip the table toward Mamma. Is it Uncle Howard?"

The room was hushed. The table did not move.

Lois tried again. "Is it our brother Ken?"

We waited. Still the table did not move.

The younger people were becoming impatient.

"They don't like to be laughed at," said Lois.

"We're not laughing at them. I wouldn't dare. We're all friends here," I said.

"Let's try again," said Lois. "Make sure all hands are touching. Concentrate. Don't push. Is it my father?"

I concentrated. Suddenly I felt a pleasant warmth all up my back and down my arms as if a loving friend had come up from behind and embraced me.

The feeling was so intense that momentarily it captured all my mind, as if I were dreaming and I forgot where I was.

"That's it. You're doing fine." The words, spoken by Lois, suddenly jerked me awake.

To my horror the table was soundlessly tipping toward me. Terrified I leaped up, the table fell back to its normal position, and I moved swiftly away.

"What happened?" Lois asked.

I told her, a bit shakily.

"You were going into a trance," she said. "You're the medium. When I spoke I broke the spell."

"Thank God," I said. "No more of that for me!"

"Perhaps we better stop. Do you want us to stop?" Lois asked.

I looked at the others. They did not seem frightened.

"No," I said. "I'm not too scared to watch. I'll have a cup of tea and a cigarette while you go on. I'm okay now. Go ahead."

They did. According to the table Father was with my brother who had been killed in the war. He was happy.

Lois began asking the force to identify people by pushing the table up to the person named. At one point the table moved toward a man in his thirties but stopped four inches away.

"Push the table right up to Eric," said Lois. "Come on. You can do it." We all watched the table. Sweat was running down Eric's face. Suddenly, unexplainably, I knew why the table had stopped.

"Eric is holding it back with his foot," I said and looked down quickly.

"I'm not," said Eric and lifted his foot from the table leg. The table shot ahead until the edge was touching his shirt.

"You're scared too," I told him, "but you don't want to admit it."

"Are you scared, Eric?" asked Lois.

"No," he answered.

"Well perhaps that's enough anyway," said Lois. "It's time for a lunch."

The table was moved back to its place by the wall. Lois and I served lunch. Jenny and I stayed a week with Mother.

Billy came home from work one day, late. He was very disturbed.

"Is Dad home?" he asked at once.

"No," I said. "Don't you remember? His shift changed. He'll be home in an hour, about 11:30. What's the matter?"

"Pack my things. I'm moving out. There's no money for board or anything, not even my debts. I dropped my whole pay in a crap game."

"You didn't! Billy don't kid like that!"

"Arrgh! You don't believe anything I say. I'm not kidding. Where's that green suitcase? I've gotta go."

"Just a minute Billy. You don't have to go out in this. You know Tom will have a fit but it isn't the worst crime in the world. I won't have you running out like a scared chicken on a night like this. Stay here until tomorrow at least."

"Okay. Well, can I have something to eat?"

"Of course. I'll get it for you."

After Billy ate he went to his room. Unable to fall asleep right away he lay in bed reading. When Tom came home his first words were, "Did Billy come home?"

"Yes," I said.

"Did he give you the board money?" Tom asked.

"No,"

"Why not?"

"He hasn't got it."

Tom was hanging up his jacket. I decided to let him have it straight.

"He hasn't got the board money, and he hasn't got the loans money either. He dropped his whole pay in a crap game, came home for his stuff and left."

"Jesus! So he's gone. That's good," said Tom, shouting the words. "He still owes me twenty dollars."

"You'll have to wait like the rest of us," I said quietly. "It was foolish but it's gone. So?"

"Goddamn him!" he said roughly, then with a sudden change of mood, "Ah, what can you do? What can I say? I've done as bad myself."

I went silently about getting Tom something to eat.

"He went out with no money?" Tom asked mildly.

"Well not exactly," I told him. "Actually I wouldn't let him go out tonight. He's in his room and don't you go hollering either so he'll take off in a blue rage."

"I'm not gonna holler. It's done. There's no changing that. Where's my tea?"

A little later Tom went upstairs to have a talk with Billy. He didn't scream. Eavesdropping, I heard him confess, "It's not right Billy. I've done as bad myself—but you should pay your debts first—gamble the rest if you want—but always pay your rent. Oh well."

"Okay, okay, I know," Billy said, thumbing his science fiction paperback.

The next morning before Billy left for work Tom had another quiet talk with him. I figured Billy needed no more advice but he listened calmly to his father's mild lecture. That evening Don and Johnny teased Billy about his lack of skill and opined that the game had been crooked and the dice loaded. Billy took the razzing in good humour.

The next week Billy brought all his pay home. When he had paid his board and debts he had little left for gambling. However his credit was good once more and he was able to borrow, but not wildly.

At the end of June Jenny was promoted to grade six. To her joyful surprise she was given an A in math.

"I never thought I'd make that," she cried in delight. "But I'm glad."

Johnny passed all his subjects and needed just one more credit for university. He planned to try for it through the Department of Education's free correspondence course, work a year, save some money, then return to his studies. After Dominion Day he went back to his job.

Around that time I had a phone call from Louise Firth, Tom's brother John's twenty-six-year-old daughter. I hadn't seen her since she was twelve. Tom had, though. He had kept in touch with her, and certain other nieces and nephews in Toronto who kept in touch with their parents and other relatives in New Brunswick. Through them Tom got most of the gossip from back east—some of it quite racy.

Louise wanted to see me and the kids. I invited her over. Billy announced he was moving out.

"How soon?" I asked.

"In a couple of days," he said.

"Where?"

"To Rochdale."

At the words my heart sank. Rochdale was a new building near the north end of our street. The people living there were supposed to be managing the building themselves. By all reports we had heard the tenants were mainly young radicals or anarchists living on welfare—or what they could beg or steal. Many of them, so we heard, used drugs often—LSD, marijuana, heroin, speed. The stuff was bought and sold right in the building, openly. But other young people had set up communes and tried to live quietly, doing "their thing", helping one another, and searching for the best way of life. Some couples were legally married, some were living common-law.

"Rochdale. Are you crazy? With them drug fiends? What's wrong with you?" Tom exploded.

"Oh, Tom," I pleaded, "calm down. More than drug addicts live there. Just because a few of them get arrested and make the news doesn't mean the place isn't fit to live in."

"Yeah, Dad. What's wrong with Rochdale? Have you been there? Have you talked with the people?" Billy asked angrily.

"No. I haven't been there and I don't want to be there. If you go don't come back," Tom said.

"I won't," Billy told him.

Before Billy moved out I gave a little party for him. I told him he could invite a friend or two, hoping he'd bring in a few from Rochdale so Tom and I could get to know them a little.

Billy brought a nice-looking girl to the party. She did not look like my image of a drug fiend or "bad" girl likely to corrupt our son.

Louise got to the party too. She and I had a great deal to talk about. She didn't seem too shocked at the idea of anyone moving to Rochdale. She had had some experience in helping disturbed young people, through a friend who was a paid social worker. I thought her attitude eased Tom's mind about Billy.

Louise was very career-minded. Inclined to support the women's liberation movement, she was by no means a man-hater. She had grown into a nice-looking woman with a petite figure. She wore fashionable, expensive clothes. She didn't work just to get money—she used the money to live well.

Living well for Louise meant she had a pretty and comfortable place and could indulge often a favourite pleasure—drinking beer. I was fascinated by her ability to drink, stay sober-sounding, and not have to go to the bathroom.

Before the party broke up Billy took some of his things and started to leave.

"Is he moving now, tonight?" Louise asked, surprised at the goings-on.

"It looks like it," I said. "He's only been waiting for a room."

"What's wrong with moving now?" Billy asked his cousin.

"Oh, nothing, I guess. Just that your mother went to the trouble to make you a party and you're leaving."

"Well she knew I was moving. But don't stop the party. You don't need me to keep the party going do you?" Billy seemed surprised by Louise's surprise.

"No, I suppose not," Louise said. "Well, good luck, Billy, in your new place. Come over and see me sometime."

"And Billy, remember if you need help let us know. And be sure to call in once in awhile," I said.

When Billy had gone our little party went on for a bit. Louise stayed the night with us.

To relieve my mind Johnny and Don made separate trips to Rochdale to check out the place. They assured me that Billy could make out all right, the whole thing depending on himself. Not every tenant there was a drug addict or pusher, and there were security guards, of a sort.

At the end of three weeks Billy grew tired of being on his own. He moved back home, to my great joy. Tom welcomed him.

Joyce moved back home.

Don got laid off. The company had to cut back production, it said. He was able to draw unemployment benefits. The payments were high enough to allow a single person to live well. Don continued his course at night school. Naturally he had a lot of spare time. To pass some of it he began painting seriously.

Joyce was able to pay board. Johnny couldn't pay his full board but he paid some. Don cut back his board too, with my permission. He needed money for brushes, paints, canvas. The big worry to Tom was that Don would lose the new car and the money already paid on it. Don seemed not to be worried.

My manuscript was rejected by two publishing companies.

The reason they gave was lack of money. I was sure they did not find the story well enough written. I decided to keep writing and re-do some parts of the book. Most of my friends and relatives began to laugh at me again but less heartily. After all, I had passed the Mensa test and turned the tables on them that time.

My critics began to express disapproval of Don's life-style also. Formerly his admirers they now became his denigrators. While it was stupid for a half-cracked old woman to waste her time on a book no one wanted to read, it was criminal for a healthy young man to waste his time painting pictures while living off the Government, i.e., "us poor hard-working taxpayers".

Even Pearl began to regard him as a bum, she told me. She was hurt and confused. Here she was slaving to earn and save money so she and Don could get off to a good start when they married, and Don was doing nothing.

"He is doing something," I told her. "He is an artist. They can be pretty hard to understand. Don't expect him to change after you're married."

"I know," Pearl told me sadly. "But I love him. Only he makes me so mad sometimes."

"So. Tom makes me mad too. But we can't expect them to spend all their time in ways that suit us. If we're gonna marry them we must be willing to put up with some faults, or get a divorce," I said.

"Well if I marry him I'll not divorce him. That's for sure. I don't believe in that. I guess I can put up with him." Pearl said it as if she were taking a vow.

To my surprise the most incensed over Don's reversion to a bum was George. A few months after Don had arrived in Toronto George had kindly taken him in hand, had taken him, without protest on Don's part, from his first Toronto job to a much better-paying one where George worked, had given him room and board for a small sum in his home, which meant the kids had to crowd up more, had helped him get a driver's license, and loaned him cars—in other words given him a good chance to be successful like George.

One fine afternoon George stopped off to see us. It was his day off and he had come into town to get something for Lee.

Everybody was out but Tom and me. After we passed a few banal remarks about the weather and our families' health George asked, "Is Don working yet?"

"No," said Tom. "Not likely. He's not looking for a job."

"Turning into a real bum, eh?" said George.

"Oh I wouldn't say that," I said. "He's getting nearly fifty dollars a week unemployment. He's okay."

"Okay! For Christ's sake. What's fifty dollars a week? If he weren't living with you he'd be starving. He was clearing over a hundred a week at Consumer's. He should have stayed."

"Sure he should have stayed," Tom agreed. "But he doesn't want to dirty his hands. He wants a job where you do nothing."

"So. If he can get a job using his brains as well as his hands I think he should be encouraged," I said.

"Sure, but encouraged in the right way," said George. "I'm glad he's going to night school but why isn't he working?"

"He doesn't have to right now," I explained. "He can stay home and live– "

George interrupted me. "Live off you. Tom you should put him out before he becomes a worse bum."

"I should, I guess," said Tom. "But she won't let me."

I laughed aloud.

"It's nothing to laugh about," Tom told me angrily. "You know he could get work if he wanted it. And he should be working."

"Why should he, Tom? He's got an income. He's going to night school. You'll be proud when he's in university," I said.

"University, hah!" Tom rejoined. "He'll never make it. He hasn't got the ambition."

George laughed. "He's got the ambition to be a bum."

I smiled at the men. "So if he's a happy bum that's okay with me."

"A happy bum," cried George. "For Christ's sake, Sophia, who wants their children to be bums? You must be crazy for sure."

"She is," asserted Tom. "She's writing a crazy book."

"What's so crazy about developing your artistic talents? You read don't you? Well if nobody wrote crazy books you couldn't waste time reading and if nobody painted pictures you'd have none to hang on your walls to pretty up your house. George I think you are just as crazy in your way as I am in mine. You're spending your life getting things you want and going to see things you want."

"But there's a difference. I work for what I want. Do you?" asked George.

"Sure I do. So does Don. Writing books and painting pictures is work."

"Okay. The point is Don is living off us taxpayers right now when he should be working. If nobody worked who'd pay the taxes? I've paid into that unemployment fund for twenty years and I never drew a cent. It's us working guys who are keeping the bums who're too lazy to work."

"So why do you do it?" I asked.

"Why do we do it? You know why we do it. The Government makes us. They take it off our pay and there's nothing we can do."

"Well maybe some of you working guys should join together and fight the Government. Look, if the Government is giving it to the bums why shouldn't they take it? It's legal isn't it?" I asked.

"Legal, yes. But is it right? Do you think it's right for the workers to have to support bums?"

"No, I don't, but do you think our bums, our unemployed, have no right to anything in this country? The natural wealth is theirs too. Their income isn't all from you taxpayers."

"What would this country be like if nobody worked? You know damn well some of us have got to work or there'd be nothing."

"Sure I know that. And I know that some workers get too damn little for what they do and some others get too much. Do you think it's fair that some men get seventy thousand a year and some get only four thousand?"

"Well of course it's fair. Some jobs are worth more. You know that."

"No I don't know that. At least I don't believe it. What in hell is it that makes one job worth more than another?" I asked.

"There she goes again," Tom warned George. "Don't talk to her."

"Sure I'll talk to her," George told him. "She needs to be educated. Sophia, some jobs are worth more because they're harder to do. Look at the Prime Minister's job. That's a hard job. He should get more'n Tom or me. And he does. It's perfectly right."

"Bullshit!" I cried. "Jobs are only important according to the dependency-support ratio of one to another. Who supports the Prime Minister while he's running the country? Who makes his clothes, grows his food, writes his books, and collects his garbage? How important are those jobs?"

"Oh they're important but not as hard as a Prime Minister's. It doesn't take much education or skill to collect garbage!"

"But it takes time. Just as much time as it takes to do a Prime Minister's job. Doesn't it?"

"Well sure. Any job takes time. Hell, Tom gets paid by the hour. What is Don getting paid by?"

"By the need I suppose. Can't you see, George, that some jobs are valued just according to the time it takes to do them and others are valued according to how important some people think they are? But some jobs have to be done before the others can be."

"Okay, I agree. So if people aren't satisfied with their wages let them form unions and fight."

"How are they going to form unions when for every man who sees the need there are fifty who don't? You call Don a bum for taking what he can get from the Government. What do you think you are, or Tom, for taking what you can get from your employers who take what they can get from the consumers?"

"The point is, Sophia," George continued stubbornly, but not so assuredly, "we do it the right way. I agree some people deserve better wages but living off the Government is not right. That way the burden is on the workers to support the rest."

"Well the other way the burden is on the low-paid workers to support the high-paid ones. It's always been that way. Now of course more and more people are refusing to work for low wages and the Government is helping them."

"She's right there, George," said Tom. "That's what the Government is doing all right. And it's a good thing some ways. Some producers are getting a damn poor deal."

"I know," George agreed. "But—well—hell, why doesn't the goddamn Government just raise the wages, make more jobs, and cut out some of the welfare?"

"It might be better," said Tom.

"But we have a free enterprise system," I laughed. "A democratic government mustn't tell employers what wages to pay."

"Free!" cried George. "Hell, is it free enterprise when we have to pay taxes to support bums?"

"That's what they call it," Tom laughed.

"Well it's too complicated for me," George laughed too. "It takes a genius to figure it out and I'm no genius. Sophia's the genius. Let her do it."

I said, "Well the trouble is we do not have true democracy in this country. When we do every man will be able to set his own wage. Now we have a bunch of men who set their own wage and the wage of other men as well and they make damn sure there's a big difference."

"Oh and what happens when every man can charge whatever he wants?" asked George sarcastically.

"We'll have more fair dealings. When a man can no longer take advantage of another man's needs he'll sit down and talk honestly about each man's worth because he has needs too."

"Yuh. Sure. Sophia you're talking through your hat. I can just see some lazy slob asking a million dollars to cut your lawn. Great," said George.

"So what if he does? Then when he goes to buy the other guy asks a million too. Is that any worse than a man asking ten dollars an hour and paying only two dollars an hour to someone else?"

"Ah she's crazy," said Tom. "You can't talk sense to her."

"Sophia, we can't all be millionaires," said George patiently. "If everyone had a million who'd do the work?"

"Everybody. At least everybody would do their own. We'd no longer have poorly-paid maids and garbage men cleaning up other people's messes, scrubbing floors for them, cooking for them, and washing their dirty dishes. If you were a millionaire, George, and couldn't get a servant would you do your own work, look after your own lawn, make your own clothes, grow your own food?"

"Sure. Our ancestors did. I don't because I live in a different time."

"But the time isn't so different that a man is essentially worth more than he can produce from his own labour, or worth less. George, maybe for all your work you deserve two houses. Are you sure you're getting paid enough?"

"I'm getting enough. I'm satisfied. I figure I'm getting what I'm worth," George spoke very solemnly.

"How do you figure that?" I asked, baiting him. "What measurement do you use to decide how much you are worth? You know some men in your plant who are getting less than you. Are they getting all they're worth?"

"Goddamn it Sophia, I don't know," cried George. "I don't set the wages. That's the way the system works. I didn't make the system."

"You didn't make it but you keep it going and you want Don and the others to keep it going. You never try to find out if there could be a better one. Well I do. I think this economic system is unfair and stupid and I don't want to keep it going with the rich getting richer and the poor getting poorer. I want a more democratic system where all people have more say in what work they'll do and for what wages."

"Oh is that what you want? Well I just hope you'll get it. What are you doing about it at present?" asked George with a smile.

"She's wasting her time and my money," growled Tom. "Going to meetings, making speeches, and writing crazy books."

George gave a hearty laugh. "Oh is that how you expect to get your fair system? Have you got a union yet?"

"Go ahead and laugh," I jeered. "You don't even understand what's happening in your own society. You know the country's in trouble and you can't see where we're heading, but stick around a few years and you'll see some good changes made. Now you and Tom talk. I've got to go out for meat for supper."

I left them. Before I closed the front door behind me I heard Tom ask, "What do you think of the third horse in the first race?"

On one of Tom's days off Lee invited us over for the evening. I went with Tom in happy anticipation of a good time.

The evening began nicely. Lee's mother was there. I liked her.

After supper George went to work and the older children went out with friends. The used dishes were cleared away, the younger children sent to bed and Lee, her mother, Tom and I got into a card game.

Now euchre is not my best game but Tom and Mrs. Campbell (Lee's mother) play carefully and seriously. It wasn't long before Tom was growling at me for not playing right. That angers me at any time but in that case even more because I was Lee's partner and she wasn't kicking.

But no way would he let me play my dumb way in peace. As he growled at me like a petulant child, I chose to imitate him and growled back.

Perhaps that set the mood for what followed.

We finished the game and Lee prepared to put the cards away. As she gathered them up she laughingly remarked, "So Johnny's almost ready for university. Too bad you wouldn't come up here twenty years ago, Tom. When we advised you. They'd have all got a good education. But then you were scared Sophia might find out about your other wife, eh, Tom?"

To my astonishment Tom flushed, then growled, "Awhrr."

I gave him a critical look. His reaction disturbed me. Years ago Tom had told me that for a time he had lived common-law with a girl when he was in his early twenties. He had never married, he said, until he met me but rumour had said otherwise, except that the gossips could not say what became of the "wife". Naturally, being in love, I believed Tom. Now his reaction to what I thought was plain kidding puzzled me.

Lee went on, "That's right, eh, Tom? Sophia doesn't know about her but I do. So does George, we found out. All your excuses for staying in New Brunswick were just excuses weren't they? You didn't dare bring Sophia to Ontario did you?" She was laughing gaily.

"Bullshit," muttered Tom, seemingly discomfited. I stared at him, confused and suspicious.

"Now Tom, it's no bullshit," Lee said. "You know you have another wife in Hamilton. We know. After all I come from there."

"Bullshit," cried Tom again—but not very convincingly. He got up from his chair and went to the living room and scrunched down in a big padded chair in the corner.

"What's the matter, Tom?" I called, irritated. "Don't tell me that old story is true, after all."

"Sure, it's true," Lee said. "Well, I'll get a lunch. What kind of sandwiches do you want Tom, cheese or bologna?"

"Don't want no lunch," Tom growled. "I'm going home. Sophia—call Don. He should be here by now. If he doesn't soon come I'll take a streetcar."

"Call him yourself, you bigamist, or are you even worse? Perhaps you've been married three or four times. I'll have a lunch, Lee. Give Tom bologna. He's so full of it a little more won't be noticed."

At that I saw Tom smile but he didn't speak. Inwardly I had begun to seethe. Why if he had married before hadn't he told me? Or if he was innocent of Lee's charge why didn't he defend himself? Why didn't he demand that Lee bring out her facts and figures, name names, places and dates. I thought he was acting very guilty and cowardly too.

Lee continued to tease Tom as she fixed a light lunch.

"You didn't think we knew, did you, Tom? Well we can prove it. Someday I'm going to take Sophia to Hamilton and show her the place where you lived."

"Sure. I'd like that, Lee," I said. "Tom, what is the matter with you? Why don't you come out here with the people? You're acting just like a little boy caught in the jam jar. I'm beginning to think you do have another wife."

"Not true," said Tom, the picture of guilt and dejection. "Where in hell is Don?"

"Don't worry about Don," I cried. "You better start worrying about your tangled web. How come you're in such a hurry to leave all of a sudden?"

"I've got to work tomorrow," he snarled. "You can sleep all day. I can't. Not if we're gonna pay the rent."

"Ah! Who pays the rent for the first Mrs. Tom? Huh! You're not worrying about me."

"Unh. Shouldn't have come out here tonight," Tom growled. "Well if he doesn't come I'm goin' home anyway. You can stay if you want."

"Oh no, Mister Bigamist. The boys have got to hear about

this. And you won't tell them. So I'll have to go and break the news. After all!" I said, laughing to keep Tom and Lee from seeing how serious I really was.

"Ah, bullshit," growled Tom.

"Bullshit, is it?" I asked. "Well I'm tired of your bullshit. After twenty-four years it gets kind of boring. Lee, are you making Tom a lunch?"

"Well, poor Tom must be hungry," Lee explained. "He's too embarrassed to come out here in the light so I'll take it to him."

"Yes, take the sooki-baby a lunch," I said. "I wonder where his other wife is."

"Oh, she's still in Hamilton," Lee said. "Tom knows, eh, Tom?"

Tom didn't answer. He accepted the sandwiches and tea Lee took in to him. While Tom ate in silence Lee and I chattered on. We dropped the subject of Tom's other wife but I couldn't forget it.

When Don finally arrived, Tom wanted to leave for home immediately. But Lee made Don a cup of coffee and he sat down to drink it. All the while Tom fumed and growled.

"What in hell is the matter with you?" Don asked.

"I got to go to work in the morning," Tom snarled. "I had no sleep yet. None of you give a damn." Lee was almost in stiches from laughing. Don must have sensed something odd.

"Well, why did you bother to come?" he asked Tom.

"I guess I should have stayed home," Tom answered. "Well hurry up, will you?"

"I'm gonna drink this coffee," Don said firmly. "And I'm not gonna pour it down. If you're in such a hurry to get home take a streetcar."

"I think I better," Tom said.

"Go on then," I said, "or better yet–take a bus and go right on to Hamilton."

We quieted down for a few minutes. On the way home I felt sick. I was puzzled and angry. More and more Tom's actions convinced me that he had once been married to another woman, and just might still be. And the more I thought about it the angrier I became.

The idea that he had kept such an important thing as a previous marriage from me was incredible.

Once home the other kids noticed at once that Tom and I were at odds again.

"What's the matter, Mum?" Johnny asked.

"Yes, what happened to Tom?" Don asked. "He's all riled up about something. What was Aunt Lee laughing at?"

"Tell them, Tom," I commanded. "Don't be such a lousy chicken."

"Tell them nothing," Tom growled. "I'm going to bed. To hell flames with you all."

"What's he so mad about?" the kids chorused, laughing.

"Oh, Aunt Lee got teasing him about his other wife," I said sourly. "The one in Hamilton he married when he was young. The one he said he just shacked up with."

"Oh, were you married before, Dad?" Johnny called gleefully. "Did you get a divorce? Did you have any children? I'd like that—to discover a new brother, half-brother or half-sister."

The clunk of Tom's shoe on the bedroom floor was all the answer he got.

"What are you gonna do now?" Billy asked. "Leave him?"

"What else? How can I live with a low-life like that?"

"Well you have for a quarter of a century, what's wrong with keeping on?" Don asked.

"What's wrong is I didn't know how downright low and stupid he could be," I said.

"Is it stupid to get married?" Johnny asked.

"No—but not to tell me was stupid. To let me believe all this time that I was married to him, then to discover in such a way that maybe I'm not is a lousy trick. How do you think I feel to have been duped like that—especially by a so-called husband and honourable man?"

"It's funny," Don laughed.

"Funny! Hell. It sure wasn't funny the way he acted at George's. If it's true he could have admitted it like a man, or if it's a lie he should have defended himself. After all. God damn!"

"Oh, don't take it so hard, Maw," Don cajoled. "Thousands of people are living in sin."

"Hell, I know. But they know what they are doing. They aren't being made a fool of," I growled.

"I don't believe Dad's got another wife," said Jenny. "Do you believe it, Mama?"

"I don't know for sure," I answered, "but I'll find out."

For three days I stayed so angry at Tom that I wouldn't do a thing for him. He got his own meals, and packed his own lunches, and went to work without a fuss. That I took to be another sign he well knew he had treated me very shabbily.

At 5:30 in the morning of the fourth day, Tom came to the living room where I had been sleeping.

"Are you awake?" he asked. "Are you still mad?"

I heard him but I didn't answer.

"We're legally married," he said. "I have only one wife, you."

I turned to face him.

"How long were you married before?" I asked.

"Uh, not long. She left me, then got a divorce. Are you gonna leave too?" he asked.

"I'm thinking it over," I said. "Where are the papers? Why didn't you tell me?"

"Who wants to keep junk papers? I thought you wouldn't marry me. What are you gonna do?"

"Never mind," I growled. "I'll let Lee know so she can tell you. Go away."

Tom left. It was Sunday. I stayed in bed until nine o'clock.

When I got up the house was still quiet. It was beautiful weather outside. Joyce got up.

"I'd like to go to Centre Island today," she told me. "I could take Jenny if you'd give us some money."

"Great," I said. "I want to get out too."

When the girls had gone I packed a lunch and set out for a distant park. The boys were still in bed.

At the park I sat on the warm grass and pondered my situation.

It wasn't that I was deeply hurt by Tom's deception. Oh, I had been at first but I had to admit it was in character right enough. Our marriage was in trouble because of other things—the difference in our ages and outlook and basic natures. It seemed to me that as the children grew and became more capable and independent Tom and I were thrown back on ourselves, put out of work, and had more time and energy to spend on our own individual pleasures. I could see where that could be a good thing. I didn't think my interests need by confined to the family and home. But the situation seemed to upset Tom. If I continued with him life would be hard—at least for a while yet.

And if I left him, I'd be leaving a lot of good things, a lot of valuable relationships—valuable to me. I suppose I'd not leave those entirely behind but they'd necessarily undergo a change which might not be to my liking. Certain friendships had evolved with our marriage. Tom and I had a particular image—if that were broken it would evoke a different attitude from our friends and relatives.

The thought of engaging in a whole new set of relationships with old or new friends repelled me. It would require just too, too much energy.

Outside of that there was the big question of Tom and me. What did I want from him, really? Support, care, co-operation? Yes. And I had those in good measure. Did I want total honesty? I wasn't sure. So he lied a little. How harmful was it? Didn't the answer depend on how I viewed lying? Yes it did, and since I view lying as a necessity at times to cope with problems arising from our desires and society's rules the reason for the lie can lessen its evil.

So it wasn't Tom's lying that annoyed me—but his weakness that made him lie. Okay, so he was weak—aren't we all? And I lie too—a little—and I forgive myself. So I could forgive Tom.

So why leave him then? Because for one thing I'd no longer have to explain how I waste money and my time. There I'd gain a kind of peace and freedom. And what else? Well I could perhaps marry again—or have an affair—but with whom? With what kind of man? Any man worth the effort was probably married and sitting alone somewhere pondering the same questions I was. So why not stay with Tom until I met this "other" man?

Well there's his stupid sex attitudes. Not that he isn't virile. The fact is he is far more virile than some younger men we know profess to be. I do not lack as far as the physical side of sex goes. Truthfully speaking, I can't keep up with Tom—but that's his fault. He's romantically frigid—or just plain lazy.

I know many women who claim their husbands of many years lack affection for them. Not me, brother. I suffer from an overdose of affection on Tom's part. He would ply me with clothes, flowers, candy, perfume, anything I asked for, and he'd work himself to an early grave to get the money to buy the goods, if I'd let him. I won't though, of course. All I really want are things like taking me out to lunch or to a good show with tender love scenes in it, to a dimly-lit place where we can talk and listen to music I like, even if the music be just noise to him.

Things like lying in bed and telling me little things I like to hear—like why he loves me—and why he likes certain books or places. The poor slob can't do that of course. Because he doesn't know why—he is contented with liking and never mind why. Oh, he makes sure he praises my nice complexion or nice figure or good-looking face—but hell I'm tired of listening to that.

I'd like him to say once in awhile that he enjoyed a meal I've worked hard to prepare—and he does, at Christmas time. The rest of the time he's growling because I don't put enough salt in things. For him only. The rest of us eat very little salt.

But I make my own romance. I read love poems and stories to get myself in the mood. Then I think hard about the times Tom did satisfy me romantically—accidentally—and then when finally I have worked myself into a fine passion and we are happily helping one another get relief and pleasure he says, "How's that?" or "How are you feeling? or "Jesus I love you" or "I hope I never get too old for this," or "When a man can't do this anymore he might as well be dead."

I don't know what his intention is but the effect is like a dash of cold water in the face to me and I go all frigid. Shortly he senses something wrong and he asks me "What happened? Am I hurting you?"

Brother! Hurt me? He's killed me, that's all. After all my work of getting myself in the mood, too. So then I get mad and I tell him what happened and I keep telling him and finally I ask him why. And, of course, he doesn't know. "Habit, I guess." "Where did you ever learn such stupid habits?" "Oh, around." Then he's mad and he growls, "Now you've made me lose it too, you bitch. Every time you do the same. You castrate me—just like the book says."

And he looks so mad and frustrated and depressed it is comical and I feel the urge to laugh or cry. And sometimes I do both. And then he looks worse and as I sob or chuckle he gives me one of his I-could-kill-you looks, and goes padding off to the kitchen for a snack.

When he comes back, all cheerful and confident again he says, "How are you now? Can you sleep?"

I don't answer at first. But he persists because he's scared. He doesn't understand what is happening to me and it worries him. For sake of peace I say, "I'm all right. I'll sleep after a while." But I don't say it right and he comes back sharply, "What's wrong with you?"

So I try to tell him what's wrong. How lonely I feel, how disappointed, how sad, how miserable because I have these hungers (normal or not) that he doesn't understand and can't satisfy and which I seem to be stuck with.

And the son-of-a-bitch lies there with the light in his face and goes off to sleep as relaxed as a new-born babe.

Then I get a ripping, tearing urge to jump up and pour a barrel of ice-cold water over him. Of course I can't because I'm scared I'll cause him a heart attack—so I repress the impulse and get up, light a cigarette, sit down myself and force my brain to think of mundane things like the week's laundry piling up, or what I'll cook for breakfast—and eventually I am able to return calmly to bed and go to sleep.

But that's only one aspect of married life. There are many other things. Where but in a man like Tom would I find such a combination of virtues? All things considered, he is a top-notch man as men go, and a very good father as well. So he isn't a perfect lover—so what?

So I'm not a perfect wife. So maybe I'm not a perfect lover either. The fact is that although my night-life isn't too hot my day-life is seldom dull—partly because of Tom. Even the counsellor said my husband sounded like an interesting man.

I paused in my thinking. I began to feel happier.

Sure I needed to get away from Tom and the family—but need it be forever?

Weren't modern marriage counsellors advising spouses to spend vacations separately—to get away from one another once in awhile? What had the counsellor told Tom, "Walk around the block." Good. Expand that, "Walk around the city." Sure, I could do that. Had begun to do it—had done it in the early years of our marriage in the country. Why not go on?

So now what can marriage be really?

What does it give above the legal security? It gives me emotional security since I know Tom will stand by me—and so will the kids and other family members as long as they are able. I need to belong to a family—the kind of family I have already. And our family relationships have required work on my part—and years of it.

If I leave Tom I destroy a relationship that is necessary for a number of other good relationships—for ourselves and for our children. I don't want to do that.

I just want to improve the relationship between Tom and me so that we don't stifle one another. If I could just come to a better understanding with Tom, or make an agreement.

Suppose I just go ahead and do certain things for myself—get a job—finish the book—go to bingo—what can happen? The relationship will change as we age anyway whether I deliberately change my lifestyle or not. It has been changing since we met, naturally. We are, after all, of different sexes and we've been changing year by year.

So suppose I broaden my area of activity. What will Tom do? How will it affect him? Or the kids? Will it hurt them?

Not necessarily. But a separation would. So why not continue the marriage but change myself? Why not? What have I to lose? Peace and quiet—but who wants that all the time? Not me—not yet.

When I got home Tom had returned from work. The boys had all gone out. Tom was lunching.

"Where is everybody?" he asked.

"Joyce and Jenny are over at the Island. I don't know where the boys are," I told him.

"Are you going out again?" Tom asked.

"Just to the verandah," I answered.

"Well I'm going to bed. Are you gonna get supper?"

"After a while," I said and went out into the sunshine.

Don did not go to Sudbury right away. The company wrote him that they had decided not to hire any more workers right then but they would keep his name on a list.

Don decided to go to New Brunswick for a visit and take some paintings to his relatives and friends.

"You shouldn't go," Tom warned him. "What if Manpower finds out? They'll cut you off."

"They won't find out," Don answered. "I've made my report. They won't bother me for two weeks."

"What if they find a job for you?" Tom asked.

"Mom'll phone and I can be back next day. She can tell them I'm out looking for a job," Don said.

"Okay. Go on then," Tom said, "but you'll get caught. You'll see. You're not supposed to take vacations while drawing unemployment."

"Who's taking a vacation? I'm having a vacation here. I'm going to New Brunswick to look for a job," Don laughed.

"Like shit," Tom said.

When Don came back I was ready to make some changes in my lifestyle.

As a first step I announced at a family gathering that henceforth I intended to receive a wage for my housework—especially the work I did for Tom and the working children.

That met with approval from the kids and derision from Tom.

"What work?" Tom sneered.

I smiled. "Oh, the scrubbing, the washing, making beds, cooking. This slave is rebelling."

"Good for you, Mum," chorused the kids.

"Haw!" said Tom. "Like hell I'm going to pay you to do your duties."

I let his comment pass without an answering remark and went on to explain that in addition to my wages I was going to take charge of the board money the kids paid and furthermore Tom was to pay support money for myself and Jenny, and an extra sum for his room and board.

When Tom understood my plans he really exploded. For a minute I thought he was about to burst an artery.

"Like Jesus H. Christ I am!" he roared. "You can suck my arse for all the money you'll get from me. Go on you crazy bitch. Get out. Go and live on welfare. You can't handle money. You never could."

"Rave on, Tom," I smiled. "And watch your language or you'll have another trip to the counsellor."

"Fuck the bastard," Tom answered very loudly. "No woman's gonna run me!"

"Well you're not running yourself very good," commented Don quietly.

"You go to hell!" said Tom. "All you've done is sponge off me. Twenty dollars a week board. Bullshit. That's not enough to feed you. You're all a bunch of leeches. Go on. Move out. Leave me alone."

It was a tense scene but not worse than I had expected and I was somewhat amused as were the children, but the noise began to bother Jenny.

"Do you have to yell, Dad?" she asked. "It hurts my ears."

"Go into the other room then," Tom told her lowering his voice a little. "I pay the rent here. I'll yell as much as I goddam well please!"

Raising my voice a little I said, "You pay the rent. That makes you a big man doesn't it? Well you are also a father. And what kind? It's a fine, admirable father who takes a tantrum and roars so loud it gives his little girl, his baby, a headache. Well perhaps it will be better if I take Jenny out of this atmosphere, and you know damn well if I do you'll have to support us. No way would a judge make me try to bring her up in this yelling, cursing, obscene atmosphere. It's not good for her development."

"Fuck. Take her away then. I don't care. You're making her as bad as yourself anyway. All she comes to me for is money," said Tom. His voice was far less loud and he was adopting an air of grievance. I figured he was near his giving-in point.

"You're lying again, Tom," I told him. "Jenny goes to you for math answers, and geography, and history, and stories. You have a value to her besides money. And she cares more about your health than you do about hers. When you're resting or reading she doesn't disturb you with tantrums."

"No. Because she gets her own way," Tom growled.

"Oh, is that what you're mad about? Not getting your own way anymore? You're not mad because my plan is stupid. You know lots of men who give their whole paycheque to their wives and she gives them pocket money. And the wives don't let them keep beer in the fridge either or even drink it in the house. You better figure you've had a good deal."

"And I'm gonna keep right on," said Tom, a little smile curling up the corners of his mouth.

"Yuh, a real fine deal with one room and four walls to keep

you company. No one to talk to, to argue with, to laugh with. No one to rub your back with liniment, to fix hot water bottles– "

Tom broke in to say, "And no leeches to get my money. I'd like to see how you all can get along by yourselves. You'll starve."

"Oh now, Tom dear, you wouldn't let any of us starve even if we deserve it. You're not that mean and cruel. And anyway don't you think it's a good idea for me to start learning how to manage money? How long will your insurance last me if you die suddenly before I learn? It'll be all your fault," I told Tom in my teasing way.

"Grumph," he answered and left the kitchen.

When payday came he gave me the sum I demanded, and he smiled.

The next step in my move to change my lifestyle was to join a citizens' group that was just starting to organize. The primary objective was to unite and try to unite the neighbourhood in an all-out effort to preserve our particular area for residential purposes. I liked the idea, and the chance to get involved with people on a larger scale.

In the group I met a number of interesting and capable people. A few I had seen and spoken to on the street but I hadn't been in their homes or they in mine. Now that we had a common goal and were teaming up we chose to get better acquainted. A close neighbour, Elva Grant, and I were drawn together because of our similar attitudes and viewpoints on some issues. She was younger than I, divorced and raising two children alone. Her oldest, Jerry, was the same age as Jenny and going to the same school. She painted and taught art in a high school.

Elva joined me and several other ambitious residents in creating our own small newspaper. For the first edition we collaborated on an article that poked fun at City Hall. From then on a friendship grew between us. Over a beer or coffee at her house or mine we discussed many things.

The better I came to know her the more I discovered that we differed more than we agreed. Once relaxing with a drink of wine at Elva's house we got into a discussion on the conditioning of children. She seemed to hold that society was to blame for a lot of our troubles because it had deliberately conditioned us. I held that in some cases the conditioning was accidental—and that, I said, was what happened in my case.

"I am not the product," I tried to explain, "of deliberate teaching or conditioning—but more of neglect. I am like I am because of the way I reacted to society's, that is my parents', teachers', and neighbours' treatment of me."

"You sound like Rousseau," Elva said. "Did you ever hear of him?"

"Not that I can recall," I said. "I was never very good at remembering who said what. I suppose the filter-type thing in our brain we are all supposed to have just decided names aren't as important as the ideas expressed."

"You may be right," Elva said, "but let me tell you about Rousseau. He lived in the eighteenth century. He was a romanticist. And he wrote a book, *Emile,* about a boy who was allowed to grow up very freely. His father didn't bother to teach him but he was allowed to learn whatever he wished. The idea was that Emile would, because of lack of conditioning, develop into a very free and noble person."

"Did he? I mean Emile, how did he develop?" I interrupted her.

"How did he develop?" Elva asked and seemed a bit puzzled at my question. "I don't really know. I never read the book, just studied Rousseau's theory a bit. That's what I'm trying to talk about. But anyway I think you should read the book yourself. Listen! I have a book on western philosophers. Do you want to read it?" She got out of her chair and began to search for the book. She found it and gave it to me.

"Sure I'd like to read it. I've been likened to Socrates and Karl Marx before. Now it's Rousseau. Most of the time when someone tells me I sound like so-and-so I don't know what in hell they are talking about. It's funny I'm seldom compared to a woman."

"Well because you can't be, Sophia. You are a very unusual woman. You must know that," Elva said.

"Of course I know I am different. I learned that very young. But not that different that there's never been a woman writer or philosopher a little like me."

"But then there haven't been many great women artists that we know of. They've been rottenly discriminated against. Now

I have an art magazine here with an article about that: 'Why have there been no great woman artists?' Of course we know why. Not that we don't have the talent and ability—we have—but it isn't promoted like the men, the male chauvinists."

Her last words surprised me. I thought I had read them someplace.

"Elva, are you a member of Women's Lib?" I asked.

"Why do you ask? Never mind. Yes I am. Aren't you? No, you don't need to be," she said.

"Not really," I said. "I agree with some of their causes but not their methods. I think some women don't want to be liberated."

"How can you sit there and say that? They've never known anything but the role of sex-object and slave. They won't know the difference until they are liberated."

"No, no, Elva, that's not true either. Look, I grew up with girls who could have been just as liberated as me and they chose not to be. They wanted to go along with society. They actually and deliberately sought the approval of society while talking behind its back. They didn't use their brains to reason whether the sex roles were right or wrong. They just accepted it because they got what they wanted from their role."

"But that's conditioning. Don't you see? You didn't accept it I suppose because you're so different. You have an analytical mind."

"But what I'm trying to say, Elva, is why wouldn't my schoolmates listen to me? You know people talk of kids being easily led and all that, but when they get a chance to be led in different ways why do they choose one particular way over another? Don't you think it could be because of unknown factors such as IQ, or likes and talents?"

"Oh, possibly. The whole question of the sexes and their roles is very complicated. But surely you aren't suggesting we do nothing. Or are you?"

"No, I'm not. Everybody is free to do what he chooses to do. I just think women have to liberate themselves before they can liberate others. I mean—these women's lib leaders—are they even liberated themselves?"

"Not all of them. Not completely. Perhaps not as liberated as you and me. But they are trying."

"Sure. I see that. I disagree with their methods, that's all. I don't like them putting all the blame on the men."

"But you do agree that men have put women down and do discriminate against them."

"Some men, yes. Not all men. And some women are to blame for letting themselves be put down. Besides that—I'm talking about the majority of the women I know—women are mighty quick to put other women down. You know, I have found that men are readier to let me be free than women are."

"That's probably because the men don't see you as a threat. Have you ever tried to get a job a man wanted?"

"No. Not since I was a kid. But when I was a kid I wanted to do my brothers' work and the only one who objected was my father. And that was only because he feared what the neighbours would say. However the war came along and liberated me from that."

"It was after the war that I met up with discrimination really for the first time. The first time that it made a strong impression on me. I'll tell you about that sometime, Sophia."

Elva poured wine for both of us. "I don't understand you, Sophia," she told me. "Nor Tom. Both of you are so unusual. You're both very intelligent but you don't use it."

"What do you mean don't use it? And there I go talking as if you were Gloria. You haven't met her. We use our intelligence as much as anyone."

"You don't get what I mean. Here you are living in that—that house. You don't own any furniture except for a chair or two. You don't have a TV. You don't drink much. You don't go anywhere. What kind of a life is that? Why? I just don't understand why."

"A lot of people don't. And you know that's because they don't try to understand other people. Well actually they don't even understand themselves. But look at it this way, Elva, why should we want to live like you for instance?"

She looked taken aback for a second. Recovering she said, "Well look at the freedom I have. Sure this lifestyle costs money—but it lets us do so many things. Surely you see that."

"Oh I do. But you don't see our freedom. No. Just a second.

Our freedom is inside ourselves. You are not as free as we are in fact. You are only free to buy things from others—but we are free from the want of those things. Tom and me and a hell of a lot of other Maritimers are a lot freer than most rich people because we can do without all these material goods and we have other freedoms. The freedom to tell our bosses to go to hell—to shove their job. So we'll starve a little, but— "

"Oh, I see. Well it all depends on our sense of values. And obviously yours are different. I still think I have more freedom than you."

I shrugged. "Well you're free to hold any opinion you want but I wouldn't bet on your being freer than me."

I stood up. "It's getting late Elva. I've really enjoyed talking to you, but I better go now. Why don't you drop into my place some evening or in the day? Just come when you feel like it and get to know our lifestyle."

"I will. We'll get together again. But be sure to read that book, and the magazine."

As I strolled homeward my mind was bemused. Poor Elva. She reminded me of my friend Gloria, and my brother George. I was sure she'd be outraged if she knew how alike I found the three of them. Funny how they all wanted me to wise up in a particular area: with Gloria it was housekeeping; with George it was grooming and living; and now here was Elva hinting not diplomatically that I should read philosophy.

Chauvinists. All of them, I thought.

14

It was Elva who got me interested in a Canada Council grant to get money to pay someone to type my book.

One afternoon I found myself at loose ends and strolled over to Elva's house to see how she was enjoying summer's end. She was sitting in her backyard with two painters and a poet, all unemployed, educated young people in their twenties.

Eva's front door was open. I knocked and after a while she came.

"Oh, hi, Sophia," she greeted. "Come in. We're out in the back. Leave your shoes on. The floor's wet from Brenda splashing in her pool and running about."

In the yard Elva introduced her friends and offered me a beer.

"How's the summer going?" I asked.

"Summer? Oh, hell. You know how it's going. Maddening. Listen, Sophia, we were just discussing Canada Council. What do you think about it?"

"Well I don't know much about it. Oh I have an idea what it's for and that's about all. Why, have you got a grant from it?"

"Grant!" Elva laughed. "I wouldn't even apply for a grant. Do you know what you have to be to get a grant?"

"Just a promising artist, I thought," I told her. "I understand it was set up to help people like you who could probably benefit from some free time and materials to work with."

"Hah! You are really naive. None of us could get a grant from that bunch. It's only for the élite. You have to be a full-fledged artist to get anything. If you've published a book, sold a number of paintings, or been in theatre a couple of years you may get a grant. That's *may*," Elva said.

"Well I said I didn't know much about it. But that policy seems kind of unfair to me. I thought the Canada Council was set up to promote Canadian art and help talented Canadians get started," I told Elva.

"Oh I thought that too. But that's not what it does. How can you, Sophia, expect anything from our Government to be fair?"

"Well it seems to me the Government is as fair as the people are. The Government only represents the people and it can only do what the people permit."

"Do you actually believe that? Do you believe the people want unemployment and poverty such as we have at present?"

"Just a second Elva. The people may not want it but they damn well permit and encourage those things. Do you think unemployment and dire poverty are necessary in Canada?"

"Well, under this system– "

"Forget the system. Just consider the facts of geography, biology, technology and production."

"Oh then you are right. Unemployment and poverty are not necessary. They are the result of our economic system. Then we'll just have to change the system."

"Whose gonna change it Elva, and how?"

"That's the question, isn't it? That's really the question. The answer is I guess you and I will have to get more involved in politics. How about that?" Elva ended on a laugh.

I smiled at her. I thought she had become facetious and it annoyed me. The conversation moved to our educational system. I kept most of my opinions on that to myself and concentrated on trying to understand the facts behind the points of view of the others until I went home.

That evening I wrote to the Canada Council for the application forms for a grant.

Within a few days I received the requested forms, a brochure, and a letter explaining that they did not help authors get books published.

I read the brochure carefully as requested. As I interpreted it I should be eligible for a grant to buy myself some free time. Then I read the accompanying letter again. They didn't help authors get books published—they only helped them get materials to work with and get the things typed. Ha, that was help enough.

I filled in the forms and sent them back. I was sure they would give me about 750 dollars and I would be able to pay a typist.

I was fated for disappointment. Canada Council refused the grant on the grounds that I had not had a book published nor had one presently accepted for publication.

I took the news bitterly. I thought they had a stupid and unfair policy and wrote an angry letter telling them so. I wrote also to some MPs. They sent me letters of sympathy. That made me angrier.

One late afternoon Billy came home from work somewhat disgruntled. I was alone in the kitchen when he came in. In a conspiratorial manner he came close to me and took a slip of white paper from his pocket.

"Maw," he said, almost whispering, "I want you to get this filled for me. It's not my name but it's for me. Will you get it?"

"Well. But that's a doctor's prescription isn't it? Why can't you get it yourself? It isn't forged or anything for drugs is it?"

"Naw. It's legitimate. Look. I'll tell you but don't you tell anyone. See there where it says 'pubic lice'? Well I've got them. I went to a doctor today. I was really scared. I thought I had VD and I didn't want to give my own name so I made one up. That ointment he ordered is the best. So get it will you? I'm itchy. And don't let Dad know."

"Okay," I said. I took the paper and went to the drugstore. The pharmacist checked, then told me they were all out of the stuff and couldn't get anymore because it was now banned.

I returned home and told Billy.

"God damn. What am I going to do now? I've got to get it. I can't stand the itch," he cried.

"Well I'll go to another drugstore. Perhaps if you shave that'll help," I said.

"Shave?"

"Sure. They shave people in hospitals."

"Okay. But go and get that prescription filled will you?"

"I will."

Before I could get away Johnny came home. He went to the bathroom. Billy let Johnny in and told him his troubles. Johnny came downstairs snickering.

"So Billy's got the crabs," he told me.

"Shut up, Johnny," I said, "he doesn't want Tom to start screaming."

"I can't help it," Johnny said, trying to hold the laughter in.

Tom came out of the bedroom. "What's all the whish-whish about? What's Billy done now?" he asked.

Johnny laughed loudly and said, "Billy's got the crabs. He's upstairs shaving."

Tom smiled. "Shaving's no good. Why don't he get blue ointment?"

"Oh, he has this prescription," I said, producing the paper, "but it's banned."

"He don't need that. Blue ointment will do. You can get that. You got the money?" Tom said.

"Yes I got the money. How do you know blue ointment is good enough?"

"Christ, woman. I've used it myself. What do you think crabs are?"

At this Johnny laughed even louder.

"It's not funny," Tom told him. "Maw, go and get him blue ointment. He'll be all right. He'll have to change his underwear every day."

"Oh, blue ointment, blue ointment, the crabs' disappointment," Johnny chanted, still laughing and started out of the room. "Oh it burns and it itches but it kills them sons-a-bitches. Blue ointment— "

For a couple of weeks I changed Billy's bed every day and washed his clothes as soon as he took them off. After he used the bathroom I would go in and disinfect. The crabs didn't spread.

Then I was offered typing services free. One pleasant September evening Elva came over for a chat. When Elva had been seated my niece Louise phoned to ask if she could join us. Of course we'd be happy to have her, we said.

When we were all together we talked about many things. Then we got around to our individual pastimes.

"With your kids getting so big and independent you must have a lot of time to yourself," Louise told me. "What do you do for pleasure? Do you go out a lot or do you knit or sew?"

"Knit or sew? Haw!" Tom answered for me. "That's what she should be doing. She won't even sew a button on my shirt. She's too busy running around the neighbourhood and scribbling a lot of bullshit."

"Tom, your damn shirts are worn out. You can afford to buy new ones now. Louise, I don't knit or sew much anymore. I've got a more interesting thing going. I'm writing a book."

"You're writing a book?" Louise asked with interest. "What's it about?"

"About us. Yes. About my family and friends and what we've been doing in the big city."

"Have you seen a publisher? Or is it not typed yet?" Louise asked.

"It isn't all typed, but I've seen a publisher. Two in fact. They both rejected it. That was a long time ago. But it wasn't all typed then. Perhaps they couldn't really judge it."

"I'll type it for you if you like. I have some spare time," Louise offered.

"Great! I'd really appreciate that. Before I take it to another publisher I want the first chapter done. I revised it a dozen times and now I think it's the best I can do."

"You're not letting everyone read it?" Louise asked. "You shouldn't. You should make them buy it."

"Well I let my friends and relatives read parts. It's about them and they're sort of curious and scared. So I let them read the good parts just to relieve their minds," I laughed.

"Yes," Joyce laughed. "But those are the parts the publisher will discard. I've seen some."

"Don't worry," I said. "There's only good parts to my book."

"Bullshit," said Tom. "If you don't put sex in it, it won't sell. No publisher'll take it."

"Bullshit, yourself," I cried. "People can't indulge in sex

twenty-four hours a day seven days a week. I'm writing about what they do between sex orgies, besides eating and sleeping."

"And eliminating," added Johnny, laughing.

"She'll never get it published," Tom pronounced loudly. "And she'll not get any money from Canada Council, either."

"How do you know? You always say that," Joyce cried angrily.

"Now, Joyce. Let him say what he likes. An opinion doesn't make facts, only in Tom's mind that is. Tom's just scared that I will get it published and that I've made him out a villain."

"Bullshit," said Tom. "I'm not scared. I'd really like to see you get it published. But I know you won't. Those publishers are all out to make money and sex makes the money."

"It doesn't matter anyway," I said. "Someday I'll get enough copies printed for all my relatives and friends. They'll enjoy it and all the kids, mine and Gloria's, will have it to look back on in their old age."

"Yeah. Where you gonna get the money?" Tom asked sarcastically. "I won't give you a cent to waste on that bullshit."

"You haven't been asked yet," I told him coldly. "Don't think I'm gonna stick around here nursing a house the rest of my life. I'll find a part-time job one of these days."

At that point Gloria and Bob arrived.

As Gloria joined the group she exclaimed, "What's the argument about now? We heard you outdoors. Every time I come here there's an argument going on. Well go on. I like to hear you. Is it about Sophia's book?"

"She's fighting with the Government again," Johnny laughed. "If you wake up some morning to find all our MPs have resigned you'll know who did it."

"What are you mad at the Government about now, Sophia?"

"Discrimination," I said.

"Against you, I suppose," Gloria smiled as she spoke.

"Yes, me and other Maritime artists."

"How? How is the Government discriminating against you?" Gloria asked.

"It won't give her any money," Tom said.

"What money? Why should the Government give you money and not all of us? We need it just as much as you," Gloria said.

For the next few minutes I tried to explain to Gloria about the Canada Council. When she finally decided she understood she said, "Well they must know what they're doing. It's their job."

"Oh they know what they're doing all right," Elva told her. "They're running it to suit themselves."

"Well isn't that their job?"

"Not necessarily," Elva explained, "The Government set it up and gave them a charter. Now if they don't run it the way the Government intended they can lose their charter."

"Oh, and you and Sophia, I suppose, don't think they're running it to suit the Government."

"Well they may be running it to suit this Government but not to suit me, no. As a matter of fact they aren't running it to suit a good many artists," Elva said.

"And maybe not a large section of the Canadian people who pay for it," I added.

"No government is ever gonna run anything to suit all the Canadian people," Gloria said. "But we have to put up with it. What else can we do? Before election they make all kinds of promises but as soon as they get in they forget what they said."

"Well they might not forget so easily if the people didn't let them," I said.

"You don't, for sure," Gloria said. "Ever since I've known you you've been fighting the Government and what has it got you?"

Before I could answer Tom said, "Trouble. That's what it's got her and me. She'll get herself locked up for good sometime."

Then Elva spoke, "Oh Tom, you shouldn't say that. You don't even understand what Sophia is doing. She's right of course. This system is rotten. Just rotten. It's simply got to be changed. I see that and I should fight more. Sophia is trying to change it democratically. I agree with her but I don't think she'll have much success. But then you never know. Sophia is far more optimistic than I am, and she has more ego strength. You all have incredible ego strength. And poor people need more of that. They're the ones who could change it."

"And we are," I said, "slowly, naturally. Look at the school system for instance."

"Yes," Elva laughed, then quickly said, "Oh no, let's not look at that. It's garbage. Just garbage."

"But you are aware that there are people who want it changed," I reminded her.

"Oh yes and they're doing it but not for the better. I'm in it. I know," Elva said.

"Well it's the aggressive ones with ego strength who do the changing. If we don't get together and change things for the better the others will win. And who is to blame? Them because they went after what they wanted or us because we didn't try to stop them?" I asked.

"You're right, Sophia. We've got to stand up and be counted. That's the only solution," Elva said.

"That's all right for you to say, Elva," Gloria cried. "You've got education and a good job. What have we got? Whose gonna listen to people like us?"

"Good job! That's all you know. If you knew the shit we teachers have to take. Sophia says the parents and society, of course, are to blame. Maybe she's right."

"No. You haven't got that quite right, Elva," I said. "Society is not entirely to blame. Would you say you or I are entirely to blame for our own faults? No you wouldn't. You don't. We can't be. For instance Gloria knows I don't blame her for her attitude. It's a product of her environment and education plus inherent ability. I just believe we can change our attitudes a little if we can learn more facts."

"Learn more facts. What good is that? The Government must know the facts. Why don't they change them?" Gloria asked.

"I don't know. Who knows all the reasons other people do things? I'm trying to find out. That's why I write to the Government to try to find out why they have a certain attitude and whether they'll change it or not."

"But why should they change their attitude?" Johnny asked. "You don't seem willing to change yours."

"I'm not, Johnny, and the reason is I think I'm right," I said.

"There you are," Gloria cried, "you think you're right. Maybe they think they're right too. So why should they listen to you?"

"Because they want me to listen to them," I said, "and that brings us to the question of what is our responsibility, yours and mine, to ourselves and the Government. Why should anyone listen to or obey anyone else? Why should we let our elected representatives or kings and queens and dictators impose laws on us?"

"Well we've got to have some laws. How could we live together without laws?" Gloria asked.

"Mum knows that," Joyce said. "But who has the right to make laws? Why should we obey a law we don't like?"

"Good question, Joyce," Elva cried. "Answer that, Gloria."

"Well," Gloria spoke more slowly as if puzzled, "the Government I suppose. That's what we elect them for."

"Oh yes. You're right. But we're supposed to be a free and democratic country," Elva said. "How free are you, or any of us? Do you know what would happen to me or Tom or Bob or any working person if we spoke our mind? Yes you know. You've had jobs. Free? Bullshit! Like hell we're free. Democracy. It makes me laugh."

"Cool down Elva," I cried. "Theoretically we are free. The trouble is we want to be free and right and secure. We can't be all that yet. But we can be freer if we are willing to give up some things. We can speak our minds and stay poor and unemployed. We can dress the way we like, wear our hair the way we like and stay poor and unemployed. Oh yes we can be free."

"And dead!" said Elva.

"Time for another beer," said Tom.

"Well I think Sophia is right," Louise said. "I work so I can be free on weekends. Then nobody tells me what to do."

"Nobody's gonna tell me what to do," Joyce said passionately. "I've got to be free. I can't stand being bossed around. I never could."

"Joyce, now you calm down," I admonished. "None of us can be totally free. What I feel is this: that our elected leaders are just people like we are and it's natural for them to try to run things as they see fit. But it's just as natural for us to resent their control and to rebel. And our forefathers must have felt that way too. Probably that's why we can mail letters to our House of Commons without a stamp. The ones who made that law must have wanted to make it easy for poor people to speak their mind to their governors."

"Probably they thought the Government would need help and that was a cheap way to get some good ideas," Johnny laughed.

"Well by God if it doesn't cost me money to mail letters to that damn Government I'm gonna write some too. I've wanted to tell them a few things for a long time," Gloria said. "Why don't we all write? What about you, Tom? Have you written to Trudeau?"

"Gowan," Tom growled. "It's a waste of time and paper. They won't even read it."

"I don't care," Gloria laughed, "I'll get it off my chest anyway. Write on, Sophia. I'm with you now. Fight. I hate peace."

"Oh I intend to. The way I see it, we're victims not just of our present leaders' hang-ups but the hang-ups and ignorance of their parents and grandparents as well. We're being ruled, in fact, by dead men through the laws they made and through the values and fears they pounded into their descendents."

"That's right. Of course it's right. And it's too much to expect them to change. We'll just have to get more involved and oppose them more actively. We artists can no longer be an élite group living in our own world. Oh I'm with you, Sophia. I really am."

"We're all with her, aren't we Bob?" Johnny cried cheerfully and gave Gloria's husband a friendly back-slap.

"I don't know," Bob said. "Whose side's she on, Liberal or Conservative?"

Bob hadn't been able to follow the conversation very well because of his limited English. We sat quietly for a while as Gloria explained my point of view in French. Then switching back to English she said, "So Sophia's not for any party. She's on the poor people's side."

"That's my side. I'll drink to her," Bob laughed and lifted his glass of beer in a toast.

"No. Drink to democracy," I said, "and to Canada including Quebec, and to poor little New Brunswick."

"And to all the Maritimers stuck in this goddamn city," cried Gloria.

"And especially to the Maritimers that conquered it," cried Johnny.

"Bullshit," cried Tom and Elva nearly choked on her beer. "Yes. Let's drink to that too," she said.

We drank our toasts, then Gloria went on laughing, "I still think it's a damn waste of time. People like us haven't got the brains or the power to change this system, this fuckin' rotten system as Elva calls it."

"You're right, Gloria," Tom said. "The working class hasn't got a chance. But it's no good to tell Sophia that. She's a dreamer."

"Oh so I'm a dreamer," I said. "And do you know what you are? You are an inferiority-complexed man. That's what you are. You and a lot of others are more worried about your image than about your rights and responsibilities. You are scared of being laughed at by those you esteem as superior, the people with education and money. It doesn't seem to bother you that I laugh at you does it?"

Everybody looked at me thoughtfully, as if at a loss for words but in a moment Gloria attempted to explain, "We know you don't mean it when you laugh. You are our own kind."

"You're way off base, Gloria," I said. "I am not your own kind and I do mean it when I laugh at your attitudes. I don't agree that having brains and education and money automatically gives people the right to rule. They can have all that and be damn poor rulers."

"I suppose you'd rule better," Gloria cried. "So why don't you run for Prime Minister?"

"Ah, now you're getting personal, Gloria," Elva said. "You are missing the point."

"No she isn't, Elva. She's getting the point too well. It's making her uncomfortable and since she can't attack the idea she attacks me in self-defence."

"What? I'm not attacking Sophia," Gloria cried. "I think she would make a good Prime Minister, or MP at least."

"But we're not talking about Sophia, or me, or even you in context of what we could be," Elva explained. "We are talking in general about theories and rights. Specifically the right of people to rule themselves. Don't you see the point of Sophia's argument?"

"Oh yes, she does," I directed my words to Elva. "But she can't quite accept the idea that dumb and ignorant people should fight for what they want. She thinks the Government is to blame for bad rules, not the people who elect the Government and/or put up with bad laws. She can see dumb and ignorant people fighting for their country but she can't see them running the country."

"I can't either," exploded Johnny. "Who wants to be ruled by dumb, ignorant bastards who don't know their heads from a hole in the wall?"

"Obviously you'd prefer to be run by smart élitist bourgeois bastards who know everything and care nothing for anyone but themselves," Elva laughed.

"Now who's attacking?" Gloria cried.

Elva smiled at her, "I know, Gloria. I shouldn't have said that. I was being bitchy that's all. I apologize."

"Okay, okay now, let's get back to people's responsibilities to themselves. Or do you want to drop the subject?" I asked.

"No, let's talk," said Joyce. "This society is so messed up it scares a lot of us young people, but it's our responsibility to make things better. Most of the older people have been so brainwashed they can't do anything. The parents teach the kids what they believe and if the kids don't go along with it they're punished. The parents withdraw love or support of some kind the kids need."

"You're talking about conditioning. Is that it?" Elva asked.

"Well it's the same thing. The older generation is conditioned to believe and act in a certain way and they can't change. Their grandparents were the same and they passed it on to their kids. And Gloria, and people her age and Dad are doing the same. Not Mum so much. She grew up with us."

I interrupted Joyce.

"Wait a second," I said. "I didn't grow up with you kids. I grew up by myself. I wasn't brainwashed. What I did was wait for you and try to help you grow more free."

"Yes you did, Mum. But society still gave us a hard time. I remember what the neighbours said about you and how the kids treated me. I had a lot of conflict in my life. Now I'm between the straight culture and the alternate culture. I like some things of both and I don't want to give up either completely. I can't."

"Well you're not so different from us older folk, Joyce," I said. "Don't think you're the only generation that inherited a messed-up world. We did too. And a lot of us did our best to clean it up. We've made some improvements and we're still working on the problems, but we don't have the fire and energy of youth anymore."

"Oh shit. Don't try to tell me the old ones are working on the problems except for two or three like you. But the majority don't give a damn. They're making the problem worse."

Johnny jumped in, "And you're making it better I suppose? You're only one person just like the rest of us. What are you doing to make it better besides talk? What can anyone do?"

"Ah now Johnny, that's the question every individual asks. And who knows the answer?" Elva said solemnly.

"We all know the answer," I said. "It's really very simple. Everyone is limited to what he can do with what he's got. As far as I'm concerned I think everyone here has been doing all he can, all things considered."

Elva laughed lightly. "I don't know about that. There's things I see that need changing and I could do something about it but I don't."

"Don't forget it takes time to grow, and to learn. And we all have the problem of trying to survive not just physically but in other ways. But now Elva, you and I and Gloria are getting to the point where we can become more involved. Our kids are growing up and we have more time to do things. Elva, you and I have gotten involved in a lot this past year."

"Oh we have. We really have. And we must keep on. Run for Parliament if we have to," Elva cried.

"Yeah. There's our first woman Prime Minister," Gloria cried. "Let's drink to Elva. Tom, any more beer?"

"I'll see," Tom said. "What a bunch, eh Bob? Talk and drink beer. That's all they like."

"And play cards," Gloria laughed. "C'mon, let's have a game. I'm tired talking about hang-ups and brainwashing and solving the world's problems. C'mon, Sophia, clear the table. Why do you always leave your coffee and jam on the table? Here Johnny, put them up in that cupboard. I'll clear the table. Get the cards, Joyce."

"I have new cards," Louise said, "Here, I'll get them out." She began rummaging in her handbag.

The atmosphere was suddenly lighter and gayer. We all joined in readying the kitchen for a game of cards.

15

Don got a job in Sudbury and moved there.

Not long after Don had moved out Joyce told me she was going to get married. One day she went downtown and had a quiet ceremony performed. She married an American draft-dodger from New York. She wouldn't let me give them a party.

"We don't want all that fuss," she explained. "The people who'd come wouldn't care about us. I've heard how they talk about draft-dodgers. I don't want their presents."

Joyce's husband had a job. The apartment they rented was near us.

Louise's sister, Barbara, came to Toronto. The two girls decided to try living together, although they did not get along really well. They moved into an apartment in a new building. Both of them took a strong interest in Jenny and started acting like big, kindly sisters to her. They began to shower her with clothes, money, and other gifts, and had her over for weekends. Jenny enjoyed the attention and visits. Louise had a new TV and Jenny was allowed to monopolize it quite a bit. We had no TV, nor had Joyce.

There were families with children in my nieces' building. On her visits to her cousins Jenny met some of the children and started making friends. I was glad of that. Tom said he would get a television set for Christmas.

With my household growing smaller and Jenny needing less and less attention from me I had more time and energy to apply myself to the book.

One evening while talking with a young girl who had worked with a group of us on our little area newspaper the name of Peter Martin Associates, publisher, came up. The young girl knew him personally. She suggested that I try his company. I did, the next day.

A week later I got the good news: Peter said he would publish the book, or rather he would help me make a book out of the manuscript and publish that.

Immediately I reapplied to the Canada Council for the same grant but this time I asked also for the fare to New Brunswick and back, first class. Soon the word came back that now that I had a publisher I was found to be eligible for a grant and would I please send them a substantial part of the manuscript for adjudication purposes. I did without delay.

Then I took a break from working on the book. Lee and I decided to go to New Brunswick for a couple of weeks.

The evening before we were to leave I suddenly became homesick and found myself unable to find anything of interest to do to pass the time. Finally I arrived at a point with a few hours to go before bedtime where I was just sitting listlessly in my kitchen reminiscing.

The doorbell rang. I went to answer it and was greatly pleased to see Elva. She had her daughter Brenda with her.

"Hi," Elva greeted. "I heard you are taking a vacation. I suppose you are pretty busy."

"I'm not busy at all," I said. 'C'mon in. Yes, I'm going to see my mother. My sister-in-law and I are going. I've got everything packed and was just sitting around feeling lonesome."

In a few minutes Brenda was off to see Jenny in her room and Elva and I were seated by the kitchen table waiting for the water to boil for coffee.

"Well now Sophia, you know I've quit my job," Elva said.

"Well I had heard, yes," I answered. "But you'll teach until June?"

"Yes. I'll do that. I told you I could go to Europe next year? I'd love to go to England and study. I'd like to learn to work in bronze but Jerry doesn't want to go. He wants to stay here in that house and I guess we could if we take in a roomer."

Tom joined us.

"I just came over to talk to Sophia a minute," Elva told him. "I have something very important to talk about. Important to me anyway."

"Okay Elva, go ahead. Let's talk," I said.

"Wait now till I get a beer. I want to hear this too," said Tom.

"What's happening with the Residents' Association? Since school opened I've been too busy and too tired to keep up with it. Is there anything planned?" said Elva.

"You've got me there, Elva," I said. "I don't know. They aren't too eager to let me know what they're up to. Of course I know by now they don't want me in it. That is, Lil and her supporters."

"Oh I know Lil doesn't like you or me either. We threaten her in some way, I think. Lil seems to want some kind of power but I don't understand her that well to see what it is."

"She's just jealous," interjected Tom. "She knows you're superior."

"Oh come now, Tom. How are we superior?" Elva asked.

"You're better looking. You have a better command of the language. You both have a higher education," Tom said.

"Oh but those things don't make us superior," Elva cried in exasperation.

"Wait a second, Elva," I cried. "They do though. They give us a greater ability to project our ideas and relate to other people, politicians, and the professionals. How Lil dislikes to hear me speak of you and Julia, and the professor as professionals."

"Oh, I know." Elva laughed. "Us and our hundred-dollar words. There's definitely a problem. I can see that. So what do we do?"

"Well I think we should just go ahead and do what we believe in and not worry about Lil and her type," I said. "I think we'll have to call meetings, run them, and tell people our ideas and see what reaction we get."

"Yes, I think you're right. Now I have a problem about what to do about my own life. We had something last summer but if I went to England to study I'd have to drop it. I want to get things changed. Our system is just too rotten. I think you and I can help change it. And I know the time I'd spend in England would be just groovy. We'd rent a house and I'd have more time for the children. But Jerry is twelve. He wants to stay here and I hate to disrupt his life now. It doesn't matter so much about Brenda. She's much younger. I could study here just as well I guess."

"Well but where would you have a better chance to save a little money, or earn it?" I asked.

"Oh, here. I could do better here financially. But I have friends over there and they want me to go. They think it's stupid for me to stay in this rat-shit when I don't have to. Maybe they're right."

"But how can they know what's right or best for you? You are most likely to know more than anyone else about yourself. How much self-studying have you done?"

"Self-study?" Elva smiled. "Not much."

"But you must have some idea of your limits and abilities. If you have a good idea of what you want, not just for a year but for later, and what you can do and how much rat-shit you can take then you'll probably make the right decision for you. I can't. I'm trying to find out what is best for me now. My life is changing. I'm finding myself with time and energy to do un-family things like trying to get Dan Heap elected," I said.

"Sophia I think you should go into teaching or politics. You'd be good," Elva said.

"Ah but I can't," I said. "I can't hack either one much. I get too emotionally involved. The rottenness in both systems shames me. But I am in politics. I'm just trying to decide how deep to get in. I wouldn't be a candidate for some office. I couldn't stand the stress."

"There'd be stress in politics all right. Probably too much for either of us. But that looks like the best way to make the changes."

"Well I want the changes to come through government and they will if people demand it. I don't think all of the people have to rise up in a body and demand things. A few can probably get the changes."

"You are certainly optimistic, but perhaps I'm too cynical.

You remember the McCarthy era? That was bad. Well I think it's getting as bad now and it will be worse."

"Elva, you are definitely too pessimistic. Remember Bob Dubé? Well for years he kept telling us there was going to be a depression. Well we have it but it isn't as bad as he predicted. We have a welfare system of sorts, and pensions, and the CYC, and the retraining programs which ease the shock of mass unemployment."

"And prevent a revolution. But how can we counter the rigid rightists who'd suppress everyone?"

"By keeping cool ourselves while we fight it. If we are sure our ideas are good and can defend them logically people will listen. Some people."

"Some people! How many? Anyway how do we contact those few who'll support us?"

"Through the media. Just as the suppressors do. By writing and talking."

"That's right. I agree. I liked the idea of a play to expose the rottenness. But when you said these parents have grade three or four education I couldn't continue. That's just too appalling."

"But it's true Elva. There are lots of people like Lil, too."

"Then what do we do? Become dictators? Oh I wouldn't want to do that."

"But you do do it. We all do. Wait—as a mother you must find yourself forced to dictate to the kids sometimes."

"Yes, of course. You're right. I see what you mean."

"Okay. The dictatorship I'm thinking of would be in self-defense. If we don't dictate to people like Lil, they'll dictate to us. Once I was told I talked like John Stuart Mill in that everybody should be free to do whatever he wants as long as he doesn't infringe the rights of others. And I finally decided that there may always have to be a degree of tyranny; that there'll always be a small percentage who'll try to infringe on the rights of others, and this percentage will have to be dictated to to protect the others. So I opt for the least tyranny and the greatest freedom. The problem is: Where does self-defense end and exploitation begin?"

"That's right. That's great. That really is the problem isn't it?"

"Sure it is. Has always been. And more and more people are

realizing it. Just a few days ago Johnny and I were discussing the same thing in different words. He pointed out that if we change the stimuli in society for some groups we automatically change it for the opposite groups. He said that supposing we do change the stimuli for the underprivileged and the people who become antisocial and criminal so that they become well-adjusted and law-abiding, what happens to those who under the present system are happy and doing fine? That latter group, or some of them, may go psycho under different stimuli. So where does that leave us?"

"But that wouldn't necessarily happen. Why, for instance, would I go psycho just because people in the Maritimes were getting a better deal?" Elva asked.

"If their better deal meant a worse deal for you. Taking from the—uh—privileged and all that. Don't you see the increased demand to cut back welfare or cut people off altogether is a result of the underlying, probably unrecognized, fear that some are gaining privileges at the expense of others? That, in fact, while we change the stimuli and opportunities for some people and increase their powers and social ability we decrease the powers of others—specifically the powers of others to exploit. And that increases their hostility. Oh they don't think they are exploiting anyone. They actually and firmly believe what they are getting they are earning. And when I try to get them—the privileged—to talk about their value and their rights they become very angry—at me. And they end the discussion by calling me nuts."

"Oh yes," Elva said laughing, "I can just hear them. And you have to take it—just like I do."

"Sure. That's the way people are. And that's the kind who would have to be dictated to in order to defend the right of all of us to a good education, a fair wage, more material goods—like a decent house, food and clothes—and personal freedom."

"That's right, I guess. Obviously what we've been doing last summer is right. But isn't there more we can do?"

"Well we can develop ourselves more, possibly. A year's studying might be very good for you. I've considered going to university myself but I'm not ready yet. Studying could be just the thing, and when you come back— "

"Oh, I'd not come back. That's why it's hard to decide. If I leave, that's it. I'll be out of it. That's what my friends did."

"Oh. I thought you were just taking a year off to study. Now I see your problem differently. So you wouldn't be coming back?"

"No. Hell no. I thought you knew that."

"No. You never told me about your plans beyond the year of studying. So you're in the kind of thing I was before we left New Brunswick. Except of course we had to leave. We had to get money for food and clothes and the basic needs. In your case it's a matter of choice."

"Yes, it is. There's a moral question that bothers me. So many need help. I know I can help them, but there's my own life. I want to do something for me."

"Well what about your free school? That's a terrific idea. Does it still appeal to you? Would it satisfy you—totally, I mean, to get into something like that?"

"Yes. Possibly. I think it would. Perhaps I should stay. I've enjoyed the past summer certainly. Do you realize how long I've been working for Dan Heap?"

"No. You didn't tell me that either. But how do you find that work?"

"It's been quite interesting. I'll keep on with it for a while. Through the winter anyway."

"And you'll be able to think everything over very carefully. I don't see any great need for you to decide right now. Perhaps something'll happen in the next few months to greatly influence you. Things could get a lot better."

"Or worse. Oh I know I'm just being a proper pessimist. But that school is just so depressing. There must be a better way to teach these children. Well actually there is. It has been proven in studies you are probably not aware of."

"But our bureaucrats won't try it. I know."

"Right on, Sophia. And I can't hack it to watch what that bastard is doing to my kids."

"Then you'll have to fight. Perhaps we'll form an organization to really attack the educational problems. An organization of our own."

"What? A PTA?" Elva said sarcastically.

"Perhaps," I told her seriously, letting the sarcasm pass. "We'll have to do some thinking and discussing. Perhaps we could call a residents' meeting and see what others think of a PTA."

Elva became serious.

"That would be a start, yes. Right," she said.

All the while Elva and I had talked, Tom had quietly listened and drunk beer. When Elva started gathering her own and Brenda's wraps to leave he got up, wished them goodnight and went to our bedroom.

I walked Elva to the street. As we parted Elva said, "Goodnight, Sophia. We must talk some more."

"Yes," I answered. "When I come back."

The two weeks Lee and I spent in New Brunswick were very pleasant.

The first night I was home from my trip Tom told me sheepishly in the privacy of our bedroom that he had done a very foolish thing while I was away.

"Well what was it?" I asked unperturbed, but wondering if he had been found drunk on the job and got fired.

"I tried to make out with Elva," he said. "I'm telling you before she does."

At once bitterly angry, I asked, "Why? How did it happen?"

"Well there was a political rally for the NDP and I went to it. Then a bunch went to Grossman's. I walked Elva home and she invited me in. I was pretty drunk. After we talked awhile I asked her to let me fuck her. She said no and I came home. You're mad."

"Of course!" I said between gritted teeth. I wanted to smash him. "How'd you like to hear about me running around down east? The least you could have done was go a little farther from home to act the fool, you lecher. How can you expect me to get passionate for you when you're so disgusting?"

Tom said nothing.

"Don't talk to me!" I cried. I was seething because he had broken the private contract we had made to avoid sex with others. I took a pillow and went to another room. The day was near I could see when we'd be living apart.

One night a month later the front doorbell rang and I answered it to find Elva and Brenda there. I invited them in.

"Keep your boots on," I said. "It won't hurt these old floors. Anyway who cares? I'll run the wet mop over the floors someday soon. C'mon, right through to the kitchen."

In the kitchen I took Elva's cape and offered her a chair. Jenny took care of Brenda. Tom and Joyce were sitting in the kitchen.

Tom offered Elva a beer but she gruffly refused it. She appeared quite drunk already.

"I came to see Sophia," she said. "There's something I must talk to her about."

Elva had moved to a chair at one end of our table. Tom was sitting at the other end. Elva was standing. Anger was in her voice as she looked across at Tom and bitterly cried, "And listen Tom, if I ever hear again that you're saying you made love to me, I'll, I'll– "

Elva shook a fist at Tom. Tom appeared shocked. He said, "What? I never made love to you."

Elva managed a little laugh. She said, "I know you didn't and you never will. But you said you did."

"No, I didn't," Tom told her.

"Yes you did!" Elva screamed at him. I stepped into the adjoining room to get my cigarettes.

I heard Elva say, "Just don't say anymore. I want Sophia to hear this."

Then I was back in the kitchen. I pulled up a chair and sat down near Elva. I gave Tom a hard look.

"Okay, Elva," I said lighting a cigarette. "I'm ready."

"Well," Elva said trying to speak calmly, "I didn't want to mention this. But now I have to. Something's happened. I'm hurt and very upset. Do you know what I'm talking about Sophia? Did Tom tell you anything?"

"Well he told me he got fresh with you, if that's what you're talking about," I said.

"There's more to it than that," Elva cried, angrily. "He actually tried to rape me! Do you believe that?"

Tom was keeping very quiet at his end of the table. I thought I knew more about the incident than Elva expected Tom to tell me, but I didn't intend to let her know how much I knew. Tom knew he'd have a chance to defend himself to me in private later.

"I believe you'd see it that way, yes Elva," I said, trying to seem undisturbed. "But he didn't succeed did he?"

"No," Elva laughed. To Tom, "You bastard. I thought you were my friend. But now you've done this terrible thing."

Tom said nothing.

"What terrible thing?" I asked. "Propositioning you?"

"That was bad enough," Elva said. "But to talk about it, and make it worse than it was. Tom just has no loyalty."

"Talk about it. Where?" I asked. "Is it someone we know who told you?"

"Yes. You both know him." I was not surprised when she continued. "It was Bob."

"Oh ho!" I laughed. "When did he tell you?"

"A few nights ago. I've been trying to see you all weekend. He just came to the door. I didn't expect him and when I opened the door he just barged in. He had been drinking."

I smiled as I pictured the scene.

"It's not funny," Elva told me coldly. "It was very upsetting. But maybe I'm too sensitive."

"Maybe you are," I agreed. "It is sort of funny. An old guy like Tom trying to rape you. And then Bob coming around to tell you what Tom said. I can understand Tom's purpose and method but what did Bob have in mind?"

"The same thing," Elva said, glancing bitterly at Tom. "They see us as sex objects only. But I thought Tom saw more than that. It's so disappointing."

"Well, Elva, I thought you could handle men like Tom, and Bob isn't my problem," I said. "Actually they paid you a compliment."

"A compliment! You call that a compliment? I call it an insult," Elva growled.

"I don't call it a compliment. They do. Okay? So they aren't subtle, nice gentlemen. But you turned them on. You heated up their glands and they reacted crudely. But sex is crude and basic. Surely you've been asked to go to bed with men who aren't married to you?"

"Well, yes, but not like that. Like, like animals. Tom tried to grab me!" Elva complained.

"Well then, look at it like this: the intention of the crude men and the polished men, and the feelings of both are the same. The method of expression is different. Gloria and me and our class wouldn't be shocked or deeply upset over such an incident."

"What would you do? And what do you mean by 'your' class?" Elva asked.

"Our class is the one that hasn't time for pretense and all beautiful manners. And what we would have done would first of all not let our class of men get us alone. Secondly we'd have clobbered them if there was something handy. And thirdly we'd have reported the 'dirty son of a whore' to another male relative if we had one and he'd take it from there. At our parties and get-togethers the men keep the men in line and we women look after the women," I explained.

"Then you get this behaviour quite often?" Elva asked. She was in good control of herself once more.

"Not me. I discourage it from the start. The thing never goes beyond hinting, and within the group yet; all open and above-board attempts at mild flirting."

"Oh," said Elva unhappily. "I guess I should never have let either of them in the house then."

"Right. But you didn't know and Tom and Bob didn't know. That doesn't excuse them of course. They are married after all."

"Right," Elva said. "It's so maddening to have to take such shit. Sex-objects. Damn!"

Tom smiled, got up from his chair and went to another room. Joyce spoke then. "All men don't have the same attitude. Some of them build their egos around sex. They have to always be chasing women and trying to prove their ability."

"I know," Elva said. "But it's so horrible. Surely there's something we can do about it."

"What?" I asked. "Change the men? Not the old ones. But we might be able to change our own attitudes towards them and their ideas. We could laugh at them."

"Well of course I did," said Elva. "But to be talked about and lied about. It's so—so—degrading."

"Yes," Joyce agreed. "It used to get me boiling mad when I heard what someone said about me. I don't mind so much now. We can't stop them so I don't worry anymore."

"You're right, I guess," Elva said. "What do you think, Sophia?"

"I gave up worrying about what people said or thought about me decades ago. It's more important what I think myself. Our fortunes no longer depend on everybody's opinions. We can't please everyone. However we still have to guard our reputations somewhat and the only way is to stay clear of certain types. They may make up lies but they have no proof or witnesses so our word is as good as theirs," I answered.

"I see. Yes. I agree," Elva said. "It's the way I figured it about Tom. Forget it—it was nothing. It was Bob that upset me so much. That Tom would lie or exaggerate. I'm very disappointed in him. I thought he was my friend."

"But maybe Bob lied," Joyce cried. "I know him. He could easily say Dad said something. Bob propositioned me one time and I was only sixteen. I told him I'd tell Gloria but he told her himself and he said he was only testing me to see if I was a good girl or not. Bullshit. If I had agreed to do what he asked he'd have kept on. I know."

"Well maybe they were both testing me then," Elva laughed. "I'll forget the whole thing. Okay. Let's talk about something else. How have you been since your marriage, Joyce? Do you have a nice apartment?"

The conversation was kept light from then on until Elva decided it was time to take her daughter home.

Two weeks later Joyce came home for another visit. Her husband was at work, as was mine. I had been alone until Joyce came and I was very glad to see her. We were having a happy conversation when Bob and Gloria arrived.

For a few minutes the four of us talked together then Gloria asked, "Got any beer Sophia?"

"Not a drop," I told her. "And no money to buy any."

"Oh, we've got money," Gloria said. "Bob, go and get something to drink for us."

"You go," Bob said. "You and Sophia. She knows where, on Spadina."

"Oh I'm not staying alone with Bob," Joyce said with a teasing laugh.

"What?" Bob asked as if hurt. "What you mean, you won't

stay alone with me? I won't hurt you."

Joyce continued laughing, "I've been hearing stories about you, Bob. You've been up to things."

"For Gawd's sake," Gloria cried. "There's always stories. What did you hear?"

"Oh nothing," said Joyce. "You wouldn't be interested, Gloria. I'm talking to Bob."

"What about?" Bob asked. "What did you hear?"

I tried to change the subject. "Come on Gloria. Let's go get something. Joyce is only teasing."

"No," Gloria said. "I don't feel like going over to the Liquor Commission. Not in these old slacks. Bob you go."

"No," said Bob. "You go with Sophia."

"Oh give me the money and I'll go alone," I said. They gave me the money and I left the house. Hell, if they were gonna fight let them, I thought.

When I returned, I realized at once that the three had had a hot argument. I gave Bob his change and laid his bottle of rum on the table in front of him. He made no move to open the package.

"Is it true a woman came here complaining about Bob?" Gloria asked me excitedly.

I hesitated.

"Well did she?" Gloria pressed. "Joyce told us. I don't think it's her business. It's your house."

"Well Joyce was here. She heard the woman herself. That makes it her business," I said.

"It's my business when Bob molests my friends," Joyce cried angrily. "Mum didn't know about the time Bob put his hand on Janie's leg here in the kitchen. That was before I was married, Mum. Sure he was drunk. That's no excuse."

"So why didn't she stop him?" Gloria asked.

"She's only a kid," Joyce answered. "Mum and Dad were in bed. Janie didn't want to make a scene."

"Scene. Scene. So now you make a scene," Gloria cried in exasperation. "A year later."

"No one's sleeping now, and Bob's sober," Joyce yelled. "And it isn't a year either."

Bob put his money in his pocket and picked up his bottle of rum from the table.

"C'mon Gloria. Let's go home," he said.

"Oh are you leaving?" Joyce asked. "You can do your thing but when you're told about it— "

"Yes I'm leaving. And I won't come back here again if that's the way you treat me," Bob told her.

"So you didn't treat my friend very well," Joyce told him. "How do you think she felt?"

Bob was moving through the hall. Gloria was walking behind him. She turned back to Joyce and me and grimacing ferociously she made a hitting gesture at her husband's back. Silently she mouthed the words, "the son of a whore".

When Gloria and Bob had gone Joyce said, "Are you mad, Mum? Do you think they'll visit again?"

"I'm not mad. Bob deserves it," I said. "Why should we have to listen to the complaints of the women he chases? If they don't come back I'll get used to it."

A bit later Joyce went home and Gloria called me.

"Goddammit," she said. "Now Bob won't let me go to your place anymore. Why didn't Joyce keep her mouth shut?"

"You've got it wrong, Gloria," I laughed. "Why didn't Bob keep his shut and stay away from the women?"

"It's not a bit funny," Gloria cried over the phone. "I didn't do anything and now I've got to suffer. Yours is the only place I had to go and now I can't. I should leave the son of a whore. Bastard."

"He must be out now, is he?" I asked. "He can't hear you?"

"Yes he's out. He can stay out and never come back."

"Don't take it so hard, Gloria."

"Well who wouldn't? Goddamn. Here I was set for a nice visit and look how it ended? I am stuck home now with no company again. Oh here he is back. I saw his car go by the window. I'll call you another time. 'Bye."

She hung up.

That night I told Tom and the kids what had happened. Billy and Jenny were not impressed.

Johnny laughed. "Poor old Bob. I hope he's not mad at me. Oh the poor guy. All the women mad at him. He's just like me. I think I'll have to go see him and cheer him up."

"They left mad?" Tom asked. "That goddamn Joyce. Can't

keep her mouth shut. Always causing trouble with her big mouth."

"What?" I laughed. "And what were you doing while I was in New Brunswick? Who did Elva come to to complain? Oh yes, Joyce caused the trouble all right. You and Bob are just innocent victims of malicious gossip."

"Awhr!" Tom growled and turned his attention to the daily paper.

"You can say *awhr,* you damn lecherous old bastard," I cried. "Causing me to lose all my friends. Some husband you are."

Tom didn't answer.

Johnny said, "Poor old Mother. Well when you get your grant take off and take Gloria."

"I think I'll have to," I said. "I'll go back to the hills and hide. And write another book."

Johnny and I each picked up a section of the newspaper and settled ourselves to read.

Bob didn't stay angry long. Christmas was coming and I guess the spirit got to him. That and Gloria's coaxing. About two weeks after the row with Joyce they came down and made peace.

"Well Bob decided maybe he was wrong," Gloria explained. "Anyway it's nearly Christmas and what's the good of staying mad?"

"That's right Gloria," I said. "Life has its ups and downs. Maybe next near it'll be up all the way."

"Up where?" Bob asked. "To heaven?"

"No," Gloria laughed. "To Ottawa to get Sophia some money."

In December Tom's brother John's wife Henrietta came up to visit Louise and Barbara. Louise talked Barbara into holding a family reunion-type party Christmas Eve. Tom and I, Johnny, Billy, and Jenny went to it. There were nieces and nephews there with friends, and friends of their friends.

The party started out quietly happy. Louise had a very good record player and sufficient records. The young people danced and sang. Tom, Henrietta and I talked, and drank. Well Tom drank. Henrietta and I merely tasted our drinks from time to time.

Soon Tom was drunk and very obnoxious. After some cajoling

I got him to lie down in Louise's bed. He was fully dressed. I sat on the bed talking to him until he fell asleep.

I returned to the party in the living room thinking Tom was good for the night.

An hour later we heard an unusual racket in Louise's room—a body stumbling around, and some crashing things and cursing. I went in and found Tom on his hands and knees trying feebly to extricate himself from Barbara's wooden clotheshorse.

Suppressing the urge to laugh I helped him to his feet and tried to steer him back to the bed. He resisted my help and began fumbling with the front of his pants. I tried then to lead him out to the bathroom. Johnny came in and took his father's arm.

"Let me help you, Dad," Johnny said. "The bathroom's out this way."

"Leave me alone," Tom mumbled. "I've got to piss. Let me go." He struggled weakly against our pulls, and with the zipper he couldn't operate.

Johnny grew weak with laughter. He let go Tom's arm and left the room. I saw that Tom was about to urinate on Louise's wall-to-wall rug. I was horrified. Desperately I looked around for some waterproof utensil.

In the corner by the dresser there was a tin wastepaper basket.

I grabbed it up and ran to Tom as he sat down on the edge of the bed. Just in time I got the basket to him. He relieved himself in the basket that I held in position, zipped up his pants, and lay back on the bed, asleep instantly.

I took the basket out, emptied it into the toilet, washed, dried and replaced it.

Back to the kitchen where Henrietta and her girls were waiting to hear what had been going on with Tom.

"The drunken slob," Barbara said. "He'll have to get me a new clothesrack. I'll see to that."

"If he had ruined my rug I'd kill him," Louise said, but she laughed. "Goddamn. Danny's girl friend has been sick all over the floor in Barb's room. The last goddamn party I'll give."

"It's a good thing some of us don't drink," Henrietta commented mildly. "You got a way home Sophia?"

"Oh we'll take a taxi," I said. "But Tom's okay for a while

now. Next time he wakes up he'll have to eat."

"Just like John," Henrietta laughed. "Goddamn if I'd hold a basket for John."

"Oh well," I murmured.

"I don't think I'll give him anything to eat, even a sandwich," Barbara said, but she was smiling.

"Now, Barbara," her mother admonished.

Around three a.m. we were all home. Tom, as he had promised months before, had bought a new television set. Jenny stayed up to watch the late, late show.

Early in the new year Johnny was given a small car that was about ready for the scrap heap. Johnny determined to fix it. A friend towed it to our place and put it in the lane.

Tom told all of us more than once that Johnny was very foolish to spend money on "that piece of junk" but he joined Billy and me in helping Johnny to get the thing running.

The motor had to be taken out, cleaned, given new parts, and put back in. Even Bob Dubé helped with that.

The work I helped with was not physically strenuous. Mainly it was pushing pedals or pulling levers while Johnny made adjustments. I put in a lot of time holding nuts in place with a wrench while others were tightened. One day while thus engaged I was head and shoulders on the floor of the car with the rest of me stuck out in the beating rain. That night I quit my mechanic's helper job.

I got a small standard typewriter and started learning to type—slowly, with one finger. It was something to pass the time.

Spring drew near. To the proud satisfaction of the whole family Johnny succeeded in making his "pile of junk" roadworthy and I received a nice cheque from the Canada Council.

The first bank I took the cheque to would not cash it although Tom and I had a small account there.

"We'll have to keep it for five days," the manager said.

"Why?" I asked.

"Well, how do we know they've money up there?"

I laughed at him.

At our Toronto-Dominion bank I had no trouble.

With the money I paid the fine I had owed the library for

so long, and my overdue Mensa fee. I had the house fumigated because we had seen a few cockroaches around. I paid Louise some for typing. I sent John the twenty-five he had lent Tom to come to Toronto, and sent some to Lois whom we had owed even longer.

And some I used to throw one last party since I figured that after the book came out I'd have no friends left, and only cold relatives.

The party was great. By three a.m. most of the people had gone to bed or gone home. Tom, Joyce, Elva, and I were left alone. We sat in the kithcen, smoking cigarettes, and drinking lightly.

"Did you look at the book I gave you, Mum?" Joyce asked.

"Not deeply," I told her. "Just enough to see that it's a good one and has poems I like."

"You got her a book of poetry, Joyce?" Elva asked, pleased. "That's probably the best gift she received. May I see it Sophia?"

"Sure," I said.

I gave Elva the book.

She began thumbing through it. Stopping at a particular page she said, "Listen. Here's a poem I've always liked. Want to hear it?"

We did. Elva read the poem. We discussed it awhile—and literature in general. Joyce left the room to get more books and Tom said, "Let me see that book, Elva."

Elva gave Tom the book. He looked up a poem he liked and began reading aloud. Joyce returned with a load of books.

From then until five a.m. we took turns reading poetry to the group. Then we discovered we were out of cigarettes. Tom was okay though. He doesn't smoke.

"I think there are some at my house," Elva said. "Want to come over?"

"Oh I do," said Joyce.

"Well-ll, I think I'll go to bed," I said. "I like this. Sitting around, reading together and talking, but I'll get a headache if I stay up much longer."

"Go to bed then," said Tom. "I'm going too."

"Well then I better be going," Elva said.

"Oh no," said Tom. "You don't have to go. Joyce is here."

"I'll go with you Elva," Joyce said. "I'm not tired. Besides I want a cigarette. Don't you?"

"Yes," said Elva. "Let's go, then."

The two gathered up books and left. Tom and I saw them to the door. Walking ahead of me to the bedroom Tom quoted, " 'Let me live in a house by the side of the road and be a friend to man.' Know who wrote that?"

"No," I said. "Who?"

"Bliss Carman. You don't know anything. He was New Brunswick's greatest poet."

"So," I said sleepily. I was walking behind Tom down the hall.

"So New Brunswick produced some great people: Bonar Law, Beaverbrook, Bliss Carmen. You don't know. You don't care. G'wan to bed," he growled drunkenly.

It entered my mind to retort, "Does that make up for the good ones it starved, the kids it left cold, hungry and sick, and the old people it's neglecting?" But I did not want to set off another battle; not just then. I was enjoying a buoyant feeling of having got my own back on society and I did not want to lose it.

Tom turned into our bedroom still growling about my ignorance. I contir ued on to the living room and the couch.

My dreams were sweet.